NIGEL JONES is a historian, biographer and broadcaster, and former Assistant Editor of *History Today* and *BBC History* magazines. He has written lives of the writer Patrick Hamilton, Rupert Brooke, and Oswald Mosley, and his study of the Great War, *The War Walk*, is being reissued in 2004. His latest book is a re-examination of the Edwardian era for BBC Books.

A BRIEF HISTORY OF

THE BIRTH
OF THE NAZIS

Nigel Jones

Foreword by Michael Burleigh

ROBINSON

ROBINSON

First published in Great Britain in 1987 by John Murray (Publishers) Ltd

This revised and updated edition by published by Robinson,
an imprint of Constable & Robinson Ltd, 2004

Reprinted by Robinson in 2017

10

Copyright © Nigel Jones, 1987, 2004
Foreword copyright © Michael Burleigh, 2004

The moral right of the author has been asserted.

A CIP catalogue record for this book
is available from the British Library.

UK ISBN: 978-1-84119-925-2

Printed and bound in Great Britain by
CPI Group (UK) Ltd., Croydon CR0 4YY

Papers used by Robinson are from well-managed forests
and other responsible sources

MIX
Paper from
responsible sources
FSC® C104740

Robinson
An imprint of
Little, Brown Book Group
Carmelite House
50 Victoria Embankment
London EC4Y 0DZ

An Hachette UK Company
www.hachette.co.uk

www.littlebrown.co.uk

To Ernst Jünger (1895–1998)
Fighter & Writer

ACKNOWLEDGEMENTS

I would like to express my thanks to the following institutions and individuals for help in the writing of this book: Herr Ernst Jünger, Professor Horst Muhleisen, the staff of the Staatsbibliothek für Zeitgeschichte Stuttgart, the London Library, the Wiener Library, and the Imperial War Museum; also my editors Antony Wood and Roger Hudson, my colleague Colin Parkes for suggesting the title, Ms. Elaine Koster for typing the manuscript, and the staff of the *Berliner Morgenpost* newspaper.

NIGEL JONES

CONTENTS

List of Illustrations and Maps   ix
Foreword by Michael Burleigh   xi
Introduction   xvii

1 Birth of the Stormtrooper   1
2 Collapse of an Empire   14
3 'Revolution or Republic?'   32
4 The First Freikorps   47
5 'Spartacus Week'   60
6 The Twin Murders: Liebknecht and Luxemburg   70
7 Maercker's March   84
8 Strikes and Street Fights   95
9 The Freebooting Spirit   107
10 The Baltic Campaign   123
11 The Munich Soviet   139
12 Versailles: Resistance or Submission?   159
13 The Kapp Putsch   170

14 The Red Army of the Ruhr 192
15 The Politics of Murder 203
16 Enter Hitler: The Beerhall Putsch 230
   Epilogue: The Fate of the Freikorps 261

   Afterword 271
   Appendix A The Main Freikorps, leaders, dates,
   fate, size, and insignia 281
   Appendix B Freikorps members later prominent
   in Nazi Germany 297
   Selective Bibliography 311
   Index 317

ILLUSTRATIONS AND MAPS

Plates

A Freikorps recruiting poster

General Ritter von Epp, Freikorps leader

Friedrich Ebert, first President of the Weimar Republic

Revolutionary Spartacists, Berlin, January 1919

Spartacist leader Karl Liebknecht, 4 January 1919

Defence Minister Gustav Noske

A Freikorps unit moves in to crush the chaotic Soviet Republic, May 1919

Insurrection in Kiel during the Kapp Putsch, March 1920

Members of the 'Red Army of the Ruhr' on parade, Spring 1920

Hitler at the time of the Beerhall Putsch in Munich, November 1923

Great War hero General Erich von Ludendorff

Nazi demonstration in central Munich during the Beerhall Putsch, November 1923

*All images are courtesy of akg-images

Maps

Germany   xvi
Berlin   46

FOREWORD

Nigel Jones's book is an important, well-researched and vividly written account of a group of men who connected the mass death of the First World War with desolation and disorder on post-war Germany's streets, and hence with the early Nazi movement that thrived in such conditions of mass despair. Jones tells the story of the Freikorps with great economy in a book that has the intensity and pace of a thriller, although its subject matter is the formation of a Fascist mind-set, not simply in Germany, but also elsewhere.

The Freikorps were born amidst the carnage of the trenches. General Erich von Ludendorff formed units of 'Storm troops' to spearhead massed infantry attacks. They wore green uniforms with silver facings, some consisting of the 'Death's Head' insignia once worn by Blücher's Prussian Hussars, and subsequently emblazoned on the caps of Hitler's feared SS.

Armed with pistols, rifles and grenades, these highly mobile units were expected to punch holes in enemy lines wide enough for massed infantry to pour through. They developed a unique esprit de corps based on their élite status and skill in inflicting maximum damage on the enemy. Some of the stormtroopers had literary proclivities too, although they included only one writer – Ernst Jünger – of near genius, producing a body of literature that glorified and mystified war as the breeding ground and school for a new élite that was aristocratic in spirit but democratic in social origins. Like the Italian *arditi* whom they resembled, the storm-troops were the prototypical Fascist 'new man', with straight jaw and empty killers' eyes staring from beneath the shadow of their steel helmet. The Nazis would regard them as their immediate precursors.

The first Freikorps, or volunteer units, were formed to assist the Social Democrat Provisional government of what shortly became the Weimar Republic in order to suppress attempts by the anti-democratic extreme Left to seize power through revolutionary violence. Many of the volunteers were newly demobilised storm-troops, their ranks augmented by middle class youths and students with the right-wing nationalist sympathies common to their age and social class at the time.

When the hard-core Spartacist Left attempted to seize power in central Berlin, volunteer Freikorps – under the command of the Social Democrat's Defence Minister Gustav Noske – blasted and shot their way into the heart of the city, and massacred any Spartacists they found alive. The Spartacist leaders, Karl Liebknecht and Rosa Luxemburg, were tracked down and killed after being interrogated in the Eden Hotel. Nigel Jones tantalisingly suggests that they may have been betrayed by fellow communist Wilhelm Pieck, who after the Second World War became East Germany's first President, a state which mythologized Liebknecht and Luxemburg as Communist martyrs.

Worryingly, for Germany's fledgling democracy, the Freikorps were almost as hostile to their Social Democrat masters as they were to the 'Red rabble' they had wiped out at the former's behest. As one Freikorps leader wrote in his diary: 'The days of the revolution will forever be a blight on German history. As the scum hate me I remain strong. The day will yet come when I will knock the truth out of these people and tear the mask from the faces of the whole miserable, pathetic lot.' Another described the Ebert government as 'A miserable socialist rabble'. In the meantime, the Freikorps exacted their vengeance on the working class quartiers of eastern Berlin, bombarding the suburb of Lichtenberg, before running amok and killing between twelve and fifteen hundred people. By March conditions were sufficiently stable for the Assembly at Weimar to promulgate a constitution. The SPD newspaper *Vorwärts* retrospectively exculpated the Freikorps, when it editorialised:

> In a struggle to the death in which the Spartacists gave no quarter, it is only natural that the volunteers should fulfil their duty with resolute firmness. They have performed a very difficult task, and if isolated acts of brutality have occurred, our judgement can only be that their actions were only human.

Freikorps units were next recruited to intervene in the Baltic region, where the peace of Brest-Litovsk had vastly extended Germany's control. German dominance was jeopardized by the Bolsheviks, Poles, and the governments of the newly proclaimed republics of Latvia, Lithuania and Estonia, which were supported by the western Allies, who included Britain. Latvian troops, backed by British naval guns, proved a rather different proposition than German urban radicals, and the Freikorps suffered humiliating defeat. The Freikorps attributed this to the cowardly authorities in Berlin, giving themselves further grounds for diffuse resentment as misunderstood and misused heroes. A desultory struggle against insurgent Poles also took place in Upper Silesia.

In Germany, the Freikorps were used to suppress the abortive Munich Soviet and figured in the armed resistance to French occupation of the Ruhr in 1923. They were involved in every prominent political murder and nationalist plot that the Weimar Republic experienced, so their history also sheds light on paramilitary terrorist violence in general. Their most prominent victims were the Catholic politician Matthias Erzberger and the Republic's Jewish Foreign Minister Walther Rathenau. Erzberger was killed on a hiking holiday. Two young hikers he encountered pulled pistols from their rucksacks and killed Erzberger who was armed with a rolled umbrella. Rathenau was shot in the face and then blown up with a grenade in the back of his open car. Seven hundred thousand people lined the streets for his memorial service, a reminder of the extensive basis for democracy in Germany, notwithstanding the activities of small undemocratic minorities.

As this suggests, the Freikorps final mutation was to become members of shady paramilitary death squads, from whence they debouched into the rough-house security organisations of the early Nazi Party where there was unlimited demand for their absence of scruples or squeamishness. They were among those who participated in Hitler's abortive 1923 Beerhall Putsch. Although in 1934 many Freikorps men who had joined the strong arm SA would be murdered by the SS – chiefly to placate Hitler's conservative partners – others would go on to enjoy notoriety under the Third Reich, something Jones discusses in his newly written Afterword. By this time, Hitler had no need of the buccaneering mentality that the Freikorps embodied, preferring the more disciplined and bureaucratised killers of the SS for the enormities he then committed. Some former Freikorps veterans figured in German resistance to his rule.

Jones has written an extremely accomplished book that clarifies a very confused and turbulent period in German history, and which vividly illustrates a particular Fascist mind-set based on experience of mass death, intense camaraderie and a democratic form of elitism to which Jünger and other radical rightist intellectuals attempted to give shape. I am sure many readers will enjoy this remarkable book that is a major contribution to the history of paramilitary violence and to the shocking consequences of the First World War.

Michael Burleigh,
London
December 2003

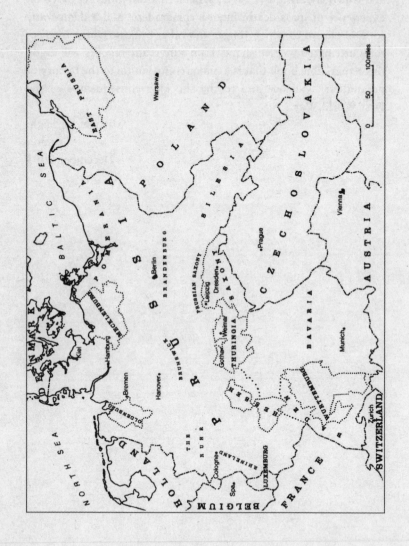

INTRODUCTION

The course of German history is like some great river, shadowed always by a darker and deeper stream, almost a sewer. The difference between these two Germanies has been conveniently summarised as the difference between civilisation and 'kultur'. There is the classic Germany of poets and thinkers – 'Dichter und Denker' – Goethe, Schiller, Kant and Beethoven, of liberal parliaments and democratic constitutions, of heroic Christians and gentlemanly officers. But there is also the older, darker Germany, reaching far back to the deep forests across the Rhine and the Teutonic tribes which resisted the Romans so savagely and successfully. In modern times this is the Germany of 'Richter und Henker' – judges and hangmen, of Prussian militarism, Hitler and Himmler, Auschwitz and the SS . . . and of the Freikorps.

Even a cursory examination of the 'lighter' phases of German history reveals that the darker strata were never far from the surface. Martin Luther, the great religious reformer of the sixteenth century, purger of the corrupt Catholic Church, was the same man who unflinchingly called for a massacre of the 'murdering, thieving' bands of peasants when they dared to rise against their feudal princes. Germany spent most of the seventeenth century in the fratricidal strife and aftermath of the Thirty Years' War, a religious conflict unsurpassed for the sheer scale of savagery and human suffering it inflicted on the country. The eighteenth century saw a nod made towards the spirit of the European Enlightenment, Frederick the Great of Prussia invited Voltaire to his court, and insisted on speaking French. But this same monarch disciplined his soldiers with pitiless brutality. 'Scoundrels!' Frederick yelled at his troops as they flinched at a crucial moment during one of his innumerable battles, 'Do you want to live forever?' It is this contempt for civilised life and individual human value that runs like a red thread throughout German history and links Luther and Frederick via Bismarck to Kaiser Wilhelm II, Ludendorff and the Freikorps leaders . . . and to their poisonous progeny, National Socialism.

In the country's intellectual history the story is the same. The most distinguished German philosophers argued in favour of absolute monarchy (Hegel and Schopenhauer), the primacy of the Will, unreason and the 'Ubermensch' or Superman (Schopenhauer and Nietzsche). The great German military thinker Clausewitz offered the cynical and classical definition of war as the pursuit of politics by other means. The mood even infected the great upsurge of German Romanticism in music and literature. The 'Sturm und Drang' movement had its roots in suicide, madness and the worship of death (Kleist, Büchner, and Holderlin). The greatest composer of the late nineteenth century, Wagner, began as a Liberal revolutionary and ended as an anti-Semitic power worshipper, lost in the misty Sagas of *Götterämmerung*.

Despite galloping industrialisation and its new-found national cohesion, the end of the century saw Germany, behind its rigid facade of a militarised hierarchy, seething with its unresolved heritage of violence and irrationalism, creating a mystic hankering after ends that were diametrically opposed to those of the rest of western Europe. These aims were all the more dangerous for being imprecise and vaguely formulated. They were deeply held and only awaiting an outlet. The Great War and the bitter taste of defeat formed the necessary catalyst for those forces of darkness to emerge from their pits, and to stream hot and destructive through the fissures of German society.

1

BIRTH OF THE STORMTROOPER

'The German people have held off a world of enemies for fifty months.
They will preserve their liberty and unity despite every kind of violence.'
Matthias Erzberger, Chief German Armistice plenipotentiary to
Marshal Foch,
11 November 1918

The German nation that embarked with blithe abandon on the war it had sought so impatiently for so long in August 1914 was a contradiction in terms. Economically it was the growing giant among the European family of nations. The productive power of its heavy industry had long since outstripped its nearest rival, Britain. From 1870 to 1914, German coal production increased eight-fold – Britain's merely doubled. Like an impatient adolescent in a cramped room, young Germany, her population shooting up from 41 million in 1870 to 68 million in 1914, was eager to flex her limbs. She cast jealous eyes on the overseas colonies acquired by Britain and France, seeing them as potential markets that she was being unfairly denied. It was unfair, too, that Britain should still lazily rule the waves. Kaiser Wilhelm II had his answer to that: the construction of a modern navy, the High Seas Fleet. Its purpose was undeclared but obvious – there it lay, menacingly riding at anchor, facing Britain's long east coast across the North Sea.

The political and social structure which held this modern young ogre in place was a complete anachronism: it was as though Germany was riding into the twentieth century in a gleaming new Daimler-Benz car – towed by a mediaeval knight in shining armour. The German Empire, inaugurated as recently as 1871 after the Franco-Prussian war, was by no means a centralised state. It was a loose confederation of nearly thirty Kingdoms, principalities, duchies and 'Free Cities' united only in obedience to the Kaiser – King of the keystone state, Prussia.

The Kaiser had autocratic powers of almost feudal strength. Wilhelm held personal command of foreign and military affairs, as well as Government and Army appointments, finance and trade. Without consulting anyone, the all-Highest could and did make and break his own Chancellors and Cabinets, Generals, Admirals and Ministers. His power was most dramatically illustrated in 1890 when he unceremoniously ditched the man to whom he owed his Imperial Crown – Bismarck. The nation's Parliament, the Reichstag, was an imposing rubber stamp – empowered to debate legislation but not to initiate or enact it.

The Kaiser's throne rested, as it had always done, on bayonets. It was the Prussian Army that had first lifted the state to prominence from the sandy wastes of Pomerania under Frederick, greatest of the Hohenzollerns. It was the army of Gneisenau, Scharnhorst and Blücher that had worn down Napoleon. It was the army of Moltke and Roon that had humbled Denmark, Austria and finally France. If his military machine failed or fell, Wilhelm would crash down along with it.

But he was surrounded by sycophantic courtiers, who had long since realized their master's antipathy to contradiction, discussion or bad news of any sort. Such a monarch was a willing and eager tool for the German military-industrial complex whose interests demanded Germany's greatness and expansion; and hence, inevitably, war.

The German people, as a whole, were distinguished – if that is the word – by blind obedience to authority, social conservatism and tenacious endurance under pressure. What opposition there was to the ruling military-industrial élite was provided by the huge Social Democratic Party (SPD). Founded on the sleeping strength of the working classes and trade unions in the industrial cities, the SPD was ostensibly a Marxist Socialist party. But in practice the party had evolved, in typically German fashion, into the mousily moderate, pragmatic and parliamentary voice of the proletariat. In Lenin's term it had become 'revisionist'; content to co-operate with the state and participate in the parliamentary game. Its professed revolutionary internationalism belied its true patriotic heart. In 1914 the SPD deputies in the Reichstag voted virtually en bloc for the credits necessary to finance the war. 'We shall not betray the Fatherland in its hour of need', said the party's spokesman, Hugo Haase. 'I see no more parties – only Germans', said the Kaiser in delight, and for once the master of bombast spoke no more than the truth. The long and shameful moral decline of the SPD had begun.

At first the Germans reacted against their mounting military difficulties with courage and success: propping up their ailing Austrian allies, by the beginning of 1917 they had brought the Tsar's empire to its knees. On the Western Front they held their own against France and Britain in the great slaughter houses of Verdun and the Somme.

But fear and pessimism as to the eventual outcome of the war were growing and led to nervous changes of command: Falkenhayn, the Kaiser's favourite General, who had master-minded the bloody and ultimately unsuccessful assault on the citadel of Verdun, was sacked as Chief of the General Staff in August 1916 and succeeded by Hindenburg and Ludendorff, who had triumphed at Tannenburg and overseen the subsequent successful prosecution of the war in the east. This marked the eclipse of the Kaiser's personal power and the replacement of the last shreds of civilian rule by open martial law. The Chancellor who had brought Germany into the war, Bethmann Hollweg, was replaced by Michaelis, a pliable tool of the Generals, in July 1917. Germany had become, to all intents and purposes, a military dictatorship. Hindenburg was the imposing figurehead, but the real political and military decisions were taken by the Quartermaster-General at his elbow – Erich Ludendorff. The peppery Ludendorff was a violent proponent of ending the war through outright German victory: not for him the peace without annexations that appeared more and more attractive to politicians of the left and centre.

Ludendorff ensured that the cream of the country's depleted and dwindling resources was reserved for the army's purposes. As a result of Britain's naval blockade, shortages were becoming serious – the bread ration was down to 100 grams a day, meat was 100 grams a week, and fresh vegetables had been replaced by pickled cabbage stalks and turnips. Fats – urgently needed for the making of munitions – were almost unobtainable. The bones of undernourished children curled with rickets, pasty faces were pinched with hunger, the chill of winter bit through threadbare clothes, and the people's discontent swelled with their distended bellies.

Their sullen grumbles found various political voices. As early as 1916, Karl Liebknecht and Rosa Luxemburg, two maverick left-wing members of the SPD, attracted thousands to an open demonstration against the war – and were jailed for their pains. From prison, they founded a new political group, the Spartacus League – named after the leader of a Roman slave revolt. The Spartacists preached international revolution and turning the 'Imperialist War' into a class struggle. Numerically insignificant at first, they exercised an influence out of all proportion to their numbers.

The Spring of 1917 was a decisive moment for the future course of the war, and of Germany's internal political development. In March, the Tsar abdicated under the combined pressure of Russia's disastrous military situation and food riots by the starving population. The following month this blow to the Allies was more than balanced by the entry of the United States into the war. Also in April, with the connivance of the German Government, a veteran Russian revolutionary, Vladimir Ulyanov, better known as Lenin, was smuggled into Russia aboard a sealed train to complete the revolution and finally remove Russia from the war. Partly inspired by the unfolding course of that revolution, and needled by the Spartacists, the strong left-wing of the SPD split away from the parent party in July and constituted themselves as the Independent SPD (USPD).

The USPD programme struck a note midway between the reformist, pragmatic policies of the majority SPD and the revolutionary extremism preached by the starry-eyed Spartacists. The USPD emphasised traditional Marxism, and secured the blessing of the old SPD's two leading intellectual ideologues, Karl Kautsky and Eduard Bernstein. Led by Hugo Haase, who had swiftly repented his reluctant support for the war, the new party eschewed the do-nothing complacency of the cautious SPD leadership and swiftly attracted support as the only legal opposition to the war with a voice in the Reichstag and the Socialist press. Though ostensibly opposed to the Leninist line of 'the dictatorship of the proletariat' associated with Liebknecht and Luxemburg, events soon propelled the USPD to the left: only a week after the new party's founding conference 300,000 workers, including munition makers, took part in a strike wave in the traditionally left-wing cities of Berlin, Leipzig, Magdeburg, Halle and Brunswick.

Later in the summer an unsuccessful mutiny broke out among the sailors of the vaunted High Seas Fleet. Marooned in the ports of Kiel and Wilhelmshaven since the indecisive battle of Jutland in 1916, the morale of the fleet had rotted on a diet of boredom, bad food and inactivity. Strained relations with the ultra-reactionary naval officer class, combined with fears that the war was being needlessly prolonged, made the sailors – like their comrades in Russia – a spearhead of revolutionary activism.

Representatives of the fleet's discontented ratings made contact with the USPD leaders who advised them to offer passive opposition to the war. But before any further action could be taken, the alarmed authorities acted to nip the incipient mutiny in the bud. The ratings' ringleaders were arrested and two of them were summarily shot, 'Pour encourager les autres'. These hasty counter-measures only had the effect of delaying the reckoning; it was as though the authorities were recklessly screwing down a valve on a steadily mounting head of steam. The mutiny was destined to break out anew just over a year later with dramatic consequences for the whole country.

The USPD was not the only new party to appear on the political scene in 1917. September saw the birth of a new party on the extreme right: the Fatherland Party, with a policy of aggressive pursuit of victory through conquest abroad, and repression of opposition to the monarchy at home. Presided over by the father of the High Seas Fleet himself, old Admiral von Tirpitz, the founder of the new party was an obscure American-born Prussian Government bureaucrat complete with shaven head and pince-nez named Wolfgang von Kapp.

The Fatherland Party was spectacularly successful in securing support from a middle class thoroughly alarmed by the subversive rumblings within the working-class movement. Within a few months of its foundation, the party was claiming a mass membership of more than a million, higher even than the pre-war SPD. More than a year before the actual end of the war we see the beginning of an extreme polarisation in German politics: the working class and the unions are moving to the revolutionary left. In reaction, the bourgeoisie, terrified by the prospect of military defeat and red-blooded revolution, run into the arms of the blackest reaction. The peaceful, moderate parties of the middle way did not, it seems, appeal to the dark Germanic 'geist'.

In November 1917, the Bolshevik bacillus injected into the Russian body politic by the German General Staff erupted in a coup which brought Lenin's little party to power in the greatest state in the world and hastened the end of the war in the east. Early the following year, the vindictive peace of Brest Litovsk was dictated to the Bolsheviks by the German military: Russia lost huge chunks of territory – about a third of her land mass – including the whole of the Ukraine, which became a German puppet state, Poland and the Baltic lands. Ludendorff now had a free hand to move the bulk of his forces from the Eastern to the Western Front to make his final bid to break Britain and France before the arrival of the Americans tilted the scales irrevocably in favour of the Allies.

A decisive showdown was now necessary both for internal political as well as external military reasons. As another strike wave in January 1918 made clear, the malnourished population had neither the physical strength nor the moral stamina to stand up to another year of hunger, hardship and war. The demands for a negotiated peace became ever louder among the Socialists and were beginning to permeate the ranks of the moderate Catholic Centre Party. The inflammatory peace-and-bread ideology of the newly-installed Bolshevik regime in Russia was heady wine to soldiers and workers who for three-and-a-half years had eked out a miserable existence on the thin gruel of war and want. The only thing that could justify the sacrifices already made and guarantee Germany's survival as a great power after the war was an outright gamble on military victory, reasoned Ludendorff. If it failed, no one, least of all the military caste, could answer for the consequences. The only question was: where was the die to be cast? After agonised indecision, Ludendorff decided to hurl the main weight of his offensive against the weakest British Army, Gough's Fifth, on the fifty-mile sector of the Western Front north and south of St. Quentin. A total of three army groups – more than sixty divisions – were flung against the British from out of a morning mist at dawn on 21 March.

Ludendorff employed entirely new tactics for the battle, that were later to be of crucial importance for the character and development of the Freikorps. He eschewed the traditional frontal assault by mass waves of infantry that had so frequently and fruitlessly dashed against solid walls of wire. The Germans had raised experimental 'Storm' ('Sturm') or 'Shock' ('Stoss') battalions. Their aim was to spearhead the attacks of the general infantry. Only the youngest, fittest and most intelligent men were selected and trained in these crack formations.

The stormtroops' training, quarters and conditions were quite separate from their former comrades' in the old regiments out of whose ranks they had been recruited. They were dressed in green uniforms with silver facings. Some of them sported the infamous 'Totenkopf' (Death's Head) emblem, originally worn by Blücher's Hussars but later to become the badge of many Freikorps, and later still the symbol of Himmler's SS.

The arms of the stormtroops were also different: they were allowed the officers' privilege of wearing pistols, carried short carbine rifles, and slung on their belts their favourite weapon of all – the distinctive 'potato masher' hand grenade. The men of the squads owed a special loyalty to their commanders and this, along with the unique cameraderie born of belonging to a select élite, was to carry them through into peacetime and render them immune to the germs of mutiny and revolution.

Officers and men in the storm battalions had a freer and more equal relationship than the stiff-necked Prussian discipline that prevailed in the traditional army. The storm soldiers called their superior officers by first names, or addressed them with the intimate 'Du' (Thou), an unheard-of familiarity. Gratitude for their better food, quieter rest camps and longer leave furloughs, was cemented by shared sufferings and the shedding of blood in battle into a spiritual, almost mystical state of mind compounded of profound contempt for the civilian world and bourgeois way of life. At the same time there was the joy of battle, an exalted excitement that was more than mere blood-lust. These men could not believe that their sacrifices for the Fatherland were in vain. They blotted out the looming fact of Germany's imminent defeat and transformed it into an inner victory. They had won the battle within themselves so the evident collapse of the nation was clearly the fault of others: the Socialists, strikers and Spartacists skulking in safety at home; the Jewish war profiteers making Marks from their blood and sweat; the cynical politicians, bargaining away their conquests at the negotiating table.

These self-deceptions bred a murderous resentment and hatred of those who had, in Ludendorff's later notorious phrase: 'Stabbed them in the back'. A more positive, but equally insidious, delusion was that the storm battalions were more than just gallant soldiers, they were an entirely new type of man altogether. The elemental experience of combat had stripped away the deceptions and woolly comforts of the pre-war world. The fire-storm of the trenches had been a 'Great and hard school'. True, many of the bravest and best had fallen: but others had survived, tempered like steel in the furnace of the frontline. Out of the fiery maelstrom a new man had arisen, invincible, clean, ready to build a new world; but even readier to destroy the corrupt remains of the old.

The most articulate spokesman of this attitude to arise from the stormtroopers' ranks was the often-wounded and much-decorated writer-warrior Ernst Jünger. A young veteran of four years' continuous service at the front, Jünger's experience had convinced him that war and struggle were the natural condition of Mankind: 'What can be holier than the fighting man?' Jünger asked. Answering his own rhetorical question he hymned his stormtroop comrades as 'Jugglers of death', 'Masters of explosive and flame', and 'Magnificent beasts of prey.' They were the élite who had learned the war's most profound lesson: 'Man is the bearer, the constantly changing vessel, which contains everything that has been done, thought and felt before him.' Even Death was unimportant to the New Man, for from their graves they fertilised the soil that would raise up innumerable generations to follow and achieve the Germanic ideal – the union of intellect, physique, will and spirit into a dynamic, living whole.

This strange and lofty doctrine of war-worship was probably lost on the majority of stormtroopers who fought from sheer love of a good scrap, but a cruder version of Jünger's ideas filtered into their heads: they certainly had no place in the civilian world. Men snatched from the schoolbench and flung into the jaws of death could hardly be expected to settle comfortably into office routine. Men who had lived daily with the expectation of violent and agonising extinction could care nothing for peace, security, good manners or the rule of law. It was this reckless, nihilist spirit, this devil-may-care, live and die for today attitude that constituted the characteristic mentality of both the stormtrooper and the Freikorps. Brutal, ugly, uncouth but elemental, it was a world away from the civilised comfort of the bourgeois world that called it into being – and then found its spirit, once raised, so very hard to lay.

The stormtroopers were trained to move in small groups across the battlefield, probing for the enemy's weakest points like a surgeon's knife. Any strongpoints were avoided; the stormers merely skirted them and pushed onwards, leaving the essential but unglamorous mopping up to the humble infantry trailing in their wake. The stormers sped gloriously ahead, moving fastest and furthest, set apart from their former comrades even in the hottest moments of action. This conscious separation only served to further heighten the stormers' sense of being a chosen order destined to conquer and rule.

The German armies, with their stormtroop vanguard, accomplished much in the series of great offensives launched by Ludendorff. The first, codenamed 'Michael', on 21 March, put the British Fifth Army to inglorious flight, bit out a great chunk of territory and almost succeeded in severing the British from the French. The second blow, Operation 'Georgette', struck the following month over the blasted old battlegrounds of Flanders and drove the British back to within sight of the Channel. A third offensive – 'Blücher' – let loose at the end of May, utterly broke the Franco-British forces along the Aisne, and brought the Germans, as in 1914, back to the banks of the Marne and within artillery range of Paris. For a moment, it looked as if these superhuman efforts would break the Allied lines, and the French firebrand General, Foch, was appointed as supreme Generalissimo to co-ordinate counterstrikes.

The appearance of German victory was deceptive. In truth the advancing German armies were more dismayed than elated. Their casualties had been extensive, and the losses were increasingly being made-up by the old, the battle-shy and the very young. The draft-dodgers joined the leaders of recent strike waves in the big cities in forced and disgruntled conscription. Even the keenest soldiers in the front wave of the advance were awed by the piles of abandoned Allied food and booty they found. Having been told for months that unrestricted U-boat sinkings were slowly strangling Britain, such abundance was both dispiriting and tempting. Many broke aside from their forward march to gorge themselves, an ominous indication of the sliding state of military morale. Some of the reinforcements who were shipped from the eastern front to the west were infected by the spirit of revolution sweeping Russia. A whispering campaign against the war started to rustle up from the rest-rooms and the troop trains taking new drafts to the front. 'The war is being prolonged', the whisperers told their far from unwilling listeners: 'Down with the dictatorship, away with the ruling caste responsible for all our suffering.' Spartacist sympathisers working in the Imperial Post Office began to insert their inflammatory leaflets into the mails bound for the trenches. The distant voices of Karl Liebknecht and Rosa Luxemburg were heard loud and clear by the war-weary front-line men.

For all the territory won, the enemy seemed as strong as ever. Indeed, with the well-fed Yankee doughboys flooding into France at the rate of 100,000 every month, the balance of military might was tipping ever more dangerously against Germany. Ludendorff's fourth and fifth offensives, launched against the French in June and July, ground to speedy halts in the face of unexpectedly fierce resistance. Ludendorff simply did not possess enough reliable troops, untainted by revolution and defeatism, to make the difference. After Foch launched the first of his counter-attacks on 18 July, the military initiative passed finally and irrevocably to the Allies. Relentlessly, allowing his failing opponents no respite, Foch pressed them ever backwards towards the Rhine. When the British joined in on 8 August with a tank-led offensive in front of Amiens, Ludendorff's last remaining hopes of eventual victory dissolved. He called the day 'The black day of the German army in this war', and noted the ominous reports that new troops going up the line had been greeted by taunts of 'Blacklegs' by the sullen returning soldiers.

Sensing victory before winter, Foch orchestrated a series of lightning 'Tapping' attacks. Switching swiftly from front to front, catching the enemy by surprise, then breaking off the assault and striking somewhere else, the Allies bent the German lines backwards towards breaking point. At Army HQ, Ludendorff's manic moods lurched from depression to absurd optimism. At times, he seemed to his long-suffering staff to be on the very verge of insanity. Finally, on 29 September, his tautened nerves snapped.

2

COLLAPSE OF AN EMPIRE

'I implore you to cherish hatred – a profound, abiding hatred for those animals who have outraged the German people. But the day will come when we will drive them from our Germany. Prepare for that day. Arm for that day. Work for that day.

Capt. Hermann Goering,
speech to officers, December 1918

Germany's mounting woes swarmed around Ludendorff; they could no longer be merely brushed aside. Germany's ally, Bulgaria, was facing complete military collapse in Macedonia. Austria was being pressed backwards into the Alps by the Italians; she had already put out independent peace feelers and her patchwork empire was splitting apart, each race seeking its own salvation. At the end of September, simultaneous attacks on the Western Front by the Belgians, the Americans and the British brought matters to a head. At his headquarters in the pleasant little Belgian town of Spa, Ludendorff at first stormed at the 'Betrayal' he was suffering at the hands of the whole world. His staff were so embarrassed by the outburst that they shut the door of their Chief's room and let his rage burn itself out.

When he recovered some semblance of composure, Ludendorff made his way to Hindenburg, his nominal superior, and peremptorily demanded that terms for an immediate armistice be sought from the Allies. The pliable Commander-in-Chief concurred. Ludendorff had already cleared the way for his plan by summoning the Imperial Chancellor, the elderly Count Georg von Hertling, together with his Foreign Minister, Paul von Hintze. When the puzzled pair arrived in Spa the next morning, they were astounded to be told by the Quartermaster-General that the war was as good as lost and, if the army was to be preserved, an immediate peace must be concluded. In order to speed the peace process, the Government had to be restructured on a broader basis. In other words, the whole High Command, led by Ludendorff, had undergone an overnight conversion to what more rational Germans had been saying for many months. To curry favour with President Wilson and his allies, Ludendorff and Hindenburg accepted the need for a democratic – perhaps even a republican – facade, under cover of which the Army could withdraw from an untenable front, and recoup to enable it to fight another day.

Last and least, there remained one man to be told of Ludendorff's plans: the Kaiser himself. Wilhelm listened meekly when he was summoned that afternoon. In the following days, Count Hertling quietly resigned, and was succeeded by Prince Max of Baden. The Prince was a first cousin of the Kaiser, but he was an intelligent liberal with advanced, some said neo-socialist, ideas. A war veteran who had become chief of the German Red Cross with responsibility for looking after Allied prisoners of war, Max, speedily nicknamed 'Max-Pax', had the right credentials to impress the Allies, yet his Royal blood would reassure worried monarchists and conservatives. Upon his appointment at the beginning of October, Max sent a note to Wilson asking for the Allied armistice terms. At the same time he formed a new coalition Government spanning the National Liberal and Progressive parties of the moderate right, the Catholic Centre party and – for the first time – the Social Democrats. In his reply, Wilson called for more clarification of Max's first peace note, and when the Chancellor wrote back accepting the President's 14 points as a basis for a permanent peace, Wilson upped the ante and demanded that Germany rid herself of her ruling autocracy before the dove of peace could descend.

In the face of this, Max vacillated; he was a Hohenzollern himself and, keen on reform as he was, he could hardly ask his cousin to abdicate outright; things were not yet quite so desperate. For its part, the Army Command reacted to Wilson's demand with fury. Ludendorff and Hindenburg had regained some of their nerve and swung again towards optimism – perhaps they could hold out until the Spring after all. A proclamation was drawn up over Hindenburg's signature, spitting defiance at Wilson and ordering the troops to fight on until the end, to defend the Fatherland's sacred soil. This was suppressed before it could be read out, but an alert telegraphist who sympathised with the USPD copied out the text and sent it to his party in Berlin. When the proclamation was read in the Reichstag, it caused a sensation. Max, furious at the High Command's latest volte face, threatened to resign unless Ludendorff was dismissed. Obedient again, the Kaiser held an audience on 26 October with Hindenburg and Ludendorff. Summoned to the Imperial Bellevue palace in Berlin, Ludendorff was trapped into offering his resignation. It was accepted. The following day, another note to Wilson was despatched by Max. This time there were no quibbles: the German Government was ready to accept virtually any peace terms. But by then it was too late. It took the fallen leader, Ludendorff, to perceive what lay in store. 'Just wait,' he told an aide on his return from his final confrontation with the Kaiser. 'In two weeks we will have no Empire – and no Emperor.'

*   *   *

The scene now shifts, in the dying days of October, away from Berlin, where the Kaiser boards his Royal train bound for his beloved army's HQ at Spa, for the last time. Where Prince Max, stricken like so many others with Spanish 'Flu, lies helplessly awaiting Wilson's mercy, and where Ludendorff packs his bags and dons a pair of blue sunglasses as he prepares to flee into Swedish exile. The action moves north, to the port of Kiel, main home of the High Seas Fleet, fogbound in the autumn mists, but seething with the spirit of mutiny – and revolution.

On 28 October, Admiral Franz von Hipper, hero of Jutland, gave the order to his Fleet to assemble in the Schillig Roads ready for a major offensive operation. As the twenty-four capital ships of the Fleet's three squadrons nosed reluctantly out of harbour towards the rendezvous, wild rumours swept the decks. No one knew exactly what sort of operation the Admiral had in mind: some said that the officers were intent on one last do-or-die confrontation with the Royal Navy. Others opined that old Admiral Tirpitz – or even the Kaiser himself – was personally leading the Fleet out for its *Götterdämmerung*. In reality, the confused intentions of the Admirals were to lure the British Grand Fleet south by means of mine-laying and destroyer raids on the Thames estuary, and then engage them in a battle, which would, hopefully, result in a German victory and vastly improve the prospects for favourable peace terms, or at least save the honour of the Fleet, mothballed in harbour since Jutland in 1916.

But to the sailors on the big ships, the mission meant destruction at best, senseless provocation that might well prolong the war, more likely a one-way ticket to the bottom of the North Sea. The ratings decided that they had had enough; enough of their officers' vainglory and absurd arrogance; enough of hanging around in the dull northern ports, scraping barnacles and painting the hulls of the unused ships; enough of lousy food and ferocious discipline. In a word: enough of the war.

As daylight dimmed, unauthorised signal lights winked out along the dark superstructures of the battleships and cruisers riding at anchor in the Jade estuary. The crews were communicating their discontent. When Hipper summoned his Captains to a pre-mission meeting at eight o'clock, sailors manning some of the skippers' boats had mysteriously vanished and had to be rooted out.

At ten, just two hours before the scheduled sailing time, Hipper realized that he could not lead such an unreliable fleet into action. Acts of sullen indiscipline were turning into open mutiny. On board three ships in particular, the *Thuringen*, the *Helgoland* and the *Markgraf*, stokers threatened to draw their boilers rather than put to sea. Hipper was forced to postpone the mission, using the excuse of foggy conditions to hide the climbdown.

At dawn on 30 October, the crew of the *Thuringen* refused renewed orders to set sail and gathered below decks for an unauthorised meeting. That afternoon, Hipper again tried to get the recalcitrant crews to move. The stokers' response was to carry out their threat, and boilers were doused on board the *Thuringen* and the *Helgoland*. When orders were given to weigh anchor, capstans were jammed and the ships immobilised. Hipper had no alternative other than to back down; he cancelled the operation completely and gave orders for the Fleet to disperse to its home ports.

Hipper then made a successful attempt to arrest the main instigators of the mutiny. Under the threatening torpedo tubes of loyal U-boats and destroyers, squads of marines were able to board the *Thuringen* and the *Helgoland* and remove some 500 of the most mutinous men. As the Fleet sailed for home, the disaffected Third Squadron, consisting of the *König*, the *Markgraf*, the *Kronprinz Wilhelm* and the *Grosser Kurfust*, was directed to the large industrial port of Kiel, where a new Commander, Admiral Souchon, had just taken office. The decision was a major blunder by the

Admirals: ill-fed, made idle by the Fleet's lack of action, Kiel's dockers had become thoroughly radicalised, and the port was a stronghold of the USPD.

When the vessels arrived in Kiel early on 1 November, 180 more mutineers were taken off the *Markgraf* and locked up in the town's naval prison. The following day, Saturday 2 November, Stoker Karl Artelt, a lower deck agitator, led 500 of his comrades to hold a rally in a park known as the Exercise Place. For the first time, the sailors were addressed by a civilian, an ally of Artelt named Artur Popp, who led the local USPD branch in Kiel. The sailors resolved to meet again the following day in the same place and in greater numbers, to compel the release of their comrades.

When the meeting went ahead the next day, it became clear at once that it was beyond the power of the officers to stem the flood of revolt: more than twenty thousand men, sailors and workers, thronged into the Exercise Place to hear Artelt's and Popp's harangues. The speakers renewed their demands for the freeing of the arrested men, but also – again for the first time – made specifically political demands as well. Calls for a Republic were made, and a resolution was passed setting up a Workers' and Sailors' Council – a Soviet – to by-pass their officers. Another sign of the influence of the Russian revolution came when the crowds, waving red flags, struck up the 'Internationale' as the meeting broke up. This time, the sailors did not disperse and meekly return to their ships. Emboldened by their numbers they marched through the deserted Sunday streets to the Feldstrasse where the Naval jail was located. The prison was protected by a thirty-strong naval platoon drawn from the still loyal ranks of the smaller ships, under the command of a Lieutenant Steinhauser. As the roaring crowd bore menacingly down upon him, the Lieutenant ordered his squad to fire over the heads of the advancing column. The marchers slowed, but continued to edge ever closer. Steinhauser gave his men the order to fire directly into the mob. Immediately, the march scattered in confusion, leaving eight dead and thirty wounded on the street behind them. Steinhauser himself was shot and severely wounded in the ensuing chaos; the revolution had drawn its first blood.

The sailors knew now that they could expect no mercy from their officers if they drew back and gave in. They elected their own representative councils on each ship, raided the vessels' armouries and disarmed their officers. Ashore, the Kiel workforce declared a general strike and public transport ground to a halt. The loyalist smaller ships slipped out of harbour.

Admiral Souchon, by now thoroughly alarmed, summoned help from the army base at nearby Altona – one infantry company marched into town and managed to reach him, but another detachment was disarmed by the sailors as its train rolled in. By Monday afternoon, 40,000 mutinous sailors and their worker allies ruled Kiel. Souchon sent for Artelt, who had been proclaimed leader of the Kiel Workers' and Sailors' Council, and suffered the supreme humiliation of having to ask to know the ex-stoker's demands.

Artelt's list of grievances was surprisingly moderate, considering the blood that had already been spilled and the armed power that he now wielded. He asked only that the Fleet not be ordered to sea without consultation with the crews, and that the mutineers already arrested be freed. (This was granted.) The other demands focussed on old grumbles like the quality of food and excessive deference to officers in speech and saluting. Souchon played for time by meeting some of the demands and issuing an order to his few remaining loyal men not to fire on the mutineers. In the meantime, he sent a telegram to Berlin asking urgently for a Government representative to come to Kiel and calm the situation.

The man picked for this delicate task was a shambling 50-year-old bull-necked SPD veteran named Gustav Noske. As Noske played the key role in reversing the course of the German revolution, it is worth describing him in some detail. Originally a basket-weaver from Brandenburg, Noske has risen through the party hierarchy as a political journalist by dint of energy, hard work and steadfast loyalty to the cautious party line. As a Reichstag member before the war, Noske had made a special study of military matters and acquired the reputation of being the SPD's expert on questions of defence and the armed forces. During the war, he assiduously courted the Army officer corps by frequent visits to the front. What little trace of orthodox Socialism he had ever possessed was, by 1918, thoroughly expunged. The man who came to Kiel was as patriotic and chauvinist a German as the most hardened militarist could wish for. Barely concealing his contempt for the mutinous masses and his loathing of the left, Noske was nevertheless a decisive and formidably energetic leader of men; a powerful Trojan horse of the right inside the SPD camp. He exemplified the readiness of the majority Socialist leaders to betray their revolutionary followers into the hands of militarism and reaction.

Noske was unsure of the reception that he and his fellow delegate, the Progressive Party chief, Konrad Haussmann, would receive. As his train steamed into Kiel station on the evening of 4 November he was amazed to be greeted by a vast throng of cheering sailors who welcomed him rapturously and – much to his embarrassment – chaired him shoulder high to a waiting car, bedecked with a huge red flag. Noske was driven slowly through streets filled with cheering crowds to a mass meeting on the Wilhelmplatz. The dazed plenipotentiary was hoisted on to a rostrum and invited to address the enthusiastic audience. Hastily casting aside a symbolic sword that had been thrust into his hands, Noske made a lightning assessment of the situation.

He could see that the sailors were a dangerous rabble, yet they were still unsure of themselves and politically ignorant to the point of naivety. (Why else had they greeted Noske, the pillar of reaction, as though he were Lenin, arriving at the railway station to usher in the revolutionary apocalypse?) Noske's oafish appearance concealed a quick and shrewd brain as well as an unbridled self-confidence and appetite for power. He perceived that the fluid mob, correctly handled, could be pacified, rendered harmless and quietly suppressed. No false modesty blocked his assumption that he was the ideal man to reverse the revolutionary tide. Noske told the crowd that there must be a restoration of order before their demands could be considered. But even as he spoke, the sound of a stray sniper's shot echoed around the square. 'What kind of "Schweinerei" is this?' demanded the outraged Noske. Affronted by the breakdown in discipline, Noske realized that he was treading on eggshells; one false move and his counter-revolutionary intentions would be exposed. In order to channel the revolutionary flood into quiet waters he would have to play along with the prevailing militant mood.

Hastily finishing his speech, Noske moved on to Kiel's Trade Union headquarters where he met the Sailors' and Workers' Council and learnt their demands. Noske sent the first of a barrage of telegraphed reports to Berlin. He assured the Government that he could handle events provided that the Army authorities refrained from sending more troops to combat the well-armed sailors. Noske also asked that the ships which had left Kiel should return and embark the mutineers before the revolutionary contagion spread further inland. He then returned to the railway station where Admiral Souchon was being held hostage in the second class waiting room, which was littered with confiscated officers' daggers and epaulettes which had been torn from the shoulders of their uniforms. Noske negotiated the humiliated Souchon's release, and advised him to leave town. Throughout the night, using a mixture of pleas, threats and wheedling cajoling, Noske strove to damp down the still tense atmosphere. During that edgy night, the commander of the Kiel fortress, Captain Heine, was shot dead by mutineers and two officers on the *König* met a violent end.

The following morning, a haggard Noske met Artelt and demanded that the bloodshed should cease. The same day he formed his own pliable nine-man 'Supreme Sailors' Council' – ostensibly to help him run the city, actually to provide a cloak of revolutionary legitimacy to cover his own designs. The Council obligingly made Noske Governor of Kiel and then counter-signed every order he made. With feverish energy, in pouring rain, Noske hurried from meeting to meeting, exhorting, hectoring, bullying the sailors back to the path of duty. His policy combined the stick – threats of retribution, and English invasion – and the carrot – acceding to the more moderate demands, and flying in a planeload of back pay from Berlin. By these means, within a few days, Noske single-handedly restored law and order to Kiel. He persuaded the crews to man their deserted ships, got the citizens to take down the red flags and even persuaded his political rival, the USPD leader Haase, to leave town when the latter arrived to re-ignite the guttering flames of revolt. Noske, the one-man counter-revolution, had, by sheer force of personality coupled with political skill, succeeded in turning the tide in the revolution's own birthplace. But even he could not manage to contain and confine the revolution to Kiel, and within days the inflammatory spirit was spreading throughout Germany.

On 5 November, the port of Lübeck was seized by revolutionary sailors. On the 6th, Cuxhaven, Bremen and the huge port-city of Hamburg fell into the hands of Workers' and Sailors' Councils. In Hamburg the USPD called a general strike and turned the local paper, the *Hamburger Echo,* into the *Rote Fahne* (Red Flag). On the following day, the revolutionary fever had spread inland to Hanover, Oldenburg and Cologne, and by the 8th, revolutionary councils controlled all major west and central

German cities including Frankfurt, Leipzig, Munich and Magdeburg. Every train brought 'Red' sailors streaming into the German capital, and on 9 November, the revolution reached Berlin.

November 9 was the decisive day of the German revolution. The old German order – Kaiser and Army – crumbled away and the only question left to resolve was: what sort of republic? Was it to be the proletarian People's Republic preached by Liebknecht and Luxemburg and to a lesser extent by the USPD, or the pragmatic, moderate and eventually fatally compromised Social Democracy of the old SPD leaders Ebert, Scheidemann and Noske and the bourgeois parties of the Centre?

The immediate priority which temporarily united Max, the SPD and the Army Generals was the necessity of rolling back the tidal wave of revolution sweeping across Germany, and if this objective was to be achieved, then the war must be ended – and in hours rather than days. Power, momentarily, lay in the streets with the teeming crowds of men and women, uniformed and civilian, who surged solemnly up and down in their drab grey and blue clothes, under billowing red banners.

At noon on 6 November, Max arranged a meeting between Ludendorff's successor, General Wilhelm Groener, and the SPD leaders, headed by Friedrich Ebert. Max reasoned that only a compact between the 'rational' military chiefs and the 'reasonable' Socialists could maintain some sort of order. He had chosen his men well. Ebert and Groener were both Swabians, hailing from that cosy south-west corner of Germany, renowned for its reasonableness, lack of extremism and prudent, cautious complacency. Both were the sons of humble working men who understood each other well. Groener, in his wartime capacity as supremo of railways and transport and later as organiser of economic warfare, had come into contact with Ebert the Trade Union stalwart, and both these mild-mannered men liked what they had seen.

Now the moon-faced soldier-technocrat and the roly-poly saddler's son put their heads together. The SPD chief told Groener that only the Kaiser's immediate abdication would suffice. The SPD supporters were already showing signs of slipping away to the left – into the waiting arms of the USPD or even Liebknecht's Spartacists. Groener was non-committal at first. He had only recently returned from the Russian front and was not aware how deeply the revolution was embedded. Max decided to force the issue. He had heard that very morning that Foch and the Allies were at last willing to receive a German armistice delegation. Max hastily assembled one willing to carry out the distasteful – and dangerous – duty. To head his Commission, the Chancellor chose yet another fat man from the south: Matthias Erzberger, leader of the Catholic Centre Party.

Erzberger was a peculiar phenomenon in German politics, a puffing, plump and bespectacled figure, who looked, in the words of a disdainful aristocratic acquaintance, 'Just like an ornamental beer cork'. His ruthless ambition and driving energy had led him to be elected as the Reichstag's youngest member at the age of 28, and to become his party's leader when he was 44. He had moved swiftly – and, many said, opportunistically – from a position of militant pan-German aggression and aggrandisement early in the war to one of pacifism and defeatism by July 1917 when he made a courageous pro-peace speech in the Reichstag. Erzberger's weird combination of slippery self-advancement coupled with a caustic schoolmaster's tongue and a willingness to take up unpopular positions on matters of principle had made him many political enemies. Nevertheless, he was widely acknowledged to have few masters in the arts of negotiation and debate. All in all, he was ideally fitted to be the scapegoat of the defeated nation.

The Prince lost no time in packing Erzberger off on a special train to Spa; from there he would be conducted through the front lines to his appointment with Foch. For appearance's sake, he was accompanied by a retired ambassador, an elderly general with a French wife and a junior naval officer; but the military were very careful to distance themselves from the disgrace of defeat. The main – and ultimately fatal – responsibility was to fall on Erzberger's broad peasant shoulders.

After a gloomy and hasty lunch at Spa, Erzberger and his companions set out in teeming rain for the front. Two of their five cars crashed on the outskirts of Spa, leaving the plenipotentiaries huddled in the remaining three. The incident can hardly have boosted Erzberger's already battered confidence. At Spa the General Staff had treated him almost as a leper. Various excuses were made as to why no high-ranking officer would have anything to do with the bedraggled mission. Old Hindenburg grasped the hated politician by the hand with the pious farewell; 'God go with you – and try and get the best deal you can for our country.' But for all his fair words, it was painfully clear to the shrewd Erzberger that neither Hindenburg nor any of his officers would have anything to do with the defeat that they had brought down on their heads.

At the German lines a white flag was fixed to the leading car and the little procession wobbled out over shell-cratered tracks into the darkness masking the French front. A bugler stood blowing short blasts on the running board of the car to warn of their approach. After 150 yards French soldiers emerged out of the gloom and Erzberger was escorted into the nearby town of La Capelle where a train was waiting.

By 9 a.m. the following morning, Friday 8 November, the German party had reached the forest of Compiègne, north-east of Paris. They were ushered into a railway waggon drawn up on a railway siding among the dripping trees. After a few minutes of tense waiting, Marshal Foch entered, accompanied by his aide, General Weygand, and three British Naval officers. The old Gascon savoured every moment of shame that the Boche were suffering; he put them through the hoop of pretending to cancel the conference on learning that the Germans had no concrete peace proposals to put but were merely waiting on his mercy. But, at last, Foch allowed Weygand to read the eighteen crushing clauses that made up the Allied peace conditions. They included: evacuation of all occupied territory within a fortnight, surrender of all submarines and internment of Germany's High Seas fleet, abandonment of the Brest-Litovsk treaty and crippling reparations – in both cash and kind – for damage caused during the four years of the war. As Weygand intoned the terrible terms, his voice was interrupted by the sound of muffled weeping; two of the officers with Erzberger were choking back tears. Erzberger himself remained mute. Ever the professional politician, he dealt in facts rather than sentiment, and he was too realistic a man to hide the truth from Foch. He pleaded with the Marshal to stop the fighting that very day, without waiting for the German Government to reply to the Armistice terms. 'Our armies are a prey to anarchy', he admitted. 'Bolshevism menaces them, and Bolshevism may win all over Germany and then threaten France herself.'

Back in Germany, events were bearing out Erzberger's words: in Stuttgart, the Mercedes-Daimler-Benz work-force struck; in Friedrichshafen, home of the Zeppelin airship, the workers set up their own council; in Kassel, the garrison commander himself led his troops in revolt. In Berlin, Prince Max again sent for Ebert. They shared a common objective: stopping the revolution in its tracks. It was on this occasion that Ebert made his celebrated remark that he hated Social revolution 'like sin'. Indeed, he told Max that although he thought it essential that the Kaiser abdicate, he and the other SPD leaders would have no objection to one of

Wilhelm's younger sons, Prince Eitel Friedrich, assuming the Crown in his father's stead. Only the isolated Court at Spa seemed unaware that the Kaiser's day was done.

On the 7th the USPD, seizing the chance to upstage their bitter rivals in the majority SPD, had called no fewer than 26 separate meetings in Berlin for that evening. Frightened by the spectre of imminent revolt, Ebert told Max that the Kaiser had to go in less than twenty-four hours. Failing this promise, he could no longer hold back the masses.

On the 8th, Max spoke to his cousin on the telephone in Spa. Dropping the formal mode of address, he spoke to Wilhelm man-to-man 'as a relative' in the second person singular: 'Your abdication has become necessary to save Germany from civil war.' Wilhelm would not budge. On Saturday 9 November, Max was wakened in Berlin with the news that the USPD had called for a general strike the previous night. Before seven, the SPD's number-two man, Philipp Scheidemann, was on the phone, nervous as a kitten and threatening to resign if the Kaiser did not go within an hour. Already the streets were filling with thousands of striking workers, joined by Red sailors, carrying placards reading 'Brothers, Don't Shoot' in case they met soldiers who might feel some sense of loyalty to the old regime. The message was hardly necessary, since unit by unit, the army were leaving their posts and joining the rebels. Even élite troops like the 'Naumberger Jäger Battalion' were reported to have gone over to the Reds. A meeting of the SPD presidium voted to withdraw from the Government at once. Leaving the meeting, one of the party leaders explained, 'There was nothing else to do. We were obliged to jump into the revolution if we did not want to lose leadership of the masses.'

At Spa, a thick symbolic fog hung over the sombre chateau housing the Imperial headquarters. The Kaiser chatted to his aides, optimistically predicting that the Allies would come to his aid in order to save Europe from rampant Bolshevism. At the nearby Hotel Brittanique, Hindenburg could have told a different story. Haggard after a sleepless night and clutching a sheaf of telegrams from Berlin with their stories of disorder, revolt and civil war, the old Prussian summoned Groener. The two of them drove grimly over to the Kaiser.

Tears ran down Hindenburg's cheeks and his words would not come. It was left to Groener to explain. Equably, and as gently as he could, Groener declared that not only was the home front convulsed with revolution, but there were hardly any loyal troops left to send against the revolutionaries. 'Sire,' concluded Groener bluntly: 'You no longer have an army . . . It no longer stands behind your Majesty.' Wilhelm demanded that Groener put his disloyal words in writing and asked angrily, 'Have the troops not taken their military oath to me?' Groener took a deep breath. 'In circumstances such as these, Sire, oaths are merely words.'

To the taunts of the Kaiser's sycophants that he did not understand the heart and spirit of the Prussian fighting man, Groener stolidly replied: 'I have different information.' Not only had the Kaiser's own regiment, the Second Division of Guards, flatly refused to march on Cologne and suppress the revolution there, but the reports of thirty-nine of the fifty top officers of the army who could be contacted were to hand. They had been compiled by a Colonel Wilhelm Heye who had put two simple questions to each officer in turn. Could the Kaiser lead his armies back to Germany and crush the revolution? and, Would the men fight reliably against Bolshevism when they got home? To the first question only one replied with a certain 'Yes', 23 said no, the rest were uncertain. To the second question 8 said 'Yes', 19 'No' and twelve were unsure. All ideas of the Kaiser joining his son the Crown Prince and marching back to bring his disloyal subjects to heel, dissolved in the mist like the fantasies they were.

Scheidemann's proclamation of the Republic in late morning came just in time. In a theatrical gesture Liebknecht had taken

possession of the Imperial Palace and crawled into the Kaiser's
bed to snatch a few minutes' sleep. But that afternoon, at 4 p.m.,
he roused himself to address the immense throng of people
gathered expectantly in the streets outside: 'The day of liberty has
dawned!' he hoarsely proclaimed: 'A Hohenzollern will never
again stand at this place . . . I proclaim the free Socialist republic
of Germany. . . We extend out our hands to all Germans and call
on them to complete the world revolution. Those among you who
want the world revolution raise your hands . . .' with Teutonic
obedience a forest of hands shot up to greet the revolution.

As darkness fell there were two centres of power in Berlin, both
claiming the allegiance of the people, and both insisting that theirs
was the correct way forward for the nation. As the Kaiser's
authority collapsed, the vacuum was filled – officially – by the
Social Democrats, to whom the trappings of authority had been
reluctantly handed. They held the offices of state, and commanded
the grudging allegiance of the civil service and the officers of the
army. To their left stood Liebknecht's and Luxemburg's tiny
Spartacist group, coupled with their Independent allies, the USPD,
whose might rested on the shop stewards' committees – the
'Obleute' – in giant factories. These shadowy but powerful figures
could bring industrial production to a standstill and have an army
of workers on the streets at an hour's notice. Milling somewhere
between the two power-bases were the people themselves, the
mobs of workers, soldiers and sailors who were in a state of
revolutionary ferment, but leaderless and unsure of what to do
with the power that had fallen so easily into their hands.
Parliamentary democracy or revolutionary Socialism – these were
the two ways open to Germany.

A year earlier, in Russia, a similar situation had been resolved
in favour of the revolutionary way by the ruthless action of Lenin
and Trotsky, backed by the disciplined cadres of their Bolshevik
party and an élite of revolutionary soldiers and sailors. A sudden

coup d'etat had deposed Ebert's equivalent, the moderate Socialist Kerensky, and placed power in the hands of the Bolsheviks. In Germany, the situation was different: Liebknecht and Luxemburg lacked the ruthlessness of their Russian colleagues, their followers were less organised, and, most important of all, they faced the relentless opposition of the army officers who were determined, at all costs, to stop the revolution in its tracks, and, if possible, to reverse it. Unlike the Spartacists, they had a clear plan of action and – in the bulky person of Gustav Noske – they had discovered the tool with which to carry out their counter-revolutionary scheme.

But the events of the decisive 9 November were not yet quite played out. In Spa, it was the supreme loyalist himself, old Hindenburg, who first suggested the heretical idea that now that the Kaiser's abdication had been foisted on him, he might consider crossing the nearby border into Holland, 'in dire emergency'. At five o'clock the Kaiser summoned his military chiefs to bid a fond farewell. Only Groener was bitterly snubbed: 'I have no longer anything to do with you,' said Wilhelm, refusing to shake the General's hand: 'You are merely a General from Württemburg'. Clearly, the ultimate insult to occur to his Prussian mind.

At 7.30 p.m., the Kaiser ordered his car and was driven to the Royal train, which was standing, with steam up, ready for an instant departure, at a siding in Spa station. But over dinner, he still dithered: changing his mind three times in the space of an hour. Finally, recognising the utter hopelessness of his position, he gave orders that the train should leave at 5 a.m. the next morning. The Kaiser said nothing of his going to his commanders, but when they awoke on Sunday morning, the train had left.

3

'REVOLUTION OR REPUBLIC?'

'I hate the Social Revolution like sin!'

Friedrich Ebert,
First Chancellor of the German Republic, November 1918

As dusk fell on 9 November Friedrich Ebert paced the carpet of his new quarters, the Reich Chancellor's office. The ancient dreams of Socialism seemed fulfilled, yet he was mortally afraid. When Prince Max, his predecessor, dropped by to make his formal farewell, Ebert clawed at him as a drowning man grasps at a straw. He begged the Prince to stay on in Berlin as the 'Administrator' of the new regime, a post unheard of under the constitution, which had clearly just popped into Ebert's head. Max politely declined. 'Herr Ebert,' he said gravely, 'I commit the German Empire to your safe keeping.'

'I have lost two sons for this Empire,' Ebert gloomily replied, revealing in one sentence his innate patriotism and essential monarchism. If there was ever a reluctant revolutionary, Friedrich Ebert was he.

Later that same night, Ebert received a telephone call from the

Army command at Spa. Groener was at the other end of the line. The General had two questions to put to the Chancellor. First, was he willing to restore order to the anarchic country? Ebert assured Groener that he was. Secondly, was he willing to resist 'Bolshevism' to the death? Again, Ebert asserted that the social revolution had no more bitter enemy than himself. In that case, said Groener, the new Government could rely on the Army to play its part. The Commander, Hindenburg, would stay at his post, as would all the other officers and the Army would place itself at the Government's disposal to put down any manifestations of rebellion. Ebert replaced the telephone with relief. At the heavy price of putting himself in hock to the Military for ever more, he had secured the immediate survival of his regime. From now on he conversed with Groener on the secret line to Spa almost every evening, telling him of the progress of events in Berlin, and in turn receiving advice – or instructions, depending on interpretation – on how best to deal with the unfolding situation. In reality, both the wily Swabians were bluffing each other. Groener had no means of knowing whether the rank and file of the Army, mutinous and beaten as they were, had the will or the means to put down the revolution. Ebert, for his part, had to preserve a revolutionary front to appease his left, while taking secret instructions from the remnants of the old power. Both men needed time to build up their scattered forces, and time was what their conversations bought them.

For Ebert, the following days would be occupied in bringing the revolution under control and checking it, while at the same time giving his more radical Socialist colleagues the impression that it was continuing at full throttle, and indeed, was being institutionalised as the motor of Government. Groener, not only steering the revolution into safe channels but actively countering it, had a scheme brought to his notice devised in the fertile brain of one of his military protégés, Major Kurt von Schleicher.

Schleicher was one of those men who seem destined from the cradle to play a devious, sinister and shadowy role in history – his very name, in German, means 'Creeper'. The political intrigue and plotting which he began in these November days was to lead him, eventually, to the Ministry of Defence and – briefly – to become Reichs Chancellor just before Hitler took power in 1933. His relentless conspiracies made him more enemies than friends on both right and left, and there were few tears shed for him when he was shot down by SS killers on 30 June 1934 – one of the more prominent victims of the 'Night of Long Knives'.

Schleicher's plan was for the Reichswehr to recruit 'new forces on the basis of voluntary service to protect the Government and secure Germany's menaced borders'. In other words, to junk the crumbling regular formations and to drum up a new army from scratch to act as the mailed fist of the counter-revolution. Such was the origin of the Freikorps.

The new forces Schleicher had in mind would not be entirely mercenary. Their officers were to be from the regular Reichswehr, and trusted soldiers from the front lines were to form their core and backbone. Schleicher also wanted to tap the untarnished patriotism of the young military cadets and right-wing students, born at the turn of the century, who were just too young to have fought in the war and hence to have been exposed to the debilitating experience of trench warfare, defeat, and revolutionary propaganda. Together, these two strands would prove a formidable fighting combination.

Independently of Schleicher, such formations were already coming into being. One of the first areas where they sprang to birth was Kiel. Immediately after the Naval mutiny, a member of Admiral Scheer's staff, Lieutenant Wilfried von Löwenfeld, had begun to recruit fellow officers with the aim of protecting themselves and forming the nucleus of a new and purified Navy. More concretely, in the words of one of Löwenfeld's cohorts,

U-Boat Lieutenant Lothar von Arnauld de la Perière, the eventual goal of the group was to 'Drain the Red swamp'. Löwenfeld himself blamed the Ebert government for the revolution and made little secret of his wish to 'struggle against those in power – both overtly and covertly'. Thus, even in their earliest days, these groups which were to form the heart wood of the Freikorps had secret – and sometimes not-so-secret – political ambitions directly contrary to their ostensible purpose of protecting the existing Republican regime. In reality, almost all of them were poisonously contemptuous of the Ebert government and privately resolved to bring it down once the immediate threat of Red revolution had receded.

For the moment, however, that threat was all too real. Sunday 10 November saw an uneasy calm prevailing in the streets of Berlin. In the city's prosperous West End the swirling proletarian mobs that had ruled the streets on the day before were gone. But in the crowded factories of east Berlin the workers were once more massing, this time at the bidding of the revolutionary shop stewards. Their task was the election of workers' councils – 'Räte', the German equivalent of the Russian Soviets – which that afternoon would hold a mass meeting in the Busch Circus assembly hall to install and legitimise the new People's Government. The shape of that Government was as yet uncertain, and so was the fate of the revolution.

Ebert knew that he would have to make at least a show of co-operating with the USPD and the Shop Stewards. Heavily influenced by Karl Liebknecht who was still nominally a USPD member, they held out for an all-Socialist Government, an immediate signing of the armistice and all legislative, executive and judicial power to be placed in the hands of the workers' and soldiers' councils. Desperate for time, Ebert agreed to the first two conditions. But he stolidly refused to allow power to pass into the hands of the 'Räte' unless this were ratified by the national assembly he was planning to call.

The shopfloor elections must have pleased Ebert. Influenced by heavy propaganda from the official SPD press, which called in blazing headlines for 'No Fratricidal War', and lulled into a mood of lazy generosity by the apparent ease of their victory, the mass of workers, reverting to cautious type, voted en masse for candidates who were prepared to give Ebert and the SPD the benefit of the doubt. Simultaneous elections in the military barracks for the parallel soldiers' councillors produced results even more favourable to the SPD. Influenced by the flaming oratory of Otto Wels, an SPD leader who, like Noske, had a down-to-earth manner which commended him to soldiers, the troops decided to support the Ebert line and accompanied Wels on a mass march to the Busch Circus. A solitary Spartacist supporter, sensing that the wind was turning, shouldered his way towards Wels and threatened him with a revolver. 'You dog!' he shouted, 'You are going to ruin everything for us.'

While the elections were in progress that morning, Ebert himself was chairing a Government meeting. Top of the agenda was the question of the armistice. Erzberger and his delegates at Campiègne, pens poised over the damning document of surrender, were waiting for word from the new masters in Berlin. Prodded by the High Command under Hindenburg for a speedy decision, Ebert told Erzberger to sign. This act, forced on him by a right wing too cowardly to accept responsibility for their own defeat, would cost Erzberger his life and earn himself and Ebert the stigma of 'November criminals', a phrase which, constantly repeated by Hitler's raucous voice, etched itself into the minds of the German nation. Ebert had taken yet another step towards his own eventual destruction. He was bartering away his options as the price of temporary survival.

At lunchtime, word reached the Chancellor that the USPD Independents had agreed to join his Government: a Council of six Ministers, or 'People's Commissars' was set up, comprising equal representation from the two Socialist parties. There was Ebert himself, Scheidemann and another SPD chief, Landsberg; the Independents contributed their leader, Haase, a colourless functionary named Dittmann, and Emil Barth, a representative of the revolutionary shop stewards.

The meeting in the Busch Circus that was to determine the immediate outcome of the revolution was a tumultuous affair attended by almost three thousand aspiring politicians, soldiers, workers and assorted onlookers. Although Barth was in the chair, Ebert dominated the proceedings from the start with a powerful opening speech stressing the need for unity among all strands of Socialists. Haase reluctantly backed this theme in line with his decision to participate in the Government. An attempt by Barth, on behalf of the shop stewards, to form an action committee dominated by the USPD whose real purpose would be to by-pass the Government, was defeated, largely by the bloc of 1000 pro-Government soldiers who chanted in unison 'Unity! Unity!' Liebknecht was howled down when he denounced Ebert and the SPD as traitors to the revolution. At one point, exasperated by the confusion and indiscipline of the meeting, a group of soldiers stormed the speakers' podium and proposed to install an outright military regime – a threat of things to come. Eventually, the meeting confirmed the Government of People's Commissars in office, and Ebert left, satisfied that the immediate threat to his power had been removed.

From the start the new Republic, and the Majority Social Democrats of the SPD who formed its mainstay, had earned the unremitting hostility of the Right for their supposed part in the general downfall and humiliation. The right, of course, were wilfully blind to the fact that the SPD leadership had played no voluntary part in the revolution, but had been reluctantly propelled along, kicking and screaming, in the wake of tumultuous events. Ebert hated the mob, and hated the revolution – he had said so on numerous occasions. He lost no opportunity to conspire with the blackest reactionaries to thwart all plans for revolution and even mild reform. He professed to see enemies only on the Left, whereas to anyone with even half an eye, the forces of the extreme Left were small, splintered, ill-disciplined, unarmed and pathetically disorganised. There was no tightly-knit Bolshevik party, as in Russia, tempered by years of clandestine revolutionary conspiracy and schooled to take power. There was merely the newly formed and intellectualised group of Spartacists clustered around Liebknecht and Luxemburg, and the leaderless mass of rank-and-file soldiers and sailors whose main aim was demobilisation and return to their homes, jobs and families. These pathetic particles were the reality behind the myth of the Bolshevik bogy which terrified the SPD chiefs in their beds and persuaded the good burghers of Germany that they stood on the brink of anarchy.

But it is rarely reality that motivates history. The perception of the Left's enemies was that Germany had been 'Stabbed in the back'. When it came to looking for the culprits, they lumped Ebert and Scheidemann in with Liebknecht, Barth and Luxemburg. They were all Reds – Socialists – weren't they? Then they must all hang together. To quote that old demented ruffian Ludendorff: 'The revolutionaries' greatest piece of stupidity was to leave us all alive. Well, if I ever come to power again, there will be no pardons. With a good conscience I would have Ebert, Scheidemann and company strung up and dangling.' The next few years would show how very close Ludendorff and those around him came to carrying out their threat.

When a revolution does not go forward, it begins to retreat, and in the days and weeks following 10 November, the tide turned. The bourgeoisie awoke from their stupified paralysis and began to organise against their enemies; the army officer corps recovered from the debacle of Spa and began actively to plot their return to power and prestige; the revolutionaries themselves, in the grey December light, awoke from the heady intoxication of revolt and resumed old German habits of caution and obedience.

An early manifestation of the rapidly restored confidence of the army command came on 6 December, when the first of many bids was made to overturn the new Government by means of force. This murky affair was shrouded in mystery at the time, and it is impossible now to disentangle the threads of the plot, although the main outlines are clear. They demonstrate beyond doubt that the higher echelons of the civil service, leaders of industry and the army itself were implicated up to their necks.

Soldiers from the 'Franzer' Regiment of Guards, under the nominal command of a certain Sergeant Speiro, moved suddenly to arrest the entire executive of the Berlin Workers' and Soldiers' Council, simultaneously summoning Ebert from his office to proclaim him 'President' – or dictator. At the same time the soldiers opened fire with a machine gun on a Spartacist demonstration which they encountered on the central Chauseestrasse. Sixteen people died and twelve were injured. When confronted by the soldiers, Ebert made an ambiguous reply to their proclamation and withdrew. The soldiers dispersed in confusion and released the bewildered executive of the Council. The affair was investigated and it rapidly became clear that the soldiers had been acting under the orders of a trio of right-wing aristocratic adventurers named Marten, Matuschka and Metternich, who had all conveniently and temporarily disappeared. They in turn took their orders from high-ranking members of the Foreign Office in the Wilhelmstrasse, and from officials of the War ministry directly answerable to Otto Wels who was acting as military governor of Berlin. In short, the threads in this complex labyrinth of conspiracy led directly back to the civil servants and politicians who ran the regime.

What was unclear was whether the SPD chiefs, Ebert and Wels, had directly connived in the plot as a way of eliminating the tiresome Councils. The investigation of the putsch was blocked by the SPD, its leaders went unpunished and soon returned to political prominence and the dead of the Chauseestrasse were unavenged. After Ebert's death in 1925, Groener claimed in a court hearing that the Chancellor had indeed authorised him to 'wrench power' from the hands of the Councils by marching nine divisions of the old army into the capital and occupying it. The suspicious Independents, who were watching Ebert closely, got wind of the plan, and in the event, the entry of the troops returning from the Front went ahead without incident on 10 December.

Ebert was there in person at the Brandenburg Gate to welcome the men home with the words: 'No enemy has vanquished you. As you return unconquered from the field of battle, I salute you!' These extraordinary views from a Socialist Chancellor were not only historically inaccurate, they gave a gleeful Right more ammunition to use against the Left. If the German army was undefeated, who had brought about its evident collapse? Why, the treacherous nest of Bolsheviks and traitors at home. Not that the Right needed Ebert's support to justify their hate. In the words of a witness who heard Ebert speak, Major Waldemar Pabst, 'Ebert's speech had no effect on us . . . we knew that the fight against the "masses" would be hard and bloody. It would be necessary to fight against all physical and psychological resistance, to become hard – even against ourselves – to become free of all sentimentality. A great task lay before us.' Compare these words with the notorious speech to his Generals by SS Reichsführer Heinrich Himmler in Posen on 4 October 1943: 'Most of you know what it is when a hundred corpses are lying side by side, or five hundred, or a thousand. To have stuck it out, and at the same time to have remained decent fellows . . . that is what has made us hard.' The line of descent is direct.

The Right's plans to seize power had not been stymied by the vigilance of the Left, but by the unreliability of the army. The main aim of the weary soldiers returning from the front was to spend Christmas at home. Within a fortnight of their arrival in Berlin, the strength of the nine divisions had dwindled to a mere eight hundred men. This lesson was not lost on the Army chiefs, and was one more compelling reason for them to consider seriously Schleicher's plan to raise an entirely new and reliable military force.

Meanwhile, the Reichs Congress of Workers and Soldiers, which was due to draw up plans for elections to the new National Assembly, met in Berlin on 16 December. The 500 delegates were dominated by the SPD with 299 votes, 101 were USPD Independents, 25 were liberal Democrats while 75 were politically undecided. The Democrats and the neutrals normally voted with the SPD. The Congress obediently followed the SPD leadership's line in setting an early date for elections in January 1919. But on one issue of fundamental importance, it stuck out against Ebert: overwhelmingly passing a motion, the so-called 'Hamburg Points', which called for further demilitarisation of the army, abolition of rank insignia, and more democracy leading to a new 'People's Army'. The reaction of the military was predictably apopleptic. Hindenburg, in particular, was outraged: 'What do these people dare to ask? That I should tear off the insignia I have worn since my youth? That I should surrender the sword that has served King and Fatherland through three wars? Tell Herr Ebert that I do not recognize the decisions of the Congress . . . I will fight to the last ditch.'

Ebert proposed to Groener that the General come to Berlin for a mediation meeting with selected Congress delegates on 20 December. Groener arrived, along with Schleicher as his aide. On their way from the station to the meeting they were insulted by a group of revolutionary sailors for continuing to wear their Imperial uniforms. The sailors were at once arrested. Yet another straw in the wind.

Ebert carefully concealed the meeting from his Independent colleagues, but they discovered the ruse. They arrived at the meeting just in time to prevent the complete abandonment of the Hamburg Points. The issue was successfully fudged and the whole question adjourned until after Christmas. But by then events had taken a far more serious and violent turn.

The push which sent the German revolution – hitherto a largely peaceful affair – down the road to bloodshed and civil war, was provided by a detachment of sailors, the grandiosely named People's Naval Division, which had occupied the former Royal palace and its surroundings on 15 November. The division consisted of a core of six hundred revolutionary sailors from Kiel who had been installed in the palace stables, the 'Marstall', by order of Wels who hoped to use them as an élite guard to back up the Government against possible Spartacist insurrection. The Kiel sailors had been joined by six hundred of their colleagues from Cuxhaven, and their numbers had been swelled still further over the past weeks by a motley collection of soldiers, hangers-on, women and opportunists who relished the palatial billets and the chance to indulge in some authorised looting and pillaging of the Imperial cellars.

It is difficult to sort out how culpable the sailors' behaviour was. Their opponents claim they had degenerated into a criminal gang whose main interest was blackmailing the Government and stealing. Their supporters say the Government betrayed them by withholding their pay and threatening to dissolve them. At all events, by Christmas week, the Division had become a nuisance, an embarrassment and a potential danger to the Ebert regime. A vociferous campaign was mounting in the SPD press, maligning the Marine Division and demanding its disbandment. At the same time, Liebknecht's Spartacists strove to infiltrate and win over the sailors to their cause, remembering that it had been sailors who had formed the spearhead of the Bolshevik October revolution in Russia.

The Government put pressure on the Division to evacuate the

Palace by witholding its pay. The sailors opened negotiations with the military Governor of Berlin, Wels, who demanded that the keys of the palace be handed over. The sailors refused to budge without being allotted adequate alternative quarters. On 23 December the patience of the sailors expired. They sallied out under the command of Lieutenant Heinrich Dorrenbach, a veteran of the Kiel mutiny, and surrounded the Chancellery. They gave up the Palace keys to Emil Barth, but when Ebert refused to see them to discuss the 80,000 Marks they were owed, the sailors finally saw red. Dorrenbach ordered that all entrances to the Chancellery be blocked and all telephone wires cut. The only line that escaped the Division's eagle eye was that vital link connecting Ebert with the High Command which had now moved from Spa to Kassel. Once again, the Chancellor called the military. This time it was Major von Schleicher who answered. He promised to send troops to Ebert's aid, adding ominously 'Perhaps there will now, after so many missed opportunities, come a chance to aim a blow at the radicals.'

Another detachment of the Marine Division had made its way to the building of the Berlin city command where they were resisted by force. Three sailors were shot down in the mêlée before they forced an entrance, took Wels hostage and secured their money. The enraged seamen beat Wels up, and took him and two aides under guard back to their HQ in the Marstall.

Meanwhile the troops summoned by Schleicher were marching on the Chancellery from their base at Potsdam, just west of the capital. Thanks to their ally in Government, Barth, the sailors heard of this and demanded an explanation from Ebert. The embarrassed Chancellor was trying to justify his action when the soldiers, under the command of General von Lequis, arrived. The two sides squared up to each other in Ebert's office. It looked as though the issue was going to be settled then and there by armed might, until Barth intervened once more and suggested that the soldiers go back to the Tiergarten in the west, while the sailors return to the Marstall in the east. Ebert eagerly agreed, but at 2 a.m. the following morning – no doubt after more consultations with the High Command – he gave a secret order for the soldiers to march on the Marstall and subdue the sailors, using whatever force was necessary.

The eight hundred troops – all that was left of the nine divisions who had returned from the Front to Berlin – surrounded the Marstall in the small hours. Shortly before 8 a.m. they opened a cannonade against the building with artillery and machine guns. The fusillade raged for more than an hour, with an average of one shell falling on the Marstall every two minues. But the stable walls proved stout and by 9 a.m. the sailors showed no sign of surrendering. The army was getting worried, for the streets were beginning to fill with puzzled and hostile citizens, who showed every sign of siding with the besieged sailors. At 9.30 a white flag was raised by the Marstall garrison and a twenty-minute truce ensued. By the end of the truce, the press of people – many of them summoned by the indefatigable Barth who had driven through the city in an open car yelling 'Monarchist putsch! Counter revolution! Come to the Palace and save the Republic!' – were pressing around the confused soldiers, who seemed to be wavering. Some even joined the sailors and their civilian supporters. Amidst the crowds, now tens of thousands strong, there was no question of the assault being resumed, and those soldiers still following orders ignominiously withdrew. Nine sailors and around twenty civilians had died in the battle. A bruised and frightened Wels was released by the sailors, and was promptly sacked by the ungrateful Ebert.

The lesson of the Marstall battle, if not already uncomfortably clear to the High Command in Kassel, was driven home by a telegram sent to them that night by Major von Harbou, General Staff Officer in the Marstall attack:

Troops of the General Command Lequis no longer fit for action. I see no possibility of protecting Government with the means so far at our disposal. Government can only be saved by means of an entire army. General Command Lequis impossible. Recommend dissolution and dismissal.

Groener and Schliecher turned their full attention and, indeed, pinned their final hopes of restoring order, on the volunteer troops now in the process of being formed and trained. Salvation for the Government, the Army and the whole German bourgeoisie order now lay in the rough hands of the Freikorps.

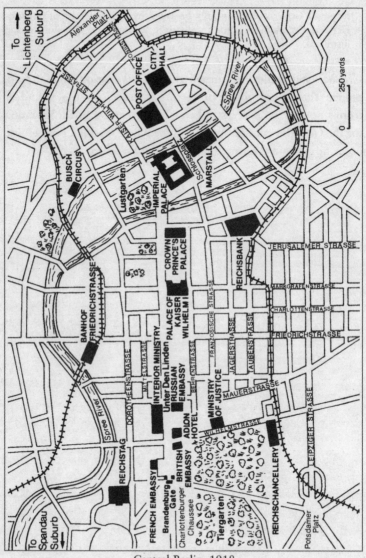

Central Berlin, 1918

4

THE FIRST FREIKORPS

'War had taken hold of them and would never let them go. They would never really belong to their homes again. The war was over . . . but the armies were still in being.'

Ernst von Salomon,
The Outlaws ('Die Geächteten')

Ebert was consumed with fear that the Reichs-Chancellery was about to come under attack. He roamed his offices and corridors repeating obsessively the refrain: 'It can't go on like this . . . no, one can't continue to govern like this.' The Chancellor was constantly on the telephone to Groener, threating to flee to Frankfurt, to Weimar – almost anywhere would be preferable to the seething atmosphere of Berlin! 'Let Liebknecht occupy the Reichs-Chancellery if he wants. He will find the birds have flown.' Lacking arms, lacking discipline, lacking numbers – above all, lacking firm leadership, Liebknecht's motley band presented no sort of threat to a Government commanding the rudiments of armed force to defend itself; unfortunately, Ebert felt himself to be naked and alone.

Liebknecht, essentially a pamphleteer and orator rather than an organisational genius like Lenin or Trotsky, was happily occupying himself over Christmas preparing a special edition of the newspaper *Rote Fahne*, with the blazing blood-red banner headline *Ebert's Bloody Christmas* – referring to the Marstall battle. As for the Spartacists' revolutionary vanguard – the People's Naval Division – they were content to rest on their laurels and spent the festive season in the traditional sentimental German way – carousing round the 'Weinachtsbaum' to the strains of 'Stille Nacht'.

As the days passed, the Government drew breath and began to regain their shattered confidence. Fortunately for Ebert the USPD obligingly decided to commit political suicide and voluntarily left the Government. The ostensible cause was the Marstall battle; the USPD were smarting under the needling of their Spartacist rivals, and felt uncomfortable at remaining inside the 'blood-stained' Ebert regime. Ebert promptly replaced them with two trusted SPD colleagues – Wissel and, fresh from his counter-revolutionary triumph in Kiel, Gustav Noske.

Noske's arrival in the capital galvanised the emerging forces of counter-revolution. He put himself forward for the vacant portfolio of Minister for National Defence in Ebert's six-man emergency Cabinet. His future policy was summed up in his words on accepting the job shunned by his more timid colleagues: 'You can count on me to re-establish order in Berlin. Someone must be the bloodhound. I am not afraid of the responsibility.' He proceeded at once to live up to his own grim job-description.

Noske's first act was to re-organise the demoralised Army staff in Berlin, surrounding himself with his own trusted officers. The Berlin Commander-in-Chief, von Lequis, whose troops had so ignominiously failed to dislodge the sailors from the Marstall, was removed and replaced by General Walther von Lüttwitz, stern, unbending, thin as a whip, 'a royalist and aristocrat to his finger-tips [who] feels a profound aversion to the ideas of his epoch. He is hostile to all politics, and his one desire is to have a country "as again in August 1914".' This was his description by one of his own officers. What was Noske, the woodcutter's son and avowed Socialist, doing in such reactionary company? The answer is that beneath Noske's rough proletarian hide beat the heart of a good German, a patriot and an autocrat who thought nothing of shedding the blood of his own class. In his own words: 'I sought out . . . the former officers and officials, beaten and spat upon as they were, and it is with their help that I averted the worst. If I had to choose between a bad Socialist officer and a good Conservative officer, I should choose the Conservative.'

Realising that the Police were as essential a stabilising force as the Army, Noske dismissed the capital's Police Chief, Emil Eichhorn, who was under suspicion as having supplied the Marstall sailors with succour and reinforcements. Eichhorn was a nominee and leading member of the extreme Left USPD. His sacking was a gauntlet thrown down to challenge the Left and the Spartacists; they could not afford to let it go by, and nor did they.

On 30 December, the Spartacists – numbering less than a thousand – formally proclaimed themselves as the new Communist Party of Germany (KPD) at a special congress marked by militant calls for action from the rank and file delegates and a more cautious approach adopted by the infant party's leaders. Rosa Luxemburg, in particular, saw the dangers of precipitate action before the time was right and warned the Congress that the struggle ahead would be long and hard, and would not be settled by a few days of street fighting in Berlin. 'Comrades,' she called, amidst a hubbub of dissent, 'you are taking your radicalism too easily; we are only at the beginning of the revolution.'

On 4 January 1919, a Saturday, the fractured forces of revolutionary Berlin assembled in the Police headquarters on the Alexanderplatz in the proletarian east end of the city. The building was still in their hands as Police Chief Eichhorn had refused to accept his dismissal and was sitting tight in his office. The executive of his party, the USPD, assembled along with representatives of the revolutionary shop stewards, the 'Obleute', and two delegates from the leadership of the newly-formed KPD: Liebknecht himself, and Wilhelm Pieck, the future Head of State of a Communist East Germany. The meeting decided to call a protest rally against Eichhorn's dismissal the following day, Sunday 5 January. On the same Saturday, Gustav Noske invited his leader, Ebert, to accompany him by car on a mystery tour out of Berlin. The destination of the SPD chiefs was a military camp at Zossen, some thirty-five miles south-west of the capital.

The sight that met the eyes of the two leaders as they clambered stiffly from the car on to the frozen parade ground must have made them blink with disbelief. For there, through driving snow, marching before them in perfectly ordered ranks, came column after column of disciplined troops, perfectly equipped, fit, eager and, above all, absolutely loyal to the Ebert Government. The officer who stepped forward and presented his compliments to his civilian chiefs, was General Ludwig von Maercker, founder and commander of the first officially sponsored Freikorps, a new kind of army, ready and able to deal with a new kind of problem.

After the defeats of November, and the recent humiliating dissolution following the Marstall fiasco, who were these men – 'real soldiers' in Noske's awed and admiring words – who had risen, seemingly like phantoms, from the ruins of chaos and disaster? Maercker was a Prussian of the old school who had spent most of the war on the Eastern Front, ending up as the relatively lowly commander of the 214th Infantry Division. But unlike most of his fellow officers, he had grasped at an early stage that the miseries of defeat offered the opportunity for a wholly new type of soldiering: 'A vast militia of bourgeoisie and peasants, grouped around the flag for the re-establishment of order.' The implied message was that this coalition of the middle-class and the rural worker would be set against the industrial working classes of the city, with their dangerous notions of democracy and socialism. As his own division began to melt away, Maercker seized the chance of preserving its loyalist kernel as the basis of a new corps of volunteers able to carry out the twin tasks of combating the Bolshevik enemy at home and defending Germany's crumbling borders from the rapacious grasp of the foreigner.

On 6 December, Maercker had called together his divisional staff and outlined his plan. To a man, his officers pledged their support, and Maercker set about the practical task of raising his Freikorps. Within a week he had mapped out his scheme in a memo which he submitted to his superior, Lieutenant General von Morgern, Commander of the XIV Reserve Army Corps. Maercker's memo dwelt on how his new unit would differ – both in structure and in spirit – from the rigid, stratified hierarchy of the old Imperial Army, with its great yawning gulfs between officers and men; the stiff-necked and stupid class distinctions which, in his opinion, had been a major contributing cause to defeat.

He believed that traditional discipline could be maintained more effectively by making constructive use of the camaraderie forged in four years of trench warfare. Maercker, a convinced monarchist at heart, was even ready to countenance the concept of soldiers' councils which had been thrown up in the bitter days of November 1918. But instead of the revolutionary Bolshevik-infected Councils that had overturned the old order, he set up elected committees of 'Vertrauensleute' (Trusted people), consisting of loyal enlisted men who would act as a channel to convey the feelings and complaints of the rank and file to the officers.

Having got the go-ahead from his superiors to set up the new Freikorps, Maercker and his men withdrew to a remote

Franciscan friary at Salzkotten deep in the Westphalian countryside to form and train the young unit in a peaceful atmosphere far
from the turmoil of the cities. From there, on 14 December, he
issued his ground orders for the unit, which he called the
'Freiwillige Landesjägerkorps' (Volunteer Rifleman's Corps):

Divisional Staff

Salzkotten (Westphalia)

Dec. 14th 1918

1. *Aim:* The Volunteer Rifle Corps is created for the maintenance of
   order within the Reich and for the defence of its frontiers.
2. *Constitution:* The Rifle Corps is composed entirely of volunteers.
3. *Discipline:* The fighting strength of a troop can only be manifested in
   its full strength if it gives implicit obedience to its leaders. This applies
   particularly to corps of volunteers. To achieve it an iron discipline is
   necessary. It is the indispensable condition of success, and is a benefit
   to everyone. Discipline should be founded upon ready and consenting
   obedience.
4. *Trusted Men:* These should be a bond between non-commissioned
   officers and subordinates. They second the non-commissioned officers
   in the maintenance of discipline, and submit the wishes and complaints
   of the men to the commanders. The finer the spirit of a corps is, the more
   closely it is allied to its chiefs and the less trusted men need to interfere.
   The trusted men carry out the following functions:
   a) They administer the private possessions of the troop, in conjunc-
      tion with the treasurer.
   b) They should be consulted by the leaders on questions of subsis-
      tence, leave and, in short, everything concerning the material
      welfare of the troop.
   c) They must undertake the complaints of their comrades when the
      latter have to complain of their superiors.
   d) They serve as judges in courts-martial.
   To avoid injury to discipline, the trusted men must in no case exceed
   the limits of their power. They have no authority as regards the
   command.
5. *Disciplinary Measures:* Punishments should only be inflicted by
   company or battery commanders and their superiors. A minimum
   delay of three hours is prescribed between the moment when the fault
   is committed and that in which the penalty is pronounced. Penalties

consisting in extra hours of drill (Strafexerzieren) are abolished. The leader of a volunteer corps must never inflict a punishment capable of touching a man's honour. For the rest, the disciplinary regulations of the Army are preserved.

6. a) Any man guilty of pillage will be condemned to death.
   b) The following offences will be punished by dishonourable dismissal from the Rifle Corps.
      1) Cowardice in the course of service.
      2) Theft.
      3) Deliberate damage, discarding or sale of State property. Men guilty of these offences will, moreover, be subject to the penalties prescribed by the military code in existence at the time.

7. The troop has the right to propose for the rank of non-commissioned officer any rifleman who has accomplished acts of heroism.

8. Any man having a complaint to make of his superior is to ask the advice of the trusted men in his company or battery. If the trusted men confirm the grounds of the complaint, the man concerned has the right to carry the complaint himself to his company or battery leader, or, if the complaint is directed against them, to the senior officer after them.

9. *Outward marks of respect:* Respect towards leaders is outwardly shown by the military salute. Every soldier forming a part of the Rifle Corps is bound to salute his hierarchic superiors. Every officer is bound to return the salute.

MAERCKER

Maercker chose the men of his new corps with care. In the main, he picked experienced senior officers who had seen front-line service and promoted NCO's with a similar record. He eschewed highly politically motivated officers (i.e. blatant anti-parliamentary reactionaries) and insisted that each man recruited be at least nominally loyal to the legally constituted Ebert Republican regime, and swear a fealty oath to that effect.

This fine distinction set Maercker's men somewhat apart from the majority of the Freikorps who followed them. The General, essentially a moderate man, retained the 'correct' habits of a German military gentleman of the old school: order and discipline were his watchwords, not for him the brutal neo-anarchic 'free-booting' spirit so manifest in other more notorious examples of the Freikorps genre. As a consequence, the Landesjägerkorps were a larger and more effective fighting force who bore the brunt of the often savage fighting and civil strife which followed across the country in the months ahead.

Maercker was an innovator too, in the administration of his Corps: he created a unified command, doing away with the outmoded distinctions between cavalry, infantry and artillery that had so often hamstrung the German war effort. Each company in the Corps had its own attached heavy machine gun section and mortar detachment – creating a flexible all-round force more than capable of meeting the new and testing demands of civil war. His men were drilled in the tactics of the type of street warfare they were about to encounter. On 22 December Maercker published the conditions of entry to his Landesjägerkorps:

1. Volunteers of all classes may enrol in the Rifle Corps, provided that they have completed their military training.
2. Officers, officials and non-commissioned officers receive pay according to their grade. Riflemen receive monthly wages of 30 Marks. Every man is boarded and lodged. Non-commissioned officers and men, moreover, are provided with uniform and equipment.
3. All members of the Corps of Riflemen receive a supplementary payment of 5 marks a day. These sums are not paid during punishment or time spent in hospital (except such as results from injuries received in the course of service).
4. Family allowances are continued.
5. Time of service in the Rifle Corps counts toward retirement and pensions just as time of service in the Army.
6. Upon leaving the Corps, every volunteer receives a bonus of 50 Marks, plus 15 Marks journey money, and a new suit, if he has not had it before.
7. Every member of the Rifle Corps joins for a period of thirty days. He cannot leave the Corps without giving fifteen days notice. If he has not given notice on the 15th of the month, his engagement is automatically renewed for the following month. This regulation does not infringe upon the cases of immediate dismissal referred to in p. 7. of the Constructive Order No. 1.

8. All subsidiary questions will be settled by the provisional government of Ebert, and finally by the government constituted by the National Assembly.

MAERCKER

After laying the foundations of his force, Maercker set about an intensive recruiting drive. In the troubled and uncertain conditions prevailing in Germany, secure employment, with regular wages and the chance of a scrap, enticed those men who only knew a soldiering life, and felt insecure and ill-at-ease in the civilian world. In addition, there was the extra bonus, for the patriotically inclined, of 'doing their bit' for the Fatherland. Moral probity plus one Mark a day with board and lodging thrown in, were not to be sniffed at. The recruits started to arrive in a steady flow.

Within days of issuing his original 'Founding Orders' Maercker was able to review his first fully-fledged section, consisting of three infantry companies and an artillery battery. Despite severe difficulties caused by the chaotic breakdown of the old Army and bureaucratic obstruction from Ministry officials in Berlin, Maercker managed to build up his Freikorps, and slowly but surely to equip it with uniforms, rifles, machine guns, lorries and munitions. By Christmas Eve – the day of the old Army's humiliation before the walls of the Marstall – Maercker's little band had swollen to some 4,000 determined men.

On Boxing Day, Ebert's embattled Government asked for the Rifle Corps to be placed at Lüttwitz's disposal for the defence and security of Berlin. Nine days later, the Freikorps concentrated at Zossen camp, there to be reviewed by a grateful Noske and Ebert. As they left the windswept parade ground, the two SPD leaders felt a glow of returning confidence at what they had witnessed. The giant Noske slapped the diminutive Ebert across the shoulders and guffawed: 'Now you can rest easy; everything is going to be all right from now on.' The first Freikorps had arrived and was ready for action.

It had come, from the Government's point of view, only in the very nick of time. The day after the Zossen parade, Sunday 5 January saw the mass demonstrations called for by the Left-wing press: the USPD journal *Freiheit* and the KPD (Spartacist) organ *Rote Fahne*. The ostensible purpose was to protest at the sacking of Police Chief Emil Eichhorn, but the real object was to re-assert the revolutionary way. In answer to the joint newspaper appeal, thousands upon thousands of workers flooded into Berlin from the outlying suburbs. By 2 p.m., the centre of the capital was a vast sea of swaying, murmuring humanity, standing shoulder to shoulder, packing the Siegesallee, the Tiergarten, the Unter den Linden avenue, the Schlossplatz and the Alexanderplatz. The immense throng outdid all previous rallies in the capital; not even in the stirring days of November had Berlin seen anything to equal it. The size of the crowds was conservatively estimated at 700,000. Many among them were armed; all were angry at the 'betrayals' of the SPD leadership and ready for action. Small groups of agitators took it upon themselves to occupy Berlin's newspaper quarter, the Belle Alliance Platz. Here, in Germany's Fleet Street, were concentrated the main bourgeois publishing concerns – Ullstein, Scherl and Mosse – as well as the SPD daily, *Vorwärts*, which had become steadily more vociferous in opposing the Left, even printing advertisements calling on workers to volunteer for the Freikorps. In the days before electronic communications, the newspapers were the main channel of information for the country and the capital and when, that afternoon, revolutionary groups seized control of the chief railway stations, all communications were effectively in the hands of the ultra-Left. Power was within the grasp of the crowds, but that grip never tightened.

Blame for this failure of nerve undoubtedly lies with the leaders of the three major left-wing factions; the USPD, the KPD (Spartacists) and the revolutionary shop stewards (Obleute). As darkness fell, the leaders gathered once more at the Police headquarters on the Alexanderplatz. Seventy Obleute were present, along with the ten-man executive of the Berlin USPD, two soldier delegates and Heinrich Dorrenbach, chief of the People's Naval Division still firmly installed in the Marstall. Once again, the infant KPD was represented by Karl Liebknecht and Wilhelm Pieck, while the cause of all the commotion, Police Chief Eichhorn, placidly presided. The atmosphere of the meeting was described by one witness as a trance-like state of intoxication fuelled by the heady experience of feeling the tide of revolution at full flood. Speaker after speaker vied with one another in extolling the heroic proletariat in waves of rhetorical hot air. Cool, objective analysis and discussion as to the next step was sadly missing.

The sailors' leader, Dorrenbach, kicked off by asserting that not only his men, but all the soldiers in Berlin stood ready to 'overthrow the Ebert-Scheidemann Government by the force of arms'. He was backed up by the ever-excitable Liebknecht, in a near apocalyptic state. (It was during these days that he assured one crowd, in Messianic terms, that the goal of their fight was to win 'The Gates of Heaven'.) A note of caution was sounded by the two soldiers present who expressed doubts as to the revolutionary reliability of the troops and even of the Marstall sailors, but their pessimism was airily brushed aside as the meeting voted by eighty to six to 'fight the Government until it is overthrown'. The gathering then broke up without anyone deciding on how, in concrete terms, this no doubt desirable aim was to be accomplished.

That night, leaflets were printed calling for a renewal of the mass demonstrations at 11 a.m. the following day, Monday 6 January, in order to achieve the final collapse of the 'blood-stained Ebert Government'. The proclamation was issued over the signatures of an unwieldy fifty-three-member 'Revolutionary Committee' headed by Liebknecht and the Berlin USPD chief, the veteran Georg Ledebour. The next day the masses obediently thronged the streets once again. The crowd gathered in even more gigantic force than on the previous day. This time, must have been the thought in every mind – surely we *must* prevail.

Once again individual groups went off to occupy more strategic points: this time it was the turn of the official state news agency, the Wolff telegraph office, and the Government's own print works. The only force in the entire city showing any signs of resisting the massive mob were a few thousand SPD loyalists hastily drummed up outside the Chancellery gates to guard Ebert against the people's revenge. It was November 1917 in Petrograd once again, but this time there was no Lenin or Trotsky prepared to give the hard order to seize power. Slowly, the hours passed.

The KPD newspaper, *Rote Fahne* later published an exasperated account of the scene . . .

> The crowds had been standing in the cold and fog since 9 a.m. Their leaders were seated – none knew where – deliberating. The fog grew thicker and the throngs were still waiting. Noon came; the chill and hunger grew. The people were feverishly impatient. They demanded an act, a word, anything to hush the suspense. But no one knew what, for the leaders were deliberating . . . The fog became more dense as night began to fall; sadly, the people began to drift home. Having hoped to accomplish great things they had ended by doing nothing, because their leaders were deliberating. They had sat first at the Marstall, and then at the Police Headquarters – outside in the Alexanderplatz, the proletariat stood waiting, rifles in hand, machine guns at the ready . . . behind closed doors, the leaders were still in session: they deliberated, deliberated, deliberated . . .

But, just as nature abhors a vacuum, so the political process detests powerlessness. If the so-called revolutionary leadership was unwilling to grasp the nettle of the responsibilities their fevered rhetoric had conjured up, there was one man on the Government side who was not afraid to act: Gustav Noske.

Sensing who was the strong man in their midst at this bleak-seeming hour in their fortunes, Noske's SPD colleagues invested him with virtual dictatorial powers as Armed Forces Commander-in-Chief in addition to his existing responsibilities as Minister of National Defence. Noske grimly took on board his new responsibilities and left the besieged Chancellery to organise the Government reaction. He was hoisted shoulder-high by the SPD loyalists at the gate: 'Let me down', he protested. 'I shall bring back order to Berlin'. True to his word, he melted anonymously into the crowd and made his way through the armed hosts of his enemies at the Brandenburg Gate, telling anyone who questioned him that he had an urgent errand to fulfil. Indeed he had.

Noske travelled to the prosperous west Berlin suburb of Dahlem where he established himself at the Luisenstift, a boarding school for upper class young ladies in more settled times. Here he set about organising the forces of counter-revolution. (It is an ironic historical footnote that Lenin organised the Russian Bolshevik revolution from a similar upper-class girls' boarding school in Petrograd, the Smolny Institute.)

Meanwhile Ebert, true to form, played for the time necessary to allow Noske to concentrate his forces. The Chancellor used his erstwhile USPD Government colleagues – Haase, Dittmann and Barth – as a channel to negotiate with the Revolutionary Committee. Ebert skilfully spun out the talks through the day as the crowds dithered and then dispersed. His chief demand was that the revolutionaries evacuate the press quarter that they had occupied. After more deliberation, the Committee rejected his condition and the scene was set for violent confrontation.

An uneasy calm prevailed on 7 January. The following day an ominous Government announcement appeared, proclaiming, 'The day of reckoning approaches.'

5

'SPARTACUS WEEK'

'In November I was Red, yes Red. But it's January now.'
Bertolt Brecht,
Drums in the Night ('Trommeln in der Nacht')

Just what was the nature of the insurrectionary threat against which Noske was marshalling his forces at the Luisenstift? In truth, despite the massive numbers who had demonstrated in the Berlin streets and squares on the 5th and 6th January, the revolutionary hard core who were actually prepared to stand and fight never amounted to much more than the Spartacists alone – around one thousand apparently determined revolutionaries. These were the men who, on their own initiative, had sallied out to seize the newspaper offices, the Government news agency and printing shop and the main railway termini. The force that comandeered the SPD daily, *Vorwärts*, for example publishing it briefly under the name *Der Rote Vorwärts* ('Red Forwards'), was commanded by a professional revolutionary Communist named Eugene Leviné, hailing, as did Rosa Luxemburg, from the Jewish ghettos of eastern Europe. But the seizure of the communications keypoints was the last positive move the revolutionaries made. They did not have the numbers, the weapons, or the will to convert their stated intention of overthrowing the Government into reality.

The weakness of the revolutionary position had already become plain on 6 January, when, believing Dorrenbach's extravagant promises, the Revolutionary Committee had moved from the Alexanderplatz into the Marstall, headquarters of the People's Naval Division. Here the sailors, far from giving them a warm welcome, deposed Dorrenbach from their leadership (he was later hunted down and killed by the vengeful Freikorps) and declared their neutrality in the struggle between revolution and Government. Disappointed, the Committee trailed back to the Alexanderplatz where they continued their fruitless debates as their support dribbled away with the grey January day.

To add an intolerable burden to the revolutionaries' already grave disadvantages, their political leadership was fatally split: only the hardened worker rank-and-file Spartacists were wholly committed to an outright seizure of power. The impulsive and emotional Liebknecht had been swept along with the prevailing current, to the evident dismay of the more thoughtful Rosa Luxemburg. 'Oh Karl', she is reported to have protested upon reading his signature at the bottom of the proclamation of a revolutionary Government, 'How could you?' Luxemburg, along with other far-sighted Communists, including Lenin's own representative in Berlin, Karl Radek, knew that the numerically weak KPD was nowhere near ready to assume power. Even if the revolutionaries temporarily succeeded in securing control of Berlin, how could they extend their rule throughout the rest of the country? The result could only be a bloodbath and a huge setback to the revolutionary cause; at best, a short-lived repetition of the 1870 Paris Commune, and at worst, the defeat of German Socialism for a generation.

The Spartacists' half-hearted allies on the Left, the USPD, were already involved in negotiations with Ebert for a peaceful solution to the crisis – hardly the sign of a confident revolution on the brink of seizing the state. Nevertheless, once battle was joined, 'Red Rosa' fell into line, and wrote a series of inflammatory articles in the *Rote Fahne* proclaiming her burning faith in the ultimate triumph of the cause:

Anyone who witnessed yesterday's mass demonstration in the Siegesallee, who felt the magnificent mood, the energy that the masses exude, must conclude that politically the proletariat has grown enormously through the experiences of recent weeks. They have become aware of their power, and all that remains is for them to avail themselves of this power.

The masses must learn to fight, to act in the struggle itself. And today one can sense that the workers of Berlin have learned to act; they thirst for resolute deeds, for sweeping measures.

However, are their leaders, the executive organs of their will, well informed? Have the revolutionary shop stewards, have the energy and resolve of the radical elements in the USPD grown in the meanwhile? Has their capacity for action kept pace with the growing energy of the masses?

We are afraid we cannot answer these questions with a straight-forward Yes . . .

What have the leaders done? What have they decided? Which measures have they taken to safeguard victory in this tense situation in which the fate of the revolution can be decided? We have seen and heard nothing. Perhaps they are discussing their tasks very thoroughly. But now is the time to act.

The Ebert-Scheidemann clique are not wasting their time in endless discussion. Behind the scenes they are preparing to act with the usual cunning and energy of counter-revolutionaries; they are loading their weapons for the final surprise attack to destroy the revolution.

There is no time to be lost. Energetic measures must be taken at once. The vacillating element among the troops can be won for the cause of the proletariat only by vigorous and determined action on the part of the revolunonary bodies.

Act! Act! Courageously, consistently – that is the 'accursed' duty and obligation of the revolutionary shop stewards and the sincere leaders of the USPD. Disarm the counter-revolution. Arm the masses. Occupy all positions of power. Act quickly!

(*Rote Fahne* January 7th, 1919)

But, for the revolution, time was already nearly up. Noske, upon reaching the Luisenstift, had established himself in a classroom, equipped it with a table, a single telephone screwed to a plank, and a schoolgirl's bed. From here, protected by a company of Maercker's Freikorps, he set to work. Tuesday, 7 January saw the arrival of the first mainly middle-class volunteer recruits from the surrounding suburbs of west Berlin. Close behind these civilians came lorryloads of weapons to arm them: rifles, carbines, machine guns and light artillery. A transport park was set up outside the school and filled with trucks, cars, motor-cycles and bicycles. A radio mast was installed in a nearby field.

Noske and his military lieutenants – Commandants von Hammerstein Equord and von Stockhausen – reviewed the rapidly growing forces at their disposal in the 'General Command von Lüttwitz'. In addition to the company guarding the school-fortress, two more sections of Maercker's men were stationed at Zossen, with a third section still gathering recruits in Westphalia. Two further sections were close by in another Berlin suburb.

A second Freikorps had been recruited by a regular Army Colonel – Wilhelm Reinhard, the former commander of the 25th Guards Regiment – and was occupying a Berlin barracks, 600 strong, and growing every day. By Wednesday 8 January, Reinhard's Freikorps had swelled to nearly 1000 men, and two companies of 150 men each were despatched to guard the Chancellery and the Foreign Ministry in the Wilhelmstrasse from possible Spartacist attack. A third Freikorps, calling itself the 'Potsdam Regiment', had been formed under a Major von Stephani in the old Prussian barrack-town of Potsdam, just west of Berlin, and was placed under Reinhard's command.

As news spread of Noske's intentions, more Freikorps sprang up, like mushrooms in a damp meadow: General von Roeder formed a 'Corps of Volunteer Scouts'; General von Hoffmann brought over a division of Horse Guards (the Garde Kavalrie

Schutze Division); General Held formed a Freikorps from the 17th Division of Infantry, and General von Wissel raised a similar detachment from the 31st Infantry Division. Another Potsdam General, von Hulsen, Commander of the 231st Infantry Division, was in the process of raising a large Freikorps, which took his name and eventually attained a strength of 11,000 men.

All these formations followed the pattern set by Maercker. The prospective Freikorps commander, sometimes a General, but often a Colonel, a Major or even a lowly Captain, would discreetly announce his intentions among his subordinate officers, who would spread the word to their NCO's and loyal soldiers. The Freikorps would commandeer a barracks or similar substantial building as a base headquarters and set about recruitment, equipment and training. Recruiting at first was by word of mouth among former front-line soldiers. Later, newspaper advertisements and eye-catching posters were employed, appealing to patriotism and the fear of Bolshevism among sympathetic civilians.

To bolster his forces, Noske sent word to his old stamping ground at Kiel, where he had raised an 'Iron Brigade' to help to secure his hold on that port. This unit, some 1600 strong, made its way by train to villages around Berlin, despite the obstruction of railwaymen who saw a sinister motive behind its convergence on the capital. On the morning of Friday, 10 January, while Noske was inspecting his Iron Brigade and conferring with its commander, Colonel von Roden, a scrap of paper was thrust into the hands of Colonel Reinhard. A scrawled pencil signature 'Ebert-Scheidemann' was the document's only claim to authenticity but the orders it gave were terse and to the point: Reinhard must take the 350 men he had with him guarding the barracks of the Moabit district and secure the northern suburb of Spandau, a working-class area where the Spartacists were strongly entrenched and threatening to take the huge local munitions works.

Obediently, a detachment of Reinhard's men under a

Lieutenant von Kassel seized Spandau Town Hall after a sharp bombardment. The Spartacist defenders not killed in the action were captured and shot dead while being transferred to jail – a sinister portent of many similar murders in the brutal days ahead. Major von Stephani, commanding the Potsdam Regiment Freikorps, had simultaneously received another mysterious order signed 'Ebert-Scheidemann' authorising him to mount an all-out offensive against the Spartacists' stronghold around the Belle-Alliance Platz, Berlin's newspaper quarter. Von Stephani collected his force, which consisted of around 1200 men, mostly young officers, cadets, doctors and students, organised in three companies. Like the well-trained military man he was, von Stephani had already made a reconnaisance of his objective: disguising himself as a Spartacist and actually entering the occupied offices of the *Vorwärts* newspaper to spy out the lie of the land.

At 8.15 a.m. on the morning of 11 January, Berliners were awoken by a fierce cannonade: Stephani's shock troops spearheaded by flame-throwers, artillery and machine-guns launched themselves against the Spartacist positions. Spartacist machine-gun nests in the *Vorwärts* building replied to the bombardment, but bullets were no answer to the devastating pounding of howitzers and trench-mortars brought up to point-blank range. The shells punched gaping holes in the front of the building, and nearby houses were set on fire.

Spartacist snipers attempted to answer back behind makeshift barricades formed from rolls of newsprint. After some minutes seven Spartacists left the building waving white handkerchiefs to discuss terms of surrender. The Freikorps were having none of it. One of the delegates was sent back into the building to tell his comrades that unconditional surrender alone was acceptable while the other six were brutally manhandled into a nearby courtyard, beaten up and finally shot down in cold blood. Stephani's troops then took the *Vorwärts* building by storm and captured

300 Spartacists alive. Almost all were roughed up on their way to prison and seven of them were shot out of hand. Von Stephani claimed later that Reinhard and the Reichs-Chancellery had repeatedly ordered him to 'shoot the lot' although he had declined to carry out this order.

Luckily for him, Leviné, the KPD commander of *Vorwärts* had been away from the building when von Stephani launched his assault; four months later Leviné was back at the barricades playing a leading role in the Munich Soviet Republic. This time, he would not escape the vengeance of the Freikorps.

The following day, Sunday 11 January (the end of 'Spartacus Week' as it was to be known), at the extreme west end of Berlin, Noske made his formal entry into the city. Smiling grimly under his battered felt hat, he strode on through the prosperous suburbs. The force at his back consisted of the 1600 members of his Iron Brigade from Kiel, plus another 2400 Freikorps men drawn from Maercker's unit, General von Roeder's Scouts, and the soon-to-be-notorious Garde Kavalrie Schutze Division (The Horse Guards).

As the field-grey columns crossed the suburb of Lichterfelde towards the centre of the capital, sober-sided citizens ventured out of their homes to greet their saviours; the conservative *Berliner Post* newspaper described the scene next day under the headline 'A Gleam of Light':

> Yesterday afternoon at about three o'clock many a patriotic heart could once again rejoice at a sorely missed sight. Soldiers were marching across the Potsdamer Platz . . . soldiers with officers, soldiers controlled by their leaders. An immense crowd lined both sides of the street and welcomed them with enthusiastic cheers. The press was so thick that the troops were compelled to stop. Sharp commands of 'Company halt! Slope arms!' were executed with disciplined precision. Shouts of 'Bravo!' from the public. All were looking with admiration at this first-class, impeccable, disciplined unit and its leaders.

At length, Noske's force reached the very hub of Berlin, the Brandenburg Gate. The Spartacist machine-gun nest which had, until a few hours before, dominated the triumphal arch, had already been dislodged by Government loyalists, in a gesture that symbolised the swinging of the pendulum of political power back to the forces of the Right. The relief column – for such it seemed to the battered and bewildered bourgeoisie – broke rank and took up its battle stations with Teutonic thoroughness.

The Kiel Iron Brigade relieved Reinhard's over-stretched forces in charge of the vital Moabit barracks. Sections III and V of Maercker's Rifle Corps took over Lichterfelde, while the Horse Guards Division seized the suburb of Zehlendorf. Dividing the capital like a wedge of cheese, Sections I and II of the Rifle Corps and another part of the Horse Guards took control of Berlin's southern districts, deploying along a line from Buckow to Zehlendorf by Marienfelde, Lichtenrade and Tempelhof.

That night, Noske's forces moved against the revolutionary headquarters – Eichhorn's Police Presidium building on the Alexanderplatz in eastern Berlin. The attacking section was led by one Sergeant-Major Schulze, commanding a company of Reinhard's Freikorps. The same tactics were employed which had been used to reduce the *Vorwärts* building: artillery, brought up to blast the headquarters at point-blank range. Shells crashed through the walls of the building, as the guns traversed it. At length, the entire front of the edifice crumbled and collapsed under the weight of the bombardment. The Spartacist defenders fought on with a courage born of desperation, but the struggle was hopeless. Outgunned, outnumbered and facing hordes of determined and disciplined storm troops, the defenders gave way. Those who could, fled over the adjoining rooftops to safety; the rest died at their posts or were captured and brutally despatched by the victors. The offices, the corridors and even the lifts inside the building became the scenes of gory massacre, as the revolutionaries were harried from room to room, and finally clubbed or shot dead where they stood.

The revolution had been defeated in open battle, but there still remained a major mopping-up operation before the Government could feel safe and securely in control. Once again the operation was organised as though Berlin were a conquered enemy capital. Each Freikorps was assigned a section of the city: the main Government area, lying between the Jerusalemstrasse and the Werderstrasse on one side, and the Tiergarten park on the other, was given to Maercker's men. This area included the Reichs-Chancellery, most of the Ministries, the Imperial Palace and the Marstall – still occupied bv the hapless remnants of the People's Naval Division. General Maercker installed himself in the former Crown Prince's Palace to oversee operations.

The Horse Guards Division commanded by General von Hoffmann, occupied the neighbouring sector to Maercker, comprising the Reichstag, the Ringbahn overhead railway and the Potsdamer Platz. The staff of the Division installed themselves in the palatial Eden Hotel. Roeder's Volunteer Scouts occupied the section around the Spree river, to the right of Maercker, with their HQ in the Viktoria School in the Neanderstrasse. General von Held's Freikorps held the suburbs of Neukolln and Tempelhof to the south, between the Landwehr and Teltow canals, with their HQ in Neukolln town hall. General von Wissel's Freikorps head-quarters in the Treptower park telephone exchange, occupied the sector between the Landwehr and Neukolln canals, including the Lohnmullerplatz. Finally, General von Hulsen's numerically large Freikorps, centred on the Charlottenburg Schloss, took over Spandau, Havel, Schmargendorf, Grünewald, Schlachtensee and Wannsee. General von Lüttwitz remained in general command of the military side of the occupation from his HQ in Dahlem. At dawn on 15 January, Lüttwitz reviewed Maercker's Rifle Corps at Tempelhof aerodrome. When the review was completed,

Maercker's men divided into three columns and marched to occupy, respectively, the Imperial Palace; the Friedrichstrasse railway station; and the Ministerial quarter around the Wilhelmstrasse. The marching men encountered no organised resistance, although the occasional Spartacist sharpshooter fired on them from the rooftops. (The Freikorps nicknamed these snipers 'Dachkaninchen' – roof rabbits – and presumably potted them in the same cheerful spirit.)

Once the troops had reached their objectives, they deployed, according to pre-arranged orders, in skirmishing formation and took up their posts inside the buildings. Machine-guns were set up in the streets to command strategically important squares, and heavy armoured cars prowled the city in a display of intimidating force. As night fell, searchlights were switched on, freezing the 'rabbits' in their glare, and a strict curfew was enforced in the working-class suburbs, cowing the populace. By midnight, Lüttwitz was able to report to Ebert and Noske that his men were masters of Berlin. A happy Noske wrote that night, 'The nightmare which hung over the town is dispersed.' But for the Spartacist leadership, scattered and hunted across the city, the nightmare was just beginning.

6

THE TWIN MURDERS: LIEBKNECHT AND LUXEMBURG

'Tomorrow the Revolution will rise again and say to you: "I was. I am. I shall be".'

Rosa Luxemburg, her last editorial in the *Rote Fahne* ('The Red Flag'), January 1919

'We are fighting for the gates of Heaven.'

Karl Liebknecht, speech, January 1919.

The twin murders of Liebknecht and Luxemburg are worth describing in some detail for their immense importance – both for themselves and in their historical and symbolic significance. In themselves, they were typical of many of the murders carried out by the Freikorps in the next four years. They are also politically vital as they removed the two most able and charismatic leaders of the German Left, and exposed the guilt of the SPD in condoning the elimination of their former party comrades, leaving a legacy of bitterness that was to divide and fatally weaken the forces of German Socialism for more than a generation. The murders, in the words of the radical liberal journalist Sebastian Haffner were: '. . . historically the most potent event in the drama of the German revolution. Viewed from the vantage point of half a century later, it has acquired something of the uncanny, incalculably far-reaching effect of the event on Golgotha . . .' If this mystical, semi-religious language seems a little far-fetched, compare it with Liebknecht's own words. Driven into hiding on 12 January, the day after Noske's triumphant entry to Berlin, he wrote from the underground an article for the *Rote Fahne* redolent with religious imagery:

> Where are we? Mystery. But we are not defeated. Even if they fetter us, here we are and here we remain. And the victory will be ours. For Spartakus is the fire of the spirit, the soul and the heart; it is the will and the act of the proletarian revolution. Spartakus is all misery and desire of happiness, for Spartakus is Socialism and universal revolution. The Calvary of the German working class is not yet over, but the day of deliverance draws near.

If Marxism is a substitute religion, then Karl Liebknecht must have seen himself as some sort of Messiah. This is certainly not how he was seen by his Social Democratic and bourgeois enemies, nor by his Freikorps killers; for them he was more like the Anti-Christ, the Devil incarnate. From the very earliest days of the revolution, shortly after they had both been released from the Kaiser's jails, Liebknecht and Luxemburg were targeted for destruction. An anonymous poster campaign early in December 1918 showed clearly which way the wind was blowing: 'Workers! Citizens!', the hoardings proclaimed, 'The Fatherland is on the brink of disaster. Save it! It is threatened not from without but from within: by the Spartacist group. Beat their leaders to death! Kill Liebknecht! Then you will have peace, work and bread.' (Ironically, the reactionary copy writer here appropriates Lenin's slogan which had swept the Bolsheviks to power in Russia.)

There is considerable evidence that this campaign originated from within the very highest circles of the Social Democratic Party. An SPD functionary, Anton Fischer, wrote in 1920 that his office had been instructed as early as November 1918 to 'dig out and hunt down' Liebknecht and Luxemburg, 'by day and by night, so that they had no chance to agitate or organise.' On the night of 9/10 December, soldiers from a Guards regiment forced their way into the offices of the *Rote Fahne*. Their admitted mission was to murder the paper's joint editor, Liebknecht. Their reward was to be 50,000 Marks bounty put up by a millionaire named Georg Sklarz, a bosom friend of the SPD leader Scheidemann.

As soon as the Freikorps established themselves in control of Berlin, the hunt for the fugitive Spartacist leaders began in earnest. A bulletin put out by one of the Freikorps proclaimed:

> The fear has been voiced that the Government might slacken in its action against the Spartacists. Authoritative sources confirm that what has been achieved so far is by no means considered sufficient, and that every effort will be made to act against the leaders of the movement. The population of Berlin should not feel that those who have for the time being got away can live elsewhere in peace. The very next days will show that they, too, will not be spared.

This threat was to be carried out to the letter.

That same day, 13 January, the SPD organ *Vorwärts*, newly wrested from Spartacist control, published a doggerel poem that was – literally – an incitement to murder:

> Many hundreds dead in a row –
> Proletarians!
> Karl, Rosa, Radek and Co. –
> None of them are there, not one!
> Proletarians!

The actual process that ended in murder had begun some days earlier, in Noske's battle HQ at the Luisenstift. The 'Bloodhound' himself had personally ordered a young Freikorps officer, Lieutenant Friedrich Wilhelm von Oertzen – later, under the Nazis, an enthusiastic hagiographer of the Freikorps – to tap Liebknecht's telephone by day and night. Oertzen was instructed to report on Liebknecht's movements and actions to Captain Waldemar Pabst, whom we last encountered as a staff officer at the Marstall siege. The egregious Captain was now Chief-of-Staff – and effective commander – of one of the main Freikorps, General von Hoffmann's Horse Guards Division.

As the hunt for the two leaders was stepped up, the offices of the *Rote Fahne* were repeatedly raided. Rosa Luxemburg was forced to go into hiding first. She continued to write her fiery editorials from a doctor's house near the Hallesche Tor before moving to a worker's flat in the Spartacist stronghold of Neukolln. On 12 January she was joined there by Liebknecht in heavy disguise. The behaviour of the two leaders differed strangely during this brief respite. Luxemburg, though prostrated by agonizing headaches, continued to write feverish articles in support of the revolt she had been so reluctant to back: 'Act! Act! Courageously, resolutely, consistently – that is the accursed duty and obligation of revolutionaries.' Recognising defeat looming she continued to spit defiance, and to justify the revolt in retrospect. Liebknecht, by contrast, seemed remote from the ruin of the revolt he had so impulsively helped to launch, spending most of his time reading fairy stories to the little daughter of the family that was sheltering him. Even the news that his wife and son had been seized by the Freikorps failed to arouse him from his shocked state.

The Neukolln quarter was being systematically combed for the pair, and on 14 January a mysterious warning telephone call was received: possibly its source was the telephone tappers who may still have been monitoring him. At any rate, the alarmed couple decided to move immediately to the middle-class area of

Wilmersdorf, in the very heart of Berlin and the midst of their enemies. On the face of it, this seems an odd choice of refuge, but they may well have calculated that they would be safer amongst their foes than continuing to endanger their friends and supporters by their presence. Their final port of call was the home of a relative of Liebknecht, Frau Markussohn, at 53 Mannheimerstrasse. There, early on 15 January, they penned their final articles for the *Rote Fahne*. Their tone was one of resolute and triumphant resignation.

> Liebknecht: Today's vanquished will be tomorrow's victors . . . whether or not we shall still be alive when this is achieved. Our programme will live on: it will dominate the world of liberated humanity. In spite of all!
> Luxemburg: O you thick-skulled upholders of the law! Your 'order' is built on sand. By tomorrow the Revolution will rise clanking to its feet again and to your horror will announce with a fanfare of trumpets: I was. I am. I shall be!

That very evening, while Rosa Luxemburg was resting with another splitting headache, there was a knock on the door. It was Wilhelm Pieck, another KPD leader, who had come with the galley proofs of the next day's *Rote Fahne*.

As he was going over them with Liebknecht the doorbell rang again. A tavern keeper named Mehring, a member of the local Wilmersdorf Residents' Defence Militia, was demanding to see Herr Liebknecht and Frau Luxemburg. In vain, their presence was denied. Mehring left, but shortly after he was back, together with a detachment of soldiers from the Horse Guards Division under a Lieutenant Lindner, who searched the flat and discovered his quarry. Both Liebknecht and Rosa asked to pack an overnight case with books and belongings, no doubt anticipating another spell in prison.

Together with Pieck the two leaders were rushed to the Eden Hotel, since that morning the headquarters of the Horse Guards

Division. Liebknecht and Luxemburg had been picked up some time after 9 p.m. By 10 p.m. they were in the hands of Captain Pabst in his upper floor suite at the Eden. As soon as they arrived in the hotel, the bullying began. Verbal insults swiftly turned to physical assault. Both were brutally beaten with rifle butts. Liebknecht asked in vain for bandages to dress two wounds on his head.

Captain Pabst, at the end of his long life – he survived until 1970 – claimed that the interrogation was conducted correctly, and lasted only long enough to establish the identity of his prisoners. But other testimony contradicts this. A hotel maid told the trial of the killers: 'I shall never forget how they knocked the poor woman down and dragged her around.' Pabst asked her if she was really Red Rosa: 'Make up your own mind', replied the indomitable revolutionary. Liebknecht refused to say anything, but a rough examination of his clothing revealed the monogrammed initials 'KL' stitched on his shirt. That was enough. He was hustled down the hotel stairs and out of a side entrance into a street which had already been cordoned off. A group of soldiers stood waiting. One of them, an oafish thug named Otto Runge, lunged forward with an upraised rifle and clubbed Liebknecht over the skull. Semi-conscious, the Spartacus chief was bundled into a car and driven off into the night to the nearby Tiergarten Park. The car was manned by a Naval Lieutenant from Noske's Iron Brigade, temporarily seconded to the Horse Guards, Horst von Pflugk-Hartung, together with his brother Heinz, and three other naval officers. The car left the hotel at about 10.45 p.m.

As soon as the car reached a dark part of the park, it stopped. The dazed Liebknecht, bleeding profusely from his head wounds, was told the vehicle had a flat tyre and was compelled to leave the car. He was ordered to start walking. Hardly had he stumbled a few paces when Horst von Pflugk-Hartung shot him in the back. The rest of the escort fired into the body too, just to make sure.

One of the party, a Lieutenant Liepmann, delivered the body to the nearby morgue at the Berlin Zoo, identifying it as the corpse of an unknown man.

Some minutes later, Rosa Luxemburg was brought out of the same side door. Runge ran forward again and smashed her over the head with his rifle butt. Critically injured, but still just alive, she too was carried into a car and driven away. The car slewed to a halt within a few hundred yards and shots were heard by the hotel guests. Rosa's exact fate remained unknown for some time. Her killers – an escort of five Horse Guards headed by a Lieutenant Kurt Vogel – had apparently panicked and botched the job. It was later suggested that another officer, sub-Lieutenant Souchon, had jumped on to the car running board and fired the fatal shot into Rosa's head. Other accounts say that Vogel delivered the coup-de-grace. At all events, her body disappeared and was only recovered, wired and weighed down with stones, bloated and noisome, in a lock of the Landwehr canal some five months later.

The role played by Wilhelm Pieck in the events of that night is one of the minor mysteries of the whole affair and will probably never be satisfactorily solved. Although detained at the Eden, he did not share the fate of his comrades and was later released to resume his Communist party career. Pabst later suggested that he had been spared because of his knowledge of Spartacist arms caches and other valuable information. It seems possible that he bargained his life against betraying the hiding places of his fellow Communists. (It will be recalled that the fatal visit of Mehring and Lindner's patrol followed hard on the heels of Pieck's arrival at the apartment. Was he tailed, or was he knowingly leading the Freikorps men to their quarry?) Pieck fled to the Soviet Union after Hitler took power, and remained in Moscow throughout the war, surviving the Stalinist purges to return to Berlin with the Red Army in 1945. He ended his life as the first President of Communist East Germany.

There is now no doubt that the murders were carefully organised, ordered and orchestrated by the meticulous little Captain Pabst. Indeed, he remained proud of his achievement to his dying day. Towards the end of his life he told the West German magazine *Der Spiegel* that Liebknecht and Luxemburg had represented a threat to western civilisation and that anyway their killing was justified under martial law. At the time of the crime he was more circumspect. Although he had attended in disguise demonstrations addressed by Liebknecht and Luxemburg to get the measure of his enemies and had satisfied himself that they were 'extremely dangerous', Pabst was a politically astute officer and well knew that the savage murders could provoke an adverse reaction in some quarters. Therefore he had prepared a careful cover story to obscure and obliterate the deed.

In fact, Pabst was already at work drafting his 'official version' of the deaths while his killer squads were still about their grisly task. Pflugk-Hartung was the first to return to the Eden and reported that Liebknecht had been shot dead 'While attempting to escape' – the euphemism for cold-blooded murder that was to become sickeningly familiar under both the regime of the Freikorps and the rule of their direct descendants of the Third Reich.

After some delay caused by the more complicated circumstances of Rosa Luxemburg's elimination, Lieutenant Vogel obediently came back to the Hotel with a bizarre tale to tell. According to him, he had been escorting the revolutionary leader for her own safety when a mob of civilians had overwhelmed the transport and borne Red Rosa away. He had, he said, no idea of her present whereabouts.

This, essentially, was the story that Pabst prepared in his report that was published in the Government press the following day. Far from having any hostile intentions towards the Spartacist chiefs, he asserted, he had merely taken them into protective custody for their own safety to save them from the blood-thirsty mobs of upright citizens who were crowding round the Eden to demand their heads.

Pabst's story started to come apart before the ink was dry. For a start there was the apparently unauthorised double intervention of the burly Hussar, Otto Runge. It transpired that Runge had been bribed to make his murderous assault by the Horse Guards Division's transport officer, a Captain Petri, who – unaware of Pabst's prior arrangements – had offered Runge one hundred Marks to attack the prisoners. Then there was the preposterous claim that the Eden had been besieged by vociferous crowds. Apart from the fact that a strict curfew was in force, and that anyone daring to break it would themselves have been shot on the spot, the streets around the hotel had been sealed off by barbed wire barricades and were crawling with the troops of the Horse Guards Division. There had not been a civilian within sight. In addition, there were just too many witnesses inside the hotel who had seen – and heard – the maltreatment meted out to the dead Spartacists. There was also the little matter of a tiny feminine shoe, brought back by Rosa Luxemburg's escort, and gloatingly passed around as a macabre 'trophy'.

All in all, Pabst's cover-up would not wash. But the one indisputable fact remaining was that Liebknecht and Luxemburg were dead, and in the bitterly cynical world of the Freikorps – the spirit that now ruled Berlin – 'Stone dead hath no fellow'.

Pabst personally reported the deaths to Noske. The brutal Minister did not quail at the demise of his former party comrades: 'He shook my hand', Pabst later recalled. When some members of the SPD expressed their disquiet, Noske rounded on them roughly:

'You've got nerves like hysterical old women. War's war. Ah well, you never were a game bunch.' True to form, next day's edition of *Vorwärts* justified the murders in retrospect: 'They were selfconfessed instigators of civil war, killers of the proletariat, fratricides and their ears must ring forever with the fateful words: "A fugitive and a vagabond shalt thou be on earth".'

Nevertheless, there were some, even among the military, whose consciences were evidently uneasy. On the day following the murders, the Commander of the Guards Division, General von Hofmann, who had not been privy to Pabst's plans, appointed a Military legal investigation officer, Kurtzig, to examine the evidence. Kurtzig, quite properly, immediately ordered the arrest of von Pflugk-Hartung and Lieutenant Vogel.

Alarmed, Pabst decided to put a spoke in Kurtzig's wheel by appointing another investigator, Jorns, to look into the case. The two lawyers split the case between them, with the more pliable Jorns taking over the Liebknecht investigation and Kurtzig remaining in charge of the Luxemburg case. Shortly afterwards, Jorns started a leisurely re-examination of the evidence. Witnesses came forward who had seen Vogel's men throw Rosa Luxemburg's body from a bridge into the Landwehr canal. Vogel admitted disposing of the corpse and was re-arrested on 20 February. A week later he was joined in jail by the men who had driven Liebknecht away from the hotel, and shortly afterwards by the other members of the Luxemburg escort.

Conditions inside the prison were ludicrously lax. The accused were left with their cell doors unlocked so that they had plenty of time to mingle and co-ordinate the stories they were to give at their trial. The regime was tightened slightly when a startled Jorns was surprised to see one of the supposed detainees – Liepmann, the man who had left Liebknecht's body at the mortuary – gaily hailing him in a Berlin bar! On 27 March Jorns responded by depriving Vogel and von Pflugk-Hartung of prison visiting rights and, a few days later, the simple-minded Otto Runge, who had been provided with cash and a false passport by Pflugk-Hartung's brother, Heinz, was tracked down and added to the bag.

Worried by the tightening net, Pabst appointed a close crony, Naval Lieutenant Wilhelm Canaris, as an associate judge on the court-martial that was to try the case – despite the fact that Canaris had been cheerfully visiting Horst von Pflugk-Hartung in jail and could hardly be considered impartial. Before the court convened, Canaris staged a full-dress rehearsal of the trial inside the Moabit prison. Some of the accused played the roles of judge and prosecutor while other defendants went through their own parts. The men obediently learned their lines and carefully laid their false trails. The slow-witted Runge had to be helped to memorise his part by repeating his alibi over and over again. As a second line of defence should the lies fall down, Canaris acquired false passports and boltholes abroad in case a hasty exit from the Fatherland proved necessary.

The entire General Staff of the Horse Guards Division were working flat out on the escape plans of their brother officers, and the wheels were oiled by the sum of 30,000 Marks raised as a secret escape fund by the German National Association of Officers. Sitting safely in their cells, the murderers could feel secure in the knowledge that even if the court, by some mischance, convicted them, they would not have to remain behind bars for long.

The charade of a court martial finally convened in May. The eight accused sauntered into the courtroom from the judge's chambers, medals gleaming on their chests, looking, in the words of a witness, 'As if they are bound for a wedding rather than the dock.' Grinning broadly, they took their places as the theatre commenced. The trial passed off as planned. No one implicated the chief culprit, Pabst, and Canaris skilfully obscured the proceedings so that no real light was shed on the true events of 15 January.

The verdicts reflected the farcical proceedings. Five defendants were acquitted outright, one was given six weeks jail for 'abrogating his authority'. Otto Runge – the only non-officer in the dock – was given two years inside for his murderous assault, and Lieutenant Vogel, thanks to those witnesses who had seen him dispose of Rosa's body, was dismissed the service and sentenced to two years and four months imprisonment for 'gross dereliction of duty and submitting an inaccurate report of his actions'; in other words, for failing to cover up his crime properly.

Vogel felt aggrieved at having to take responsibility alone. Having already acquired a properly stamped passport in a false name he looked forward to his early release. An Independent Socialist MP had got wind of the plan to spring Vogel and he was about to be moved to a stricter security jail when Canaris acted. On 17 May, three days after Vogel was sent down, an officer calling himself Lieutenant Lindemann presented himself at the Moabit prison with a pass apparently signed by Jorns, authorising him (Lindemann) to escort Vogel to another jail. Impressed by an officer's uniform and the flashed document, the Moabit turnkeys obediently handed their prisoner over and he and Lindemann drove off in a car.

Jorns visited the Moabit next day and was surprised to learn that the bird had flown. Naturally, he had signed no transfer order and had never heard of Lieutenant Lindemann, who was none other than Canaris himself. But by then, Vogel was safely across the border in Holland. As Canaris' biographer, Heinz Hohne, drily remarks: 'Judges who release the men they helped to convict were something new in German legal history.'

Noske treated the escape as a personal blow to his authority and ordered Canaris to be confined in the Moabit, the scene of the audacious escape. But he only languished there for four days. An old naval Comrade, Lieutenant Commander Löwenfeld, whom we last met in Kiel organising what was to become the Third Marine Brigade Freikorps, succeeded in converting Canaris' confinement to house arrest. The 'house' concerned was the former Imperial Palace, now serving as Löwenfeld's own HQ!

Meanwhile a commission of inquiry into the escape had been set up. The members of the inquiry were the very officers from the Horse Guards Division who had organised the escape. (Who says the Germans lack a sense of humour?) Naturally, Canaris was cleared of all complicity in the affair and set free to resume his career in the secret world of the Freikorps intelligence. His success in that shadowy world was later to make him an Admiral and Chief of the German military intelligence service, the Abwehr. Eventually, of course, it was also to lead him into anti-Hitler conspiracy and a ghastly end on a Gestapo gallows in the final days of the Second World War.

The double murder of Liebknecht and Luxemburg unleashed a wave of hatred and blood that had been notably absent from the German revolution until that date. Perhaps the Spartacist pair, both from good bourgeois backgrounds themselves, were naive in the extreme not to appreciate what forces their rhetoric had stirred up. To their numerous enemies, they were hardly human. Even an essentially moderate old monarchist like General Maercker almost foamed at the mouth when he spoke of them: 'Their threat is a dire one. Rosa Luxemburg is a she-devil, and Liebknecht the type who will stop at nothing.' Rosa's wartime anti-militarist diatribes, in which she called the proud German army 'the miserably beaten men of Flanders' and demanded the trial of officers before revolutionary tribunals, had not endeared her to the officer caste. A Polish-born Jewess with a Prussian passport and a rocky marital history, she represented the worst sort of subversive threat to a conservative, repressed and 'orderly' social structure. Anti-semitism, anti-feminism, anti-pacifism and anti-communism combined to produce a truly murderous hatred in the Freikorps mind.

As for Liebknecht, what did they know, or care, of the gentle bespectacled journalist whose greatest pleasure was to roll on the floor with his children? They only remembered the man who was the sole member of the Reichstag with the courage to vote against the war credits in 1914. They remembered his organisation of the first demonstration against the war in 1917. Again, this man represented to the military mind all that was rotten in the nation. In reality the couple could have expected little mercy when they fell into the hands of their enemies, nor, had the roles been reversed, would they have offered much in return. It is the combination of the revolting sadistic cruelty to the small crippled woman and the frail man, with the hypocritical injustice of the guilty in evading their responsibility that most appalls. In the words of Napoleon, it was worse than a crime, it was a blunder, and one which many Germans – before and after the Second World War – have failed to face.

In 1974, the West German Government dared to put Rosa Luxemburg's portrait on a postage stamp. A huge furore resulted. One man, asking for stamps at a post office, and receiving a batch of the 'Rosas', roared at the postmaster: 'Do you realise you are asking me to lick the backside of a bloody Communist?'

7

MAERCKER'S MARCH

'Just wait and see. Now everything is going to be all right.'
Gustav Noske to Friedrich Ebert
after witnessing the first parade of Maercker's Freikorps,
December 1918

Temporarily secure in the capital, the Government felt free to turn to two other pressing tasks: the holding of the promised elections to the National Assembly which was to draft a new constitution for the young Republic, and the snuffing out of revolutionary movements outside Berlin.

The elections were held on 19 January in a reasonably peaceful – if tense – atmosphere. Out of a total electorate of 35 million people, the SPD got 11½ million votes, nearly 40 per cent, entitling them to a dominant 165 seats in the Assembly; next came the Catholic Centre Party with 90 seats. The liberal Democratic Party, representing the more progressive elements of the middle class, won 75 seats. Thirty-eight seats went to the conservative People's Party, while the ultra-reactionary Nationalists won 22 seats – the same number scored by the Independent Socialist USPD, who could only muster just over 2 million votes – or 5 per cent of the total. The elections were a clear triumph for the SPD and their centrist bourgeois allies, and an outright rejection of the extremes of right and left.

Ebert could now claim, with some justification, a popular mandate for his previously ad-hoc Government. The voters had given him a free hand to stamp on revolutionary extremism, but they had also rejected the ultra-Right's virulent hatred of the Republic and all its works. The KPD, licking its wounds, had scornfully boycotted the poll as a bourgeois farce, a contemptuous attitude curiously shared by their sworn enemies of the Freikorps at the other end of the political spectrum. About 5 million voters boycotted the polls altogether.

January 19 also saw the issuing of the notorious 'Noske Rules' – an edict drafted by the victorious Defence supremo designed to emasculate and eventually eliminate those motors of the social revolution – the Soldier's Councils. The executive of the Greater Berlin Central Soldiers' Council promptly wound itself up. Where councils proved more recalcitrant, Noske was not above offering a bribe. If they did not take even this heavy hint, then force was frequently applied. Thus, on the same day, the two main supports of the revolution were abruptly pulled away: the revolutionaries lost their claim to popular support, and their political clout in the form of the Councils – always a major irritant to the officer Corps who saw them as an alien import from Bolshevik Russia.

Thus bolstered, the Government felt strong enough, on 20 January, to order the Freikorps out of the city they had conquered. Perhaps Ebert felt the first stirrings of unease at the anti-republican attitude displayed by the Freikorps troops. Attempts to recruit workers into the volunteer corps – for example, by advertisements in *Vorwärts* – had largely proved a failure. The workers were more inclined to join their local 'Wehr' – para-military militias, sympathetic to the Republic, but basically an amateur force used to defend neighbourhoods from possible Spartacist attacks. The rank and file of the Freikorps were, and remained, ex-soldiers or middle-class youths and students of right-wing nationalist sympathies. The attitude of these gentlemen to their avowed Republican and Socialist political masters is summed up in a diary entry written on 21 January by a one-armed Freikorps leader, Captain Peter von Heydebreck (later a top leader of the Nazi SA Brownshirt party militia, shot along with his chief, Ernst Röhm, in the 'Night of the Long Knives' purge of 30 June 1934): 'I will not forget these days of criminals . . . Lies and barbarity . . . The days of the revolution will forever be a blight on German history. As the scum hate me I remain strong. The day will yet come when I will knock the truth into these people and tear the mask from the faces of the whole miserable, pathetic lot.'

It must be remembered that this jet of vitriolic spleen was not directed at the dead Marxist martyrs, Liebknecht and Luxemburg, but at Ebert and Scheidemann – the 'November criminals' – paymasters of the Freikorps, but, in their eyes, traitors to the Fatherland and as guilty as the Spartacist 'rabble'.

Ten days later, on 30 January, an advance Guard of Maercker's Landes Jäger Schutzen Freikorps was sent to the town of Weimar, which had been chosen as the seat of the newly elected National Assembly. The choice of the small, sleepy central German town was made deliberately. Once the dwelling place of those arche-typal German poets, Goethe and Schiller, Weimar was small and easily defended. It was far away from the sprawling, dangerous slums of Berlin, and its national theatre, where Liszt had conducted the premiere of Wagner's *Lohengrin*, was a suitable site for the Assembly to sit in well-guarded tranquillity.

Maercker's men did not quite meet the warm welcome they had anticipated. At the end of their 150-mile journey from Berlin, the advance guard of 2 officers and 120 men were attacked, disarmed and taken prisoner by the local Communists. But over the next few days, the rest of the Corps – totalling more than 7000 men – arrived, surrounded the city with 'a ring of steel' and occupied the railway station, the post office and the national theatre itself. The two Brigade of the Jägers, supported by artillery batteries, were able to assure the Government that the Assembly could meet to debate in perfect safety – protected by the machine guns and bayonets of the Freikorps.

While the Assembly vacillated over signing the ruinous Versailles treaty, the Allies maintained their wartime blockade of the northern ports. The prospect of spring brought no relief to the hungry nation, and, as usual, the brunt of the misery fell on the working class. Unemployment in Berlin rose steadily: 180,000 in January, 250,000 in February, 560,000 in March, more than a million in April. A desperate new wave of strikes threatened to engulf the near-starving country.

'If this situation goes on,' prophesied the idealistic industrialist and politician Walther Rathenau, 'the cities will be deserted, the roads broken, the woods cut down, the harvests ruined, the harbours, railways and canals abandoned. The towns . . . will consist of destroyed buildings, half-inhabited by miserable wretches.'

Once again, it was Noske who took decisive action. Grasping at once that the ports would in future form the channels by which Allied food and relief would reach the interior of Germany, he moved rapidly against the Spartacist strikers. In the major port of Bremen, the Independent USPD and the Communist KPD had reacted to the subjugation of Berlin by seizing control on 10 January and proclaiming an independent socialist republic. The SPD funds in the town were sequestrated, their newspaper was seized and the banks were occupied. Loyal soldiers returning from the Western Front were met with machine gun fire in their home town and disarmed. Squads of Red militiamen patrolled the docks and shipyards along the river Weser while food ships sent with emergency relief supplies by the US Hoover Commission were unable to discharge their cargoes because of the strike.

Noske ordered Colonel Gerstenburg, commander of the Third Landeschutzencorps Freikorps, to subdue the city with a task force consisting of his own Brigade, and the Kiel 'Iron Brigade' – renamed the First Marine Brigade to distinguish it from Löwenfeld's Third Marine Brigade and the soon-to-be-notorious Second Marine Brigade formed by former Naval Commander Hermann Ehrhardt. The 'Iron Brigade' was commanded by Colonel von Roden. As they neared Bremen, the force was buttressed by a third Freikorps, 3000-men strong, raised by a Major Caspari. The task force's advance guard, a squad led by Fritz Furmann, later a notorious Freikorps killer, stormed the strikers' stronghold on the Weser on 4 February using grenades and armoured cars. After a furious battle, by the evening Bremen was in their hands. The nominal leader of the Left, an Independent USPD deputy named Henke, suddenly remembered more pressing appointments at Weimar, leaving his supporters in the lurch. For the loss of twenty-six men killed and fifty-one wounded, the Freikorps had secured the key port for the Government. The luckless strikers lost 300 men, killed and captured.

Seeing the fate of Bremen, the neighbouring ports of Bremerhaven and Cuxhaven collapsed without resistance and were occupied on the 9 and 10 February. Gerstenberg and von Roden next moved on to subdue the so-called 'Republic of Oldenburg and East Fresia': an autonomous, Communist-controlled area centred on the port of Wilhelmshaven and run by a revolutionary sailor, Stoker (First Class) Bernhard Kuhnt. Wilhelmshaven fell to Ehrhardt's Freikorps, its ruling Soldiers', Sailors' and Workers' Council was dissolved, Kuhnt fled the city and was arrested.

Only Hamburg, the largest and most important of the northern ports, remained defiant. The situation in the huge city was precarious indeed. At one stage 40,000 workers, some of them armed, were in the streets, threatening to 'defend the conquests of the revolution'. Delegates from Hamburg, and its suburb, Altona, had gone to Berlin to petition Noske to call off his northern punitive expedition. As usual, Noske stalled with delaying tactics until the position around Bremen was secure. Isolated, Hamburg fell into acceptance of the Government's rule.

No sooner was the situation on the coast secured, than the Government was faced with a fresh outbreak of unrest in the industrial heartland of the Ruhr, centre of Germany's heavy mining and steel industry, and the cradle of the country's industrial revolution. At the beginning of January, the United Workers' Councils in the region had resolved on the immediate expropriation of the area's coal mines. The Government had refused to accept this Socialist measure, claiming that they were preparing their own nationalisation laws. When news of the Bremen march of the Freikorps became known, the Ruhr Workers' Council proclaimed a general strike on 6 February, fearing, with good reason, that Noske was planning a similar fate for them. This became a self-fulfilling prophecy when the strikers were joined by the Soldiers' Council of the local Seventh Army Corps. Noske ordered the Corps Commander, General Oskar von Watter, to dissolve the Council, jail its leaders and suppress the strike. Fearing the unreliability of his own troops, who were in solidarity with the strikers, Watter turned to the Freikorps to carry out the distasteful duty.

The man allotted the task was a mere Captain, named von Lichtschlag, one of the numerous junior officers who had taken it upon themselves to raise a Freikorps to restore order in their beloved Fatherland. The Freikorps Lichtschlag, of regimental strength, simply surrounded the Hall where the rebellious Council was in session and presented it with the option of dissolving itself or being shot. The Council meekly submitted and was promptly replaced by a body loyal to the Government.

The Workers' Councils, dominated by the Independent USPD, reacted by proclaiming an autonomous republic of the Ruhr, and an embargo upon coal deliveries to the rest of the Reich. Noske at once despatched two Freikorps brigades from newly-conquered Bremen to stem the revolt. This force, two thousand strong, reinforced Lichtschlag's seven hundred and fifty men and moved towards the strikers' HQ at Mülheim, through mining villages which they subdued by terror, killing forty pitmen. Hastily, the workers organised a 'Red Army' to defend themselves. Bloody clashes took place at Hervest-Dorten and Bottrop, where the Freikorps men bombarded the town hall with artillery, killing seventy-two armed workers. The strikers got the better of this encounter, however, isolating a section of raw young Freikorps fighters, disarming them, and bludgeoning them to death with clubs. Lichtschlag's men eventually occupied Mülheim, but the strikers' spirit was not wholly crushed, and they threatened to sabotage the entire coal industry by flooding the pits. Watter, fearing the consequences of such drastic action, agreed to negotiate. Weakened by lack of food, the strikers eventually consented to return to work, light their blast furnaces and lift the coal embargo. Watter would have to wait for more than a year before wreaking a bloody revenge on the workers of the 'Red Ruhr' for their defiance.

The unrest now spread to the industrial towns of Central Germany. It was indeed fortunate for the Government that these outbreaks, each serious in itself, occurred in a serial pattern. Successive local revolts could be curbed or contained, but a massive united revolution would surely have succeeded. Once again the woeful lack of organisation among the workers was demonstrated, belying right-wing fantasies of a calculated Bolshevik-inspired revolutionary conspiracy.

The town of Gotha was the first centre of revolt in middle Germany. Here, as on the Ruhr, the local soldiers made common cause with striking workers and Gotha proclaimed itself an autonomous revolutionary city. In the nearby larger town of Halle, workers formed a revolutionary Council under a man named Killian, an energetic extreme USPD member who enjoyed near-dictatorial power, disarmed the police and handed their weapons to the workers. The Press was put under 'revolutionary censors' and middle-class burghers were detained as suspected 'reactionaries'.

The Council was not sufficiently revolutionary for Killian, who created a Red militia under the command of a deserting officer, Lieutenant Ferchlandt, primarily composed of fellow deserters from the Navy. On 25 February, a general strike was proclaimed in the region and railway communications to Berlin and nearby Weimar were cut. The middle class in the city retaliated by calling their own strike in service and professional industries. The city's administration, post and press shut down, most shops failed to open and electricity and sanitary services broke down. Strike and counterstrike provoked a situation of near-anarchy and the Government in Weimar decided on drastic measures to restore its authority.

Noske ordered the faithful Maercker, in Weimar with his Freikorps, to march on Halle and occupy the city. Maercker selected his First Brigade, commanded by Colonel von Reitzenstein, to carry out the operation. This force, 3500-strong, reached Halle on 1 March. The early stages of the occupation proceeded peacefully. One of the Brigade's three sections occupied Halle's artillery garrison barracks where they were warmly welcomed by loyalist soldiers who put the city's munitions dump, containing fifty thousand rifles, thirty machine guns and a million cartridges at their disposal. The second Section took over the HQ of Ferchlandt's Red Militia in a school, again without opposition. But as Maercker's men neared the city centre, the streets filled with hostile demonstrators.

Hoping to avoid bloodshed, Maercker summoned the municipal authorities and the Workers' and Soldiers' Council to a meeting at the town hall. He sent an advance detachment of his men, equipped with twenty machine guns, to defend the building. En route, the squad was overwhelmed by the mob and disarmed. Two officers commanding the detachment, Lieutenants Hirsch and Schmidt, were murdered and their mutilated bodies flung in the river Saale. Maercker himself narrowly escaped a similar fate while on his way to the town hall. He sought shelter in a post office which was besieged by the crowds. After several hours, when it looked as though the father of the Freikorps must be torn to bits by the enraged mob, the third Section of his force, which had been delayed on the way from Weimar by the railway strike, arrived in the nick of time and rescued their chief.

A full-scale battle raged throughout the evening and night. The 'Reds' – civilians, discharged soldiers and members of the revolutionary militia – launched wave upon wave of suicidal attacks against the barracks and school where Maercker's men were entrenched. The centre of Halle was full of burning buildings, looted shops, and bodies littering the streets and squares. Machine gun fire rattled from both sides of the barricades.

At dawn, Maercker – surely the most moderate of all Freikorps leaders – once again attempted to negotiate. But the talks were broken off at noon after a signal act of atrocity committed by his opponents. Lieutenant-Colonel Kluver, a regular army officer sent by the General Staff to observe the occupation, unwisely ventured into the streets alone, on a spying mission. Although clad in mufti, the officer was recognised, roughed up and hauled before the Soldiers' Council which ordered his imprisonment. On the way to jail, the mob seized him from his guards and beat him up mercilessly, breaking his jaw and several ribs. Twice, Kluver managed to escape his tormentors' clutches, and twice he was dragged out of the houses where he had sought refuge and was set upon anew.

Tiring of their sport, the crowd finally hurled the Colonel from a bridge into the Saale. Still conscious, the brave officer attempted to evade his pursuers by swimming for safety. But each time he made for the bank the crowd pushed him back into the water. The savage hunt was finally ended by a Red militiaman who gave the Colonel the coup-de-grace with a revolver.

Hearing the news, Maercker resolved on stern measures. He ordered his men to clear the streets and give no quarter, and proclaimed a state of siege in Halle, decreeing that anyone caught with a weapon would be summarily shot. As in Berlin in January, the city was divided into sections and systematically occupied. Five hundred looters were court-martialled. Within hours, calm reigned again in Halle. The cost of the battle was thirty dead on the rebel side and sixty seven injured, and seven dead Freikorps men with twenty wounded.

Maercker dissolved the Red militia and disarmed the workers. To ensure future order in the city, he formed a Halle Freikorps, christening it the 'Einwohnerwehr' (residents' defence). The same measures were subsequently applied in the other central German towns occupied by Maercker: Magdeburg, Dresden (14 April), Brunswick (18 April), and finally, by mid-May, the largest city in the region, Leipzig.

These civil guard units formed a valuable second arm of the Freikorps movement, and were eventually to develop into a full-blown reserve of the professional Reichswehr. Among the eager recruits who flocked to them was the teenage son of the Halle Conservatoire Director, one Reinhard Heydrich, the future overlord of the Nazi secret services.

Maercker's occupation of the capital of 'Red Saxony', Dresden, was preceded by yet another brutal murder: radicals in the city had seized arms from the main weapons depot and made themselves virtual masters of the old Baroque city. On 12 April a crowd of war cripples, inflamed by rumours that their pensions were to be cut, chased the SPD War Minister for Saxony, Neuring, and hurled him into the river Elbe. He too tried to scramble ashore and was shot for his pains. The Freikorps Gorlitz was sent to the city, under the command of Colonel Faupel. (Later a Reichswehr General and Hitler's Ambassador to Franco's Spain. He committed suicide when the Third Reich collapsed.) The disorders were suppressed with the usual brutality.

As well as the Gorlitz Freikorps, those units who took part in Maercker's march through middle Germany included the Von Oven regiment, the Hulsen Freikorps, the Ehrhardt Second Marine Brigade and last but not least, the 'Stahlhelm' ('Steel Helmet'), a recently formed organisation of front-line veterans who were eventually to develop into the para-military arm of the German Nationalist party (DNVP) and, as such, the main rightist rivals to Hitler's SA Brownshirts in the final years of the Weimar Republic.

Maercker's Spring campaign, though characterised by ruthless rigour, cannot be compared with the devastation of, for example, Sherman's 'March through Georgia' at the end of the American Civil War. Its relative bloodlessness is a tribute to Maercker's own insistence on discipline and moderation. Unfortunately, this attitude was to prove atypical of the general Freikorps mentality, which was soon to be demonstrated again in the storm centre of Berlin.

8

STRIKES AND STREET FIGHTS

'Someone must be the Bloodhound. I won't shirk the responsibility.'
Gustav Noske, on his appointment as
Minister for National Defence.

The murders of Liebknecht and Luxemburg had left the
Spartacists and Independents representing the revolutionary Left
in Berlin leaderless, bloodied – but unbowed. The working-class
tenements of the capital still seethed with revolt and the bitterness
of betrayed hope. Seeing the piecemeal defeat of revolutionary
outbreaks in the north, the Ruhr and central Germany, and the
increasingly insolent counter-revolutionary provocations of
Noske and the Freikorps, the surviving revolutionary leaders felt
desperate, not so much to extend the revolution but to defend its
existing gains. With Maercker triumphantly on the march in
middle Germany, and the Weimar assembly consolidating, the
time to move was now – or never.

On the morning of 3 March 1919, the KPD organ *Rote Fahne*
proclaimed a general strike:

Workers! Proletarians! Once again the hour has struck! Once more the dead arise! The 'Socialist' Government of Ebert-Scheidemann-Noske has become the mass executioner of the German proletariat... Wherever the proletariat rules, Noske sends in his bloodhounds. Berlin, Bremen, Wilhelmshaven, Cuxhaven, Gotha, Erfurt, Halle – these are the bloody stations of the cross of Noske's crusade against the German proletariat. Thousands of your brothers are being mistreated, thrown into jail, murdered – struck down, butchered like mad dogs! Remember Rosa Luxemburg and Karl Liebknecht. The murderers go free with the blessing of Ebert-Scheidemann-Noske while your comrades rot in Prison.

The Revolution can only go forward by trampling on the graves of the Majority Social Democrats.

On to the General Strike!

On to the new revolutionary struggle!

On to the new battle against the oppressors!

Let all work cease! Remain quietly in the factories. Don't let the troops take them away from you. Gather in the workshops. Explain things to Comrades who hesitate or hang back. Don't be drawn into pointless shooting! Noske is only waiting for you to do that as an excuse for spilling more blood. Stay together at your workplace, ready for action at a moment's notice.

Highest discipline!

Highest discretion!

Iron Calm!

But also Iron Will!

Workers! Proletarians! The fate of the world lies in your hands! Down with Ebert, Scheidemann, Noske and all traitors and killers! Down with the National Assembly! On to battle! On to the General Strike!

Noske had already hastened back to Berlin from Weimar and was organising counter-measures with his usual energetic efficiency. The troops garrisoning Berlin were placed on alert by General Lüttwitz. In response to the strike call by the Workers' Council, the Government gave Noske exemplary executive power in greater Berlin. The scene was set for a bloody showdown.

On 3 March, Noske proclaimed a state of siege in the capital, forbidding public demonstrations and suppressing the left-wing press. Rioters and looters were to be immediately court-martialled. That night, disorders broke out in several districts of

Berlin. Leftist writers allege that these riots and pillage were the work of 'agents provocateurs' in the pay of Noske, and although these may have been a factor, at least some of the troubles arose from two elements not under the control of the Government or the Revolutionaries – our old friends the People's Naval Division and Republican Soldier's Defence, a left-wing militia. These gentlemen feared their imminent dissolution by Noske and were also owed considerable sums in back pay.

At any rate, the unrest offered Noske the golden opportunity to move in and restore 'order'. On 4 March Freikorps soldiers entered the suburb of Spandau, occupying its vital machine-gun depot. The occupation was opposed by crowds of unarmed civilians. The troopers hit back hard with rifle butt and boot, but when the mob seized one of their officers an armoured car opened fire directly into the mass: first blood to the Freikorps.

That afternoon, a huge throng assembled on the Alexanderplatz in front of the Berlin Police HQ, nerve-centre of the revolution during the Spartacist days in January. News spread quickly of that morning's happenings in Spandau, and a detachment of troops who foolishly attempted to cross the giant square was halted and roughly handled. The officer in charge of the squad was dragged from a car, trampled on and stripped; half-naked and smeared with blood and bootmarks, he managed to reach the safety of the police building with his men.

Besieged inside the building by the mob, the Freikorps men decided on a sortie to try to clear the square. They burst out and opened fire directly into the crowd. The mob surged forward again and was only driven back by a group of armoured cars which rumbled out of the station courtyard, machine guns spitting from the gunslits.

The next day, Wednesday 5 March, saw worsening violence. A section of the Marine Division, which had been garrisoning the Lehrter railway station, went to the Police HQ to protest against their dissolution by Freikorps units. While they were bargaining at the entrance, a shot was fired from within the building, mortally wounding a popular sailor named Klöppel. Around lunchtime, the Freikorps garrison inside the HQ was reinforced by soldiers of the Alexander and Augusta regiments, ordered into the capital by Lüttwitz. That afternoon, the sailors of the Marine Division, enraged by the killing of Klöppel, began to abandon their neutrality and fraternise with the strikers. The crowds closed in once more round the Police HQ. All night the siege continued, with the soldiers keeping the crowd at bay with rifle volleys. They were answered by weapons distributed to the strikers by the sailors.

March 6 saw the climax of the fighting. Colonel Reinhard, whose men had broken the Spartacist insurrection in January, once more moved into the hostile city in a bid to raise the siege of the Alexanderplatz. A tank led three lorry-loads of troops towards the gunfire but the column was halted by barbed wire barricades erected by the sailors. Thwarted, Reinhard ordered his men to use wartime storm-troop tactics: breaking up into small patrols to infiltrate and undermine the revolutionaries. Battle commenced in mid-afternoon, with the Freikorps men attacking from three directions and winkling out groups of their opponents from the entrances of the underground railway. With the help of heavy artillery and a trench-mortar battery, Alexanderplatz tube station was taken, and the siege lifted. Fifty revolutionaries, who had succeeded in establishing a toehold in the Police station, were disarmed and taken prisoner.

During the battle, Reinhard's men had come under fire from 150 sailors still entrenched in their original headquarters in the Marstall – scene of the army's humiliation at Christmas. Furious to avenge that shame, the Freikorps turned their heaviest guns on the former Imperial stables, and within half an hour the building was theirs. A neighbouring building named the 'People's Marine

House' offered a stiffer resistance with the aid of 2 field guns, 126 machine guns, 4000 rifles and hundreds of small arms. For the first time in the Civil War, the Freikorps called up the air arm to their aid. A squadron of aircraft took off and bombed the building. When the sailors continued to offer defiance, Reinhard ordered the building to be taken by storm, backed up by howitzer and mortar fire. It took three assault waves before the building was finally carried. As night fell, a bitter battle continued for possession of the streets around the Alexanderplatz.

Repeating their January tactics, the revolutionaries installed machine-gun and sniper nests on the roofs of houses from which they raked the neighbouring streets with fire. Under cover of darkness, they beat a slow retreat towards their strongholds in the working-class warren of eastern Berlin. Building their own barricades with wire, overturned lorries, steam-rollers and park railings, they turned the entire suburb of Lichtenberg into an armed fortress.

One of the witnesses to the confused and ragged street fighting in Berlin that March week was the urbane and cosmopolitan Count Harry Kessler. A rare moderate in an age of extremes, Kessler observed events with a compassionate and clear-eyed detachment. A diplomat of Liberal views, he had close contact with Government circles, but also kept a foot in the leftist camp via his wide circle of artistic acquaintances such as the Spartacist-sympathising caricaturist George Grosz. His diaries are a valuable chronicle of the shattered times:

March 3rd . . . the Workers' Councils of Greater Berlin have decided on an immediate general strike. None of the Ullstein, Mosse or Scherl publications has come out, since the newspaper staffs are already on strike. The Government is showing fright by placarding walls with posters proclaiming that Socialism 'is here'. Too late, like the Kaiser's abdication in November. A large part of the SPD workers are rumoured to be against the Government. This could be the start of the second revolution.

March 4th   A state of siege has been proclaimed . . . I recall . . . that Scheidemann said he will only feel happy when a state of siege exists again. I doubt, though, whether he feels especially happy at the moment.

March 6th   In the morning I was told of severe skirmishes, with mortars, on the Molkenmarkt and Alexanderplatz, and of numbers of houses being demolished. Since yesterday barricades and wire entanglements have gone up all over the city, erected by both the Spartacists and the Government. There were no papers so I went to see how things were for myself. At the corner of Unter den Linden and Friedrichstrasse a fire-engine drove past at full speed with someone dead or wounded on top. Bullets whizz across the Alexanderplatz and from time to time a mortar can be heard. At 1.20 a force of Republican Military Guards marched with its band down the Unter den Linden, passing other troops belonging to Reinhardt's Freikorps, the officers with shoulder-straps. In their midst was an armoured car with mounted machine guns. The Republicans passed the enemy unchallenged. The walls of the city are placarded, today of all days, with posters asking 'Who has the prettiest legs in Berlin? Caviar-Mousey-Ball. Evening, March 6th.' Suddenly, at half past six, the lights went out. The strike now includes power stations. The affair gives the impression of having a much more serious character than the Spartacus uprising. A major operation instead of a guerilla action.

March 7th   The electricity has been on since the morning and the lights are still burning. The underground is operating. On the walls are SPD posters calling on the workers not to join the strike. The over-throw of the sailors by the Reinhard troops, though unconnected with the strike, is psychologically important. This morning, surveying the steel helmeted Reinhard pickets I saw for the first time since the revolution a glimmer of the old Prussian spirit again. Perhaps one day traditional Prussian discipline and the new socialist one will coalesce to form a proletarian ruling caste which will assume the role of a Rome propagating new brands ofeivilization at the point of a sword. Bolshevism or any other label will do. The poor PrussianJunker has always been a sort of prole. Let faith in Liebknecht, or whoever, take a firm root in these German masses, trained to discipline as they are, and woe betide their enemies. If not today, then in the generation to come.

The amiable Count's prophecy of a fusion of Nationalism and Socialism was to be fulfilled exactly and most terribly.

On 8 March, after a day of stalemated, desultory fighting, the strike committee ordered a resumption of work. But if they were hoping that this concession would wring a corresponding gesture from Noske, they were to be sadly disappointed. On the morning of 9 March officially-inspired rumours swept the capital that Lichtenberg Police station had been stormed by armed revolutionaries, and that seventy police officers had been massacred in cold blood. The editor of the respected *Berliner Zeitung* newspaper received a telephone call to this effect from Doyé, head of the Interior Ministry's secret services. Doyé begged him to publish the report without further delay. *Vorwärts* on 10 March reported that, 'Sixty police officers and several dozen Government soldiers have been shot down like animals.' The *Berliner Tageblatt* put the number of victims at sixty-seven, and even the liberal *Vossische Zeitung* stated that over one hundred and fifty had been shot 'in an unheard-of mass murder'. The London *Times* correspondent cabled that he had heard from a Freikorps officer that the Spartacists were slaying their prisoners in batches of eighteen. The story was a fabrication. When the fog of war lifted, it was eventually established that five policemen had died, and even then it was unclear whether they had been shot by their Communist captors or whether they were victims of the random violence in the streets. But by then, it was too late. The massacre story had furnished Noske with exactly the type of tailor-made excuse he needed to justify his own far-from-imaginary slaughter.

The 'Bloodhound' issued his notorious order of 9 March proclaiming that, because of the 'brutal and bestial behaviour of the Spartacists, any person bearing arms against Government troops will be summarily shot.' The Horse Guards Division – the murderers of Liebknecht and Luxemburg – went even further with an order that 'Any individual with weapons found in their house will be shot without trial.'

On 10, 11, 12 and 13 March, the Freikorps moved into east Berlin to take a terrible and bloody revenge: in the single most notorious incident, thirty sailors of the People's Naval Division who had gone to a Government office to argue about their back pay were led into a courtyard, then simply stood against a wall and machine-gunned. In another case a father and son were shot for the 'offence' of possessing the handle of a stick grenade they had found in the street and taken home. The brutal cleansing operation was chiefly the work of the same Freikorps who had put down the Spartacist revolt in January: a 'cordon sanitaire' was thrown around the Lichtenberg suburb by von Roeder's Freikorps, von Hulsen's Freikorps and the Second Marine 'Ehrhardt' Brigade.

With this weight of professional firepower against them, the estimated 10,000 revolutionaries entrenched in Lichtenberg stood no chance – but they put up a bloody and spirited resistance nonetheless. On Sunday 9 March, preceded by an artillery bombardment, the Freikorps storm squads swept into the surrounded suburb. The battle continued on the next day, and Lichtenberg Police station and Post Office were re-taken for the Government. The authorities on Lichtenberg municipal council made fruitless efforts to spare their quarter from further destruction by attempting to negotiate with the Government. Noske replied that only unconditional surrender could halt the fighting. As this was not forthcoming, the battle was resumed on the 11th with re-doubled ferocity. A battalion of von Hulsen's Freikorps reached Lichtenberg town centre, forcing their opponents back, barricade by barricade. On the morning of 12 March, the Freikorps broke into the nerve centre of the revolt, the building where the Workers' Council of Berlin was still in session. The Council was forcibly dissolved: the last bastion of revolutionary Berlin had fallen.

The troublesome People's Naval Division was also declared dissolved. Its leader, Heinrich Dorrenbach, veteran of the Marstall battle and the Spartacus Week, fled Berlin for Brunswick. In May he was arrested at Eisenach, where he was brutally murdered by the local Police Chief, Brigadier Tanschik, before he could be put on trial. The last surviving chief of the Spartacists, Rosa Luxemburg's one-time lover, Leo Jogiches, was caught and killed in the aftermath of the fighting.

Inevitably, there was an inquest into the blood-bath: between 1200 and 1500 had died in the week's fighting; the overwhelming majority either revolutionaries, strikers or innocent civilians caught in the cross-fire or mown down for being in the wrong place at the wrong time. In addition, between 10,000 and 12,000 people had been injured or wounded. On 13 March, Noske mounted the speaker's podium at the National Assembly in Weimar to tell the relieved deputies that the insurrection had been overcome after a week of 'horror'. He omitted to state that most of the horror had emanated from the Government's own agents: the Freikorps. The same day, the Berlin Press shamefacedly told its readers that five, not seventy, Policemen had died at Lichtenberg.

The investigation into the most horrific single atrocity, the cold-blooded murder of the thirty sailors, revealed that the orders for the killing had come straight from the top. On Thursday 11 March, the military Commander of Greater Berlin, General von Lüttwitz, knowing that sailors from the People's Naval Division were due to come to their pay office at 32 Französischestrasse to draw their pay, sent a detachment of soldiers under the command of a Second Lieutenant von Marloh to occupy the building. The sailors duly arrived in dribs and drabs, and Marloh, posing as their 'Paymaster', had them arrested and held in different rooms, covered by machine guns. By midday the number of sailors 'in the bag' totalled two hundred and fifty. They grew restless at their unjustified detention and Marloh, fearing he was about to be overwhelmed by sheer weight of numbers, telephoned Colonel Reinhard for reinforcements. Reinhard's staff told Marloh to 'make an example' of the Sailors, and reminded the one-armed front-line veteran of the fictitious 'massacre' of the Lichtenberg policemen. A second call from Marloh elicited an unequivocal response from Reinhard himself: 'Bullets are the best answer. . .' replied the future SS Commander of Berlin, 'Go ahead and shoot'. Marloh promptly selected thirty of his prisoners, more or less at random. (He said at his subsequent trial that he had chosen the sailors who looked the 'most intelligent', assuming that they were the ringleaders. The same criteria had been used by the suppressors of the Paris Commune in 1871, when marking down their victims for mass execution.)

Marloh had his captives marched into a walled yard where a firing squad was waiting. The victims were cut down with machine guns at such close range that the courtyard walls were splashed with blood and shreds of flesh. Even Noske was apparently ashamed of the atrocity, explaining that it had come about because of the 'blood-saturated' atmosphere prevailing in Berlin at the time. Other apologists for the Freikorps justified this, and other atrocities, as being the result of blunted sensibilities, the soldiers involved having allegedly been brutalised and de-humanised by their ordeal in the wartime trenches. Reinhard and Marloh himself showed no such shame. After his inevitable acquittal at his trial in December, Marloh was re-admitted to the staff of Reinhard's Freikorps as – of all things – a 'Judicial Officer'. In later life he became an ardent Nazi and a cigarette salesman. He brazenly used the massacre as a reference to prospective customers, proudly boasting of his 'Achievement'.

The only 'balancing atrocity' that could convincingly be laid at the door of the revolutionaries – apart from the unexplained deaths of the five policemen – was the bestial killing of a single government soldier who became separated from his unit. He was surrounded by a mob and beaten with rifles as he staggered through the streets. He managed to reach a hospital but the mob followed him and dragged him off the operating table. He was eventually despatched by a single rifle shot. Noske used this incident as justification for his 'Shoot on sight' order.

Kessler noted in his diary stories of soldiers being trampled to death by the wives of workers in the east end while in the prosperous West Spartacist prisoners were abused, tortured and executed in the Moabit prison, with the enthusiastic encouragement of the 'respectable' Berlin press. The whole country was now inextricably locked into a vortex of hatred and naked class warfare. As Kessler commented on 11 March:

> The brutalities and the shooting defile the moral atmosphere. [Two days later:]
> The White terror proceeds without restraint . . . the execution (of the sailors) appears to have been sheer gruesome murder. [Noske's 'victory' speech at Weimar the same day was] . . . Repulsive! Boorish and utterly deplorable in tone . . . predicting victory over the enemy at home. Every decent-minded person must spurn a Government which so frivolously and shamelessly plays with the lives of its fellow citizens. During the past week, thanks to its wanton lies and bloodshed, it has caused a breach in the nation which decades will not suffice to mend. The popular mood towards it fluctuates between loathing and contempt.

But the brutalism was not confined to the Government and its backers: Kessler's left-wing artistic contacts reported the mood among the beaten proletarians:

> Bitterness . . . so great that to plead for the life of a single bourgeois is downright dangerous. Should their side come to power, they want to exterminate the middle class, once and for all. The picture . . . is of a totally dehumanized military generating an equally dehumanized bloodthirstyness. Only a struggle waged with the most extreme means matters any more. [March 21st]

On 6 March, in the midst of the fighting, the Weimar Assembly passed, after much acrimonious debate, a Law for the Creation of a Provisional Reichswehr, the first step in the re-creation of a new national army to replace the Imperial forces that had withered away in November. The law did not do away with the Freikorps; on the contrary, it envisaged that the new Reichswehr would be built up on the basis of the volunteer formations. Further, to fill out the ranks, even more volunteer forces were to be recruited. For the first time, the Freikorps system was to be officially enshrined in law, and Germany's rulers were prepared to entrust the future of the Army itself, with all its hallowed traditions, to the hands of the Freikorps men who had proved their mettle and their spirit in battle with their own fellow-citizens on the streets of virtually every major German town. In the words of *Vorwärts,* the allegedly 'Socialist' SDP organ which had become little more than a mouthpiece for murder:

> [While] It would naturally be nonsense to deny that the Government troops have not perpetrated actions which would fill any thinking man with loathing and indignation . . . in a struggle to the death in which the Spartacists gave no quarter, it is only natural that the volunteers should fulfil their duty with resolute firmness. They have performed a very difficult task, and if isolated acts of brutality have occurred, our judgement can only be that their actions were only human . . .

9

THE FREEBOOTING SPIRIT

'The pure Landesknechte (Freebooter) didn't much care why they fought or for whom. The main thing for them was that they were fighting. War had become their career.'

Manfred von Killinger,
Chief of Staff to Ehrhardt's Marine Brigade,
Das Waren Kerle! ('These Were Men!')

As the first stage of the Freikorps campaign closes, it is time for us to stand back from the welter of events and take a considered look at what their brutal spirit was – the 'geist' that these men had imported from the savage world of the front and turned on their own fellow countrymen.

The phenomenon of the Freikorps, though representing the fiercest forces of German nationalism, was born of a spirit that was by no means confined to Germany. Indeed, in one way or another, the echoes of the Great War dominated the post-war politics of every European country. The immediate problem confronting the Governments of all the belligerent nations was what to do with the millions of men returning from the trenches: men who for four long years had not known the comforts or certainties of civilian life, whose existence had been one of constant danger and destruction, who knew no trade or way of life other than the infliction of death. This overriding problem was compounded by political dangers arising from the Russian Revolution. The ruling classes and castes of Germany, Italy, France and Britain were terrified by the spectre of proletarian revolution raised in Russia and openly threatening to engulf the war-shattered western world. The peril was all the more acute because of the economic crisis which followed the huge effort of the war.

The massive expenditure incurred in the war, the borrowing that all governments had been forced to make – in the case of the Allies, primarily from the United States – the devastation and material damage; all conspired to produce a huge trade crisis and an industrial slump. The governments' great fear, shared by the middle classes, was that the industrial work-force, always the first to feel the pinch of hard times, would be bitter at having provided the cannon fodder of the trenches and would be inspired by the example of the Bolsheviks to stage their own revolutions, actively aided and abetted by Lenin's Communist International organisation (Comintern). The very real threat of Communist revolution produced an immediate reaction among the middle classes which took the form of various varieties of Fascism.

The birthplace of Fascism itself was Italy. The idea arose from the intense nationalism originating in the Risorgimento movement which had united the country and freed it from Austrian domination in the Nineteenth Century. Italian nationalism was given a boost by Italy's belated participation in the Great War, and was further fuelled by the – in Italian eyes – disappointing results of the conflict when her territorial demands in Austria and Yugoslavia were largely overlooked by the other Allies.

The man primarily responsible for whipping up and exacerbating Italian nationalism to fever pitch was the flamboyant poet Gabriele D'Annunzio. Totally bald and with eyes which were described by one of his lovers as resembling 'little blobs of shit', D'Annunzio was a talented writer and a charismatic orator. The lover of some of the most beautiful women in Europe, he was saved from bankruptcy and middle-aged decay by the outbreak of war. Subsidised by the French secret service, he led a frantic campaign to bring Italy into the war, on the side, not of her nominal friends, the Central Powers, but of the Western Allies. When the campaign succeeded, D'Annunzio, at the age of fifty-three, formed his own air squadron, even staging a leaflet bombardment of Vienna.

Disappointed, along with the rest of his countrymen, with Italy's meagre gains from the war – he called it 'the mutilated victory' – D'Annunzio collected around his own extravagant person a motley crowd of mercenaries, ex-soldiers and political malcontents subscribing to wildly differing doctrines, ranging from anarchism to extreme nationalism. These self-styled 'legionnaires', calling themselves the 'Arditi', acquired many of the characteristics later to form the ideology of Fascism. There was the hero-worship of the leader – the 'Duce', D'Annunzio, was known as the Commandante; the war-cry – in the Arditi's case, a rousing chorus of the meaningless phrase 'Eia! Eia! Alala!'; a nostalgia for the war and a bitter contempt for the democratic politicians who had betrayed the blood sacrifice of those who had fought; and, last but by no means least, a dangerous thirst for violence and action for its own sake.

The essential elements of Fascism had already appeared before the war in the manifesto launched by the artistic group, the Futurists, led by the publicist Fillipo Marinetti. The manifesto, published in 1909 in Milan, called on Italian youth to 'sing the love of danger, the habit of energy and boldness'. Art, claimed Marinetti, 'could only be violence, cruelty and injustice.' The Futurists worshipped war, and called for the abolition of museums and the wholesale demolition of Italy's incomparable cultural heritage, which they saw as a stifling deadweight, suffocating the new age of machinery, speed and force. All in all, the intellectual Futurists did much of the Fascists' spadework for them, providing a justification for the barbaric and anti-intellectual reaction against centuries of European civilisation. Naturally, the Futurists rejected democracy, socialism and liberalism and took an enthusiastic part in the war they had brayed for. It remained for D'Annunzio, the man of action with the necessary prestige and patriotic credentials, to translate the ideology into practice.

On 12 September 1919, at the head of a thousand Arditi, the poet marched into Fiume, an important port in Yugoslavia (now named Rijeka) with a sizeable ethnic Italian population, and claimed the town for Italy. This action received enthusiastic acclaim throughout the country and the Rome Government was too frightened to remove the poet, who set himself up in a palace as Fiume's dictator. Within weeks, his private army had swelled to a force of more than 7000, and D'Annunzio proclaimed his intention of marching on Rome to overthrow the Government.

D'Annunzio devised his own constitution for his little fiefdom. Its main feature was the division of the town's entire population into ten 'Corporations' according to profession. This idea, designed to eliminate class conflict and labour disputes, added yet another component to the ideological baggage of Fascism which Mussolini would take over for himself when he came to power. The Constitution also invested the poet with supreme power as 'Commandante' in the event of extreme emergency.

Under D'Annunzio's eccentric rule (he was prone to assemble the port's population on the piazza outside his palace and subject them to lengthy harangues) Fiume's economy deteriorated. Nothing daunted, the Arditi resorted to piracy to support themselves. However, international isolation made the poet's rule increasingly unpopular and his men, following the Commandante's example, gave themselves up to pillage and sexual dissipation. Public opinion eventually forced D'Annunzio to abandon Fiume early in 1921. The torch of Fascism was passed on to a more ruthless and practical politician: Benito Mussolini.

Born the son of a revolutionary blacksmith in the Romagna, the young Duce showed an early tendency to violence and romantic political dreaming. He swiftly rose to prominence in the Italian Socialist party, becoming editor of the party newspaper *Avanti!* He parted company with the Socialists over his passionate advocacy of Italian intervention in the war, was expelled and started – with funds provided by France – his own newspaper, *Il Popolo d'Italia*, combining radicalism with intense nationalism. Mussolini fought in the war, was wounded and emerged with his nationalism more burning than ever. In March 1919 he founded the first of his 'Fasci di Combattimento' (Combat Groups) in Milan. So, at the very moment that the Freikorps were suppressing the March uprising in Berlin with their customary savagery, Fascism was officially born.

The parallels with the Freikorps were uncanny: the backbone of Mussolini's squads were ex-front line soldiers. They shared with their German counterparts the same churning contempt for civilian life, the same propensity for violence against the Socialist and Communist enemy and the same determination to turn the existing political system upside-down and substitute a new sort of state: ruthless, authoritarian, efficient and militaristic. Italy and Germany, both young states born in the Nineteenth Century, also shared a sense of fervent nationalism and grievance at the war's outcome, and the crumbs they had gained as late-comers to the colonial banquet.

The background of the times was propitious for the rise of a new extremist movement: the war had left the Italian economy in ruins, and 1919 saw the agrarian south swept by the unrest of land-hungry peasants, while the industrial north was crippled by strikes and lock-outs. Between April 1919 and September 1920, there were 320 deaths caused by political violence. Frightened, the wealthy landowners, bankers and industrialists financed Mussolini's movement as a hedge and bulwark against the Red Threat. Shopkeepers, farmers and small businessmen, with the traditional horror for disorder and socialism of their class, joined the Fascists in droves. The Fascist movement grew spectacularly: at the end of 1919 the movement had less than 1000 members; at the end of 1920 there were more than 20,000 members; by the end of 1921, almost 250,000. As he neared power, Mussolini distanced himself from the rough and radical elements who formed his strong-arm squads on the streets, in exactly the same way that Hitler was to discard the Freikorps and SA Brownshirts whose guns and fists had opened the gates of power.

At the same time, in order to gain the support of the respectable bourgeoisie, Mussolini moderated his originally socially radical party programme: dropping plans to nationalise private property, making overtures to the Vatican and the Monarchy, and even proposing to privatise the railways and telephone service. In the autumn of 1922, with his leftist enemies battered and bullied into submission and the centre parties terrified into acquiesence, Mussolini ordered his black-shirt squads to perform the much-heralded March on Rome. The Duce himself arrived in the capital by train, with a dress suit over his silk black shirt, and the King appointed him Prime Minister in October 1922. Fascism had achieved power. To his German sympathisers, the victory was a triumphant vindication of violence as a political weapon.

In France, there was a home-grown fascist movement – in all but name – already established by the time of the Great War. This was the 'Action Française', founded by the monarchist journalist Charles Maurras, at the height of the Dreyfus Affair in the 1890s which gave a boost to anti-Semitism, anti-Republicanism and excessive love of the Army.

The movement, with its savage newspaper edited by Leon Daudet, specialised in ridiculing Republican institutions and stoking up the always latent fires of Gallic xenophobia. Its members played a big part in the right-wing Bloc National coalition which swept the country in the post-war elections. The movement appealed to the army and aristocracy, who had never accepted the verdict of the 1789 Revolution, to young students thirsting for a fight and to the vast French peasantry, suspicious of the industrial trade unions and the cosmopolitan cities.

Maurras' decision to participate in the electoral politics he had always despised, lost him much support, and as the 1920s wore on, Action Française – was largely superseded by para-military 'Leagues' – right-wing movements like the Croix de Feu and Solidarité Française which were dominated by ex-soldiers who could not get the habit of authoritarian militarism out of their blood. These Leagues played a major part in undermining confidence in the admittedly mediocre politicians of inter-war France, and paving the way for the country's humiliating collapse before the German Blitzkrieg of 1940.

Even in stable Britain, Fascist ideas found ready support. An early manifestation of the phenomenon of militarism was the notorious 'Black and Tans', a special formation raised by the Government in 1919 to counter the guerilla insurgency in Ireland launched by Sinn Fein and the infant IRA. The 'Tans' – called after their dark blue and khaki uniforms – were designed as an auxiliary supplement to the regular Royal Irish Constabulary who – as in Ulster during the 'Troubles' – were finding their role as an anti-guerilla force fighting the community from which their own recruits were drawn, increasingly impossible. The Government's answer was to recruit demobilised soldiers and ex-officers straight from the trenches as an additional weapon. This served the double purpose of mopping up some potentially troublesome unemployed and providing the Government with rough, tough men who would not shrink from the harsher aspects of a guerilla war.

The Tans certainly fulfilled the task assigned to them, and made themselves a by-word throughout Ireland for their indiscriminate brutality, their habit of shooting first and seldom asking questions afterwards, and their savage reprisals after attacks by Republicans – such as the notorious burning of Cork town centre. They went to war in squads of lorries, in a manner remarkably similar to the Freikorps and the Fascist squadristi.

In short, all over western Europe the war had given birth to a new sub-class, the demobilised soldier, brutalised by years of trench fighting and sharing, in each of their different countries, a ragbag of broadly similar attitudes and problems: unemployment, disorientation, an inability to settle down in unfamiliar peacetime conditions, and a liking for discipline, which, translated into political terms, meant desire for authoritarian modes of Government. With this went a contempt for democratic politics and politicians caused in Britain and Italy by the post-war economic slump, and in Germany by the additional bitter experience of defeat and social revolution. As patriotic fighting men, the ex-soldiers were usually of a violently nationalistic disposition, reluctant to shed their uniforms, and hankering for 'strong' leaders. They were impatient of the seemingly endless discussions and meetings that were a part of democratic political processes. Some special conditions inside Germany gave this rather nihilistic philosophy a character all its own; a 'Weltanschauung' that lent the Friedkorps movement its own distinctive flavour.

The two negative strands were paranoid hostility to the political left and anti-semitism. In some cases these two attitudes were coupled as one. It never escaped the notice of the extreme right that many of the most prominent revolutionaries happened to be Jewish: Rosa Luxemburg, Emil Eichhorn, Karl Radek, Karl Kautsky, Eduard Bernstein, the Hungarian Bolshevik leader Bela

Kun and the Bavarian Marxist who brought down the Wittelsbach dynasty in Munich, Kurt Eisner, as well as the two 'harder men' who took over from Eisner after his assassination – Leviné and Levien. And was not the father of Communism – Marx himself – the grandson of a Rabbi? Lenin's three closest Bolshevik colleagues – Trotsky, Zinoviev and Kamenev – were also Jews.

To the German right, it was an article of faith that Jews and revolutionaries were synonymous. From there it was but a short logical step to convince themselves that the Jews had been responsible for Germany's decay and defeat in November 1918. These 'migrant rats from the east', as one racist versifier dubbed them, were not real Germans, but rootless cosmopolitans whose international intrigues embraced, in some unexplained way, the extremes of wealth and influence on one side and, on the other, the subversive movements that were sworn to bring the existing economic and social system crashing down in ruins.

It would not be fair to the Freikorps, however, to leave the impression that they were nothing but gangs of psychopathic killers with a primitive and brutal set of half-baked ideas. For there was an important and influential part of their thought that was by no means wholly negative and reactionary, indeed it was innocently idealistic to the point of naivety, and its social implications were almost as revolutionary as Bolshevism itself. Not for nothing did Hitler, in so many ways the chief heir to the Freikorps heritage, call his movement National *Socialism*. And it is no accident that many of the Freikorps leaders – Röhm, Ehrhardt, Rossbach and Lettow-Vorbeck – fell out with the Fuhrer over his failure to realise their ideals.

The roots of this idealism can be traced back to the German 'Jugendbewegung' (Youth Movement) which arose in the closing years of the Nineteenth Century and came into fullest flower in the decade leading up to the outbreak of World War One. On the face of it, this movement, with its associated 'Wandervogel' ('Wandering Birds' – bands of organised hikers) was a purely cultural manifestation, and early precursor of the Beatnik and Hippy crazes. Certainly the Jugendbewegung shared many of the characteristics of these later upsurges of the young: the casual dress, the contempt for middle-class respectability and the older generation in general. Shared too, were a free and easy mingling of the sexes, a distinct tendency towards vague religious mysticism, together with a corresponding hostility to officially organised conventional religion. Even the outward symbolism of the movement, the guitars and rucksacks, the campfire sing-songs and the impatience with the stifling social conventions born of too many years of peace and prosperity, were identical with later movements emanating from the very different society of post-war America. But the German movement possessed characteristics all its own that were typically Teutonic.

Essentially the movement was a revolt against the industrialisation that had galvanished Germany in the middle years of the Nineteenth Century, the huge population influx from the country to the town, the rapid mechanisation of everyday life, the teeming, anonymous antlike sprawl of the great cities. These sociological changes and their results – such as the rise of the Trade Unions and Socialism – sparked a reaction amongst the bourgeois young that was to be carried over, lock stock and barrel, into the ideology of the Freikorps and later on, of the Nazis.

The 'Guru' of the reaction was the Prussian-born philosopher, Nietzsche. His passionate demand for a new and man-made system of ideas to replace the outworn rags of the Christian religion – 'God is dead . . . I sing the Superman. Man is something to be surpassed.' – found an immense and immediate response in the hearts and minds of German youth. Nietzsche was preaching an overthrow not only of Christianity, but of the whole rationalist

Enlightenment that had held sway in Europe since the Eighteenth Century. His absurdly ambitious aim was an overall restructuring of human thought, a complete change in direction, and an outright rejection of all the values that had ruled civilisation since the end of the Dark Ages. It was the breathtaking audaciousness of this programme that caught the imagination of the young, particularly the German young, suffocating under the suppression of so many natural impulses. In England, this tension between the iron codes of social etiquette and the rampant urgings of Old Adam bred hypocrisy. In Germany, being Germany, it bred an extreme sense of romantic revolt.

If today we are inclined to smile at Nietzsche – the Christ-hating son of a Protestant pastor, the misogynist who spent his life under the thumb of his sister and other women, the hypochondriac invalid with his thrilling calls to action and excess, the apostle of war and struggle who lost his sanity in a bid to rescue an ill-treated cab horse – we must not make the mistake of underestimating the enormous impact his ideas had upon his epoch. He pioneered the way for Twentieth-Century thought: the cult of the leader; the appeal to the irrational; the harsh demand for struggle and sacrifice; the withering scorn for 'herd' democracy, security and safety; the yearning for the primitive and simple life; the detestation of the 'souless' machine and the swarming aimlessness of factories and cities. All these elements in Nietzsche were taken up and enthusiastically elaborated and propagated by his disciples. It is no accident that Nietzsche's philosophy, twisted and bowdlerised by his Hitler-loving sister and executrix Elisabeth, was taken up by the Nazis. The philosopher hated violence, detested nationalism and had only scorn for his stolid fellow-countrymen. No matter, a crude version of his complex and often contradictory thought gave the loathsome creed of the Nazis a thin gloss of intellectual respectability.

The leaders of the Jugendbewegung marched eagerly down the

path which Nietzsche had blazed. 'Waging a relentless fight against the school, the home and the church . . . tearing the youth away from all the old ties and replacing them with the free colony of the Youth spirit', as one of their leaders put it. This desire for action at any price was characteristic of the movement. Although prizing their 'freedom', the bands of 'Wandervogel' were only too eager to throw themselves at the feet of a Führer and to obey the mysterious dark forces of the 'Ur-deutsch' – the ancient Germanic 'geist' (spirit) they imagined emanating from the glades and serried ranks of forest trees where they assembled to sing, drink and absorb the legacy of their ancestral spirits.

In the autumn of 1913 – the year before the outbreak of the war – the members of the Jugendbewegung were summoned to a mass meeting on the Meissner mountain outside Kassel. The manifesto of the meeting is a revealing document: German youth, it said,

> No longer intended to remain a dependency of the older generation, excluded from public life and relegated to a passive role. It seeks, independently of the commands of convention, to give shape and form to its own life. It strives after a lifestyle, corresponding to its youth . . . which . . . will make it possible to take itself and its activities seriously and to integrate itself as a special factor in the general work of culture.

The leaders of the movement, whose highest value was 'Vitality', were seeking a rejuvenation of Germany's national life. Bored and constricted by the rigid structures of the Wilhelmine empire, finding the world of their fathers 'Cold', 'Static', 'Sterile' and 'Soulless', these young people sought, in the words of one of their prophets, Artur Moeller van den Bruck: 'A change of blood, an insurrection of the sons against the fathers, a substitution of the old by the young.'

As in Italy, the movement had an artistic parallel with the same impatient irrationalist spirit: Expressionism. In the paintings of the groups calling themselves 'Die Brücke' (The Bridge) and 'Der Blaue Reiter' (The Blue Rider), and in the plays of dramatists like

Frank Wedekind and Arnolt Bronnen (later to write the biography of the Freikorps hero Gerhard Rossbach), an ideology of primitive power was formulated.

The movement proclaimed a belief in mankind's progress towards vague concepts like 'Energy', 'Freedom' and a rejection of the ossified official Christian culture handed down by their parents. Bronnen, in his play *Patricide* (Vatermord) openly approved the image of roving bands of mounted boys and girls galloping over the older generation and grinding them to death beneath triumphant hooves, shouting that they themselves were God. So pronounced are the themes of violence, energy, revolt, war and murder in German art and literature in the years leading up to 1914 that one almost senses a collective awareness of the coming Holocaust.

When war actually came, the members of the Jugendbewegung naturally flocked to the colours in droves, eager to submit themselves to the demands of the War God and to sacrifice themselves on the altar of a new Germany. Many of them did not survive the experience. Their losses were so high in one particular action – Langemarck near Ypres – that the battle was known to the Germans as the 'Kindermord' (Child Massacre).

After the war, a collection was published of letters written home by young German student-officers who had fallen at the Front. The writers – many of them pre-war members of the Youth Movement – shared a common change in attitude resulting from their harsh experiences in the trenches. The suffering they had shared with their men had made them less egotistical but – if possible – *more* idealistic. The goal of their generation now was not the individualistic personal liberation they had pursued before the war, but the freeing of their country from its physical and spiritual shackles. Their loyalty was to the 'Volksgemeinschaft' (People's Community) of a Greater Germany – uplifted morally as well as materially. By fighting, killing and dying they had contributed to the moral elevation of the nation. In the words of one volunteer, quoted in the anthology of German students' war letters

> We fight for our 'Volk' and spill our blood and hope that the survivors are worthy of our sacrifice. For me it is the struggle for an idea . . . a pure, noble, true Germany, free from evil and lies. Even if we go down to defeat with this hope in our hearts it is better than to have been victorious and to see that it was only an outer victory without improving men from within.

These attitudes were far removed from the experience of the masses of the German people left at home in the far-from-heroic world of a blockaded country at war. Malnutrition, bereavement, no goods to buy and little money to buy them with were more likely to be the primary concerns of an increasingly war-weary civilian population. This difference in outlook contributed to the gap between the front line and the homeland which became an unbridgeable gulf as the war dragged on and the chances of victory receded.

Bewildered and angry at the inexplicable – to them – collapse of national will and morale in the autumn of 1918, the front-line fighters felt that the people left behind them had been 'unworthy' of their suffering and sacrifices. The surviving junior officers felt little compunction at turning their guns on their own people who had seemingly let them down so grievously. They shut their eyes to the real reasons for the collapse. At the end of his heroic Great War diary *Storm of Steel*, a book which perfectly embodies the spirit of defiant militarism, Ernst Jünger wrote:

> We – by this I mean those of the Youth of this land who are capable of enthusiasm for an ideal – we stand in the memory of the dead who are holy to us and we believe ourselves entrusted with the true and spiritual welfare of our people. We stand for what will be and for what has been. Though force without and barbarity within conglomerate in sombre clouds, yet so long as the blade of the sword will strike a spark in the night may it be said 'Germany lives and Germany shall never go under!'

A new generation was born of the war: the front line generation. Smaller and, of necessity, more élitist than the mass Youth
Movement, it was the bearer and guardian of the sacred grail of
an ideal. Purged and purified by the flames of the front, by virtue
of its struggle and sacrifice it believed it had earned the right to
dictate the terms of Germany's new life. Small wonder that the
members of this élite, returning from the trenches, felt
disappointed and embittered that their self-appointed mission of
renewal had been arrogated by the less than heroic figures of
Ebert, Scheidemann and Erzberger. What right had these fat,
waddling politicians to decide the forms and policy of the new
state? Where had they been when young Germany had been
bleeding to death on the barbed wire? Belching out speeches in the
safety of Berlin. From whom had they derived the legitimacy of
power for their bastard Republic? Who else, but the mutinous,
cowardly rabble who had stabbed the Army in the back so treach-
erously? Such was the myth of the front-line fighters.

These arrogant and antique attitudes are a world away from the
modern cosmopolitan bureaucratised European Union. But we
should not deceive ourselves that they were not deeply and
sincerely felt by the men who were returning home from the
trenches. And these were the men, armed with weapons and by
the self-righteous certainties of their experience, who were the true
arbiters of power in post-war Germany. They were the men who
formed the leadership as well as the fighting muscle of the
Freikorps.

One of their chiefs, Franz Seldte, founder of the 'Stahlhelm'
(Steel Helmet), the main 'Kampfbund' (Fighting League) of front-
line veterans, put their case with the direct brutal bluntness of an
old soldier: 'We must fight to get the men into power who will
depend on us front soldiers for support – men who will call upon
us to smash once and for all these damned revolutionary rats and
choke them by sticking their heads into their own shit.'

Ernst Jünger was their chief spokesman, by virtue of his valiant war record – wounded fourteen times, a Captain of élite storm-troops, holder of the Iron Cross, first and second class, and of the coveted 'Blue Max' medal – the 'Pour le Mérite'. A romantic adventurer, and an individualistic anarchist by temperament, Jünger paradoxically found the danger and excitement he sought by enlisting in the French Foreign Legion and then, during the war, in the comradeship of the trenches and the courage of his fellow front-line Germans. Living side-by-side with death for four long years, Jünger fell half in love with this dangerous companion. Returning from treatment for his many wounds to the trenches with the ardour of an addict seeking his fix, Jünger gloried in the mud and ruck of combat, that reduced a man to his bare-boned essence. In the trenches, where the next moment could bring eternity, there was no room for bourgeois hypocrisy and pretence. His best-selling books celebrated the 'Princes of the trenches, with their hard-set faces, brave to madness, tough and agile, with keen bloodthirsty nerves.' These were the men – the new generation – forged in the furnace of war and tempered like steel, who were destined to dictate the new order that must arise from the ruins of the old. In Hermann Goering's words they 'could not become de-brutalised'.

Ernst von Salomon was one of the generation who had been a fraction too young to have actually fought in the war, but who had been imbued with the fighting spirit of the front line, and who joined the Freikorps formations as soon as they appeared.

He echoed Goering:

> The war could not release them from its grip. The most active part of the Front marched simply because it had learned to march. It marched through the cities enveloped in a cloud of sullen rage – a cloud of vaulting, aimless fury – knowing only that it had to fight, to fight at any cost. This then was the one problem of the Freikorps fighter: to give his utmost so that the real meaning of the war could be made manifest to the very limit of his power.

10

THE BALTIC CAMPAIGN

'The soldiers in the Baltic had a marching song: "We are the last Germans to face the foe." We felt indeed that we were the last survivors of the German race. Outcasts, exiles, homeless, beggars – We held our torches high.'

Ernst von Salomom,
The Outlaws ('Die Geachteten')

The war to which von Salomon travelled with his Freikorps comrades in the early months of 1919 is today almost forgotten. But the campaign in the Baltic is important historically and for its contribution to the Freikorps' – and hence to the German nation's – myth. The warriors who stood at Germany's eastern gates saw themselves as the heirs of the Teutonic knights who had carved out Germany's eastern empire in the Middle Ages. Racially and ideologically they felt themselves to be the lonely protectors of German 'Kultur' against the 'ravening wolves' of the sub-human Slav Bolshevik hordes. They continued Germany's long obsession with its 'Drang nach Osten' (Push to the East) and hence towards Adolf Hitler's version of a vast 'Lebensraum' in Poland and the Ukraine: the Ostland, which was destined to be colonised by

German warrior-farmers who would make the Slav inhabitants of these lands a race of slave helots.

The treaty of Brest-Litovsk with the emergent Bolsheviks early in 1918 had given Germany hegemony over huge tracts of the former Russian empire stretching from the Baltic to the Black Sea, but with the catastrophic collapse of the Western Front all these gains were put at risk. The Poles, taking advantage of the chaos, reasserted their independence and made themselves masters of the city of Poznan (Posen to the Germans). The move infuriated all German nationalists, who had long regarded Poland as part of greater Prussia, the heart of the nation. But the Poles had the support of the Allies and the Germans were ordered to withdraw Freikorps units under General von Bulow who had re-occupied Poznan early in 1919. Frustrated, the Germans turned their attention to the northern Baltic lands where General Count Rudiger von der Goltz was already organising Freikorps forces to resist the advance of the Russian Bolsheviks who were moving in to assert their claim to the territory. The High Command under Hindenburg backed Goltz to the hilt. Hindenburg, the victor of Tannenberg, had attachments to the sacred soil of the Baltic both historical and personal. He saw the chance of victory in these distant provinces that would, at one-and-the-same time, redeem the shame of the Western collapse and give Germany the opportunity for expansion in a corner of the continent far away from the attention of the wrangling Allies at Versailles.

With this aim in view, the Army moved its HQ from Kassel in the west to Kolberg in the east, preparing for what it saw as an easy victory and ripe territorial pickings. The situation in the Baltic certainly seemed ready-made for German military intervention. At least three groups were competing for control: the Bolsheviks, backed by Soviet Russia; the newly proclaimed Baltic republican Governments of Latvia, Lithuania and Estonia which enjoyed the support of the Western Allies; and the reactionary Baltic landowning Barons who were loosely allied with the remnants of White Russian forces itching for a restoration of the overthrown Czarist Imperial order.

The Allies were not initially averse to using the German military forces as a catspaw to hold back the threat from Bolshevik Russia to the Baltic ports. Even the weak and struggling Baltic governments were ready to ask their former German oppressors to protect them against the Bolshevik menace. When the official German army refused to fight the Letts' war for them, it was left to the Freikorps to fill the gap.

Weary of war and acutely anxious about the 'red peril' from the east, Britain, which maintained a naval squadron in the Baltic under Admiral Sinclair, gave her tacit approval to the use of Freikorps troops as a bulwark against Bolshevism. Freikorps recruiting stations opened in Berlin replete with blood-curdling posters warning of the Red menace. Once again there was no shortage of volunteers. A campaign in the east offered the patriotic chance of defending ancestral Germanic lands against the rapacious foreigner with none of the dubious morality of shooting down fellow citizens in German cities that had marred the Freikorps' internal campaigns. In addition, there was the bait of free land – each volunteer was assured that he would be given ninety acres of Baltic territory so long as he served for a minimum of four weeks in the campaign. This bribe was a sheer lie. No deal had been reached with the Baltic governments about dishing out parcels of land to German mercenaries – the most the Latvian government was prepared to offer to their saviours was free Latvian nationality.

Whatever the mixed motives of the volunteers – patriotism, fear and loathing of Bolshevism or sheer greed for Baltic estates – they flocked to the colours. The more intelligent among them, men like von Salomon, were again inspired by that curious blend of

nihilism and courage that drove them to defy defeat. In the words
of one of them, Franz Buchner:

> Despairing over the collapse of Germany, the dissolution of her army
> and disgusted with conditions in the homeland they refused to give up
> the battle. In mind and deed they were determined to make this last
> attempt to resist the horror of German defeat and to hope for a better
> future. Or, even if they could not believe in that – they still felt that it
> was their German duty to risk life and limb in this last effort.

One of their leaders, Major Alfred Fletcher, expressed his hatred
of the Ebert government as 'A miserable, socialist rabble'. 'In the
common life and battle shared with the Balts,' Fletcher continues,
'my sick German heart, which had lost faith in the German people
during the revolution, was made whole once more.' There was
also a good mixture of the rough and tough front-line soldiers
who wanted to continue the profession of war for its own sake.
Men who, in the words of one of their number, Erich Balla, were:

'Primitives . . . what in normal times would be called bandit-
killers. They are men with no nerves and no moral scruples . . .
just like nature . . . instinctively good and instinctively cruel.'
Ernst von Salomon takes up the same theme:

> We were cut off from the world of bourgeois norms. The bonds were
> broken and we were free. The blood surging through our veins was full
> of a wild demand for revenge and action and adventure . . . We were
> a band of fighters drunk with all the passions of the world; full of lust,
> exultant in anger. What we wanted, we did not know, and what we
> knew we did not want! War and adventure, excitement and destruc-
> tion. An indefinable surging force welled up from every part of our
> being and flayed us forward.

The true essence of the Freikorps fighter is here openly – almost
nakedly – exposed like a grotesque wound. The twisted paradox
of a love of order as well as anarchy is frankly confessed. Above
all there is the Nietzschean appeal to irrationality and madness
that was to reach its apogee in these same eastern lands under the
Third Reich between 1939–45.

On arriving in the Baltic at the beginning of February 1919 Goltz organised his army into two main units: the Iron Division (not to be confused with Noske's Iron Brigade from Kiel) and the Baltic Landeswehr. The latter force was nominally under the control of the Latvian Government, but it soon passed into the hands of the old Barons who were happy to let its German Commander, Major Fletcher, dismiss all the native Baltic officers and replace them with Germans. The same weeding-out process was applied to other ranks, and by the middle of February Latvians comprised less than a fifth of their own 'national army'. Fletcher's chief advisor in this manoeuvre was none other than our old acquaintance Captain Waldemar Pabst, the murderer of Liebknecht and Luxemburg, who pops up like a jack-in-the-box at every twist and turn of the Freikorps story.

Command of the Iron Division fell to Major Joseph Bischoff, a veteran campaigner who had seen twelve years of continuous war service in Africa and Europe. The division was a fully-fledged fighting force numbering nearly 15,000 dedicated men, with a full staff, three infantry regiments, machine gun companies, field artillery and cavalry units, balloon and flame-thrower sections, a field hospital and even its own air arm. As an old soldier, Bischoff tried to mould his men along the lines of the wartime Imperial army, but he came up against that defiantly anarchic free-booting spirit. These mercenary men, as von Salomon affirms: 'Let their hair and beards grow long, saluted only the officers they knew and liked . . . this crazy outfit recognized none of the usual military regulations. No particular authority had formed them and they recognized none save their own. The only thing that counted was the will of their own Führer.'

The force of the Freikorps was soon felt: within two weeks of his arrival, Goltz had driven the Red Army from Goldingen and Windau. Mitau fell to the Iron Division early in March. One Freikorps which particularly distinguished itself was that formed by Major Cordt von Brandis, a war hero and one of the men who had taken the 'impregnable' French fortress of Douaumont at the battle of Verdun. He had formed his Corps by simply sitting under a tree outside a country inn near Berlin and inviting old comrades to join him in winning new glory in the east.

By April, with most of the Baltic coastline cleared of reds and rebels, and a spring thaw holding up military progress, the minds of the Freikorps chiefs turned to politics. Never before had they had such an opportunity for independent political action on their own account. The hated Berlin Government was out of sight and out of mind, the British had already apparently acquiesced in Freikorps action and were seemingly uninterested in German activity in this half-forgotten spot, and the Baltic governments themselves were not only pathetically weak and unsure of their authority but were proving in practice remarkably ungrateful, and less than cooperative with the Germans who were shedding blood to save them from Bolshevism. Poised to conquer the Latvian capital of Riga, Goltz realized that a greater prize lay near his grasp. If he could brush away the troublesome Baltic republicans, and restore the old Barons to their lost lands, he would not only provide Germany with a pliant puppet state guarding its vital eastern flank, but might also offer his country a springboard for seizing the nearby city of Petrograd (Leningrad – now St Petersburg) and deposing the Soviet regime.

Unwisely, the Latvian Government of Premier Ulmanis offered a provocative pretext for Freikorps action by arresting a German officer, Lieutenant Stock, and charging him with plotting to overthrow them. Enraged, the Lieutenant's comrades, members of the von Pfeffer Freikorps founded by von Salomon's elder brother (who was later to become head of Hitler's SA Brownshirt Nazi party militia), arrested the entire Latvian officer corps, some 550 men. Later the same afternoon, 16 April, Baron von Manteuffel personally arrested the members of the Ulmanis Government.

Ulmanis himself fled to the protection of the British. Goltz had gone on a diplomatic long walk while his subordinates acted on his behalf. When he returned, he proclaimed martial law and effectively turned the whole of Latvia into a German protectorate. At this point, prompted by the indignant Ulmanis and sensing Goltz's mounting ambitions, Britain moved sluggishly to thwart him and demanded that Berlin recall the offending General.

The Ebert Government pointed out that responsibility for defending the Baltic would fall to Britain if the Freikorps left, and a compromise was reached whereby the volunteers would stay in place – but not engage in further offensive action. The crafty Goltz got round this prohibition by ordering the Baltic 'Landeswehr' to attack. As we have seen, this force was, to all intents and purposes, just another German Freikorps. Once battle was joined, the Yorck, Brandis, Eulenburg, Rieckoff and Pfeffer Freikorps were ordered into action as 'reinforcements' and their combined army successfully stormed Riga on 22 May.

The Freikorps exalted in this brief moment of glory. One of their historians, Edgar von Schmidt-Pauli calls it: 'The symbol of the victory of European civilization over Asiatic barbarism.' Another Freikorps hagiographer, Friedrich Wilhelm Heinz wrote: 'It was as if all the stars in the heavens shone once more in the interminable night of Germany's self-imposed weakness and atrophy and illuminated the brilliance and greatness of eternal soldiery.' Bischoff, commander of the Iron Division, was more far-seeing, prophetically remarking: 'My God, we've won ourselves to death.' He was right. The signal triumph was a grave embarrassment to the Berlin Government and the Allies alike, and rang the death knell for the Freikorps adventures in the Baltic. Moreover, the usual excesses of the Freikorps – all the more unrestrained because they were fighting in a distant, backward land – had alienated the native support that they had previously enjoyed. The 'Liberation' of the town of Mitau had been attended by a massacre of 500 Latvian citizens suspected of harbouring Bolshevik sympathies. Hundreds more had been cold-bloodedly murdered in the subsequent campaign, and the fall of Riga signalled a slaughter of some 3000 people in the capital.

Stung by the open defiance of their instructions and emboldened by the withdrawal of the Red Army from the Baltic lands in the last days of May, the British gave their support to the Baltic Governments who were attempting to raise an army of their own to preserve their independence from Russia and Germany alike. When Goltz ordered his Freikorps to clear the rest of the coast in preparation for his projected drive on St Petersburg, a united force of Latvians and Estonians defeated Fletcher's Landeswehr at Wendon outside Riga. When Goltz sent the Iron Division in to teach the upstart natives a lesson they too were halted and put to flight. Already depressed by the hostility of the populace and the apathy shown by their own country, the effect of these two defeats led to a catastrophic drop in Freikorps morale.

As they lost stomach for the military fight, so the political battle swung against the German/Baronial interests. A new Allied commission, under the British General Hubert Gough, deposed the puppet Latvian Government set up by Goltz and restored Ulmanis to office. Major Fletcher's Baltic Landeswehr suffered a purge in reverse, ridding it of its German elements and restoring power to the Latvians. Fletcher surrendered his command to a British officer, Lieutenant Colonel Alexander – subsequently Earl Alexander of Tunis. Each man showed a soldierly regard for the other, Fletcher calling Alexander: 'An English nobleman and front-line fighter for the West . . . a true gentleman.' Alexander, not to be outdone, referred to the ruthless Fletcher as 'The best type of German officer . . . very helpful and a fine gentleman.' At the beginning of July, Gough compelled Goltz to sign an agreement for the total withdrawal of Freikorps forces from the Baltic.

Goltz and his men now put their last hopes of salvaging the

Baltic fiasco into the hands of one of the most bizarre figures thrown up by the whole fantastic period. Count Awaloff-Bermondt was one of those characters who often emerge during turbulent periods of history. In more settled times an obscure fantasist like him would have been the denizen of a psychiatric ward or the defendant in a fraud trial. In the tragi-comic world of the post-war Baltic, he found himself – albeit briefly – commanding an army of thousands of men.

Awaloff was a White Russian emigré who loved to sport the traditional garb of his type: a huge fur hat sat on his head, Cossack bandoliers criss-crossed his chest and his waxed moustache was permanently twisted into two bristling and upstanding points. During the chaos of the war and revolution, this poseur promoted himself to Prince and General and saw himself as the man of destiny with a self-appointed mission to roll back the course of history and restore Czarism to his native land. His first move, upon arriving in the Baltic, was to recruit wandering Russian prisoners of war into the grandiloquently styled 'Russian Army of the West'. When even the White Russian Commander, General Yudenich, rejected this preposterous force, Awaloff offered his services to the Germans. Lacking a sense of humour and of political reality, the Friekorps leaders took Awaloff at his own inflated value and appointed him nominal chief of all volunteer forces in the region. This device had the advantage of enabling Goltz to officially wash his hands of whatever triumphs or, more likely, tragedies were to ensue.

The exasperated Allies issued an ultimatum at the end of July threatening to renew the full force of the wartime economic blockade against Germany unless the Freikorps cleared out of the Baltic by the end of August. Ebert promptly ordered the Freikorps home. The order only served to heighten their feelings of isolation and alienation from their homeland. As Ernst von Salomon described:

The message seemed to have come from a distant, foreign land; from a country which was tired and grey and condemned to exist in the eternal gloom of cold, damp November fogs. It was like a country which had no real existence. After all, how did this place concern us? We looked at one another and shivered. We suddenly felt icy cold and terribly lonely. We had imagined that our country would never desert us, that we were bound to it with an indissoluble bond, that it sympathised with our innermost desires and that it justified our actions. We were cut off.

Reluctantly complying with the Government order, the first transport of Freikorps troops gathered at Mitau railway station on 24 August. They were about to board the train home when a 'tall and sunburned officer stepped on to the platform.' Salomon describes the scene:

> At his neck shone the 'Pour le Mérite'. He was the C.O. of the Iron Division, Major Bischoff. He looked at the train. The soldiers crowded round him, filled with vague hopes. Officers joined them. The Major raised his hand: 'I absolutely forbid the withdrawal of the Iron Division.' That was mutiny. In the evening we gave him a torchlight procession.

Bischoff's decision to defy Ebert's order irrevocably committed the remaining Freikorps men in the Baltic to Awaloff and the White Russian forces. The Freikorps movement had taken another step down the path of illegality and subversion. The next day, the Freikorps leaders met in Mitau and formed a 'German Legion' commanded by Naval Captain Siewert, and, after his death in action, by his deputy Captain Otto Wagener, later Hitler's Reichskommissar for economics.

The dozen Freikorps forming the Legion totalled 14,000 men. It was equipped with an air squadron of sixty-four planes, six cavalry formations, 56 field guns, tank and armoured car sections, a field hospital and 156 heavy machine guns. Awaloff boasted that the total forces under his command now numbered 55,000 – the overwhelming majority German volunteers.

Goltz, who had been in Berlin lobbying on behalf of his men, hurried back to the Baltic where he became Awaloft's 'technical adviser' – although in reality he retained the command and loyalty of his men. In an effort to justify their mutiny and 'defection' to foreign command, the Freikorps began a campaign of propaganda. Goltz himself pointed out that since they had never obeyed the orders of the 'Usurper' Ebert they could not mutiny against him. Schmidt-Pauli claims: 'If the Freikorps mutinied, it was against the revolution and against Versailles.' While in a proclamation addressed grandly to 'The German Fatherland and the civilized peoples of the Earth', the Freikorps fighters wrote:

> With heavy hearts we have decided to reject the order which our Government has issued under pressure from the Allies and have decided to stick it out on the Bolshevist front. We are soldiers trained to obey. Nevertheless we believe the commands of our own conscience are a higher authority than obedience to orders given under duress. And our conscience tells us to defend the Fatherland from the unspeakable terrors which the breakthrough of the Bolshevik hordes would bring to our people. In our ears we hear the shrieks of raped women and butchered children; before our eyes, the picture of bestially mutilated bodies! We will not aim our guns at you. No! It is for you that we stay on and fight . . . for you!
>
> What evil-minded men tell the world about our motives does not matter. Do not believe them. They are in the pay of the Spartacists who have been bought out by the Bolsheviks. They only want to slander us in the eyes of the world in order to put us aside so that they will have a free hand.
>
> We tremble for our brothers and sisters. We fear for the culture of the entire world! If the Fatherland and the statesmen of the world abandon us, then good! Then we will be the only ones who emerged from the Great War with our sense of human duty and honour unsullied. Perhaps there is still a God who will stand beside us!

Beneath the hysterical bluster, the proclamation is a plaintive document demonstrating the Freikorps' pathetic sense of grievance and hurt vulnerability.

One might almost feel sorry for these children of Germany so cruelly abandoned to their fate by a stern parent. As it is, the proclamation is a revealing statement of inner motivations. It is all there, the burnished pride in 'duty', 'soldierly obedience' and patriotism, coupled with resentment against the ingrate Fatherland. The tears for the Bolsheviks' victims seem particularly reptilian, bearing in mind the Freikorps' own behaviour in Berlin and Riga. Nor can one accept wholeheartedly these self-proclaimed barbarians' new role as the guardians of world civilisation and culture. It is as if Attila the Hun had suddenly evinced an interest in the conservation of Rome.

Much more convincing are the words of Ernst von Salomon:

> In those days the soldiers in the Baltic states had a marching song which began: 'We are the last Germans who stayed to face the foe.' We felt indeed that we were the last survivors of the German race. We were almost grateful to the Government for shutting us out of the country. For, since the connection had been officially severed, our actions need not be influenced by troubles at home. We should in any case have acted as we did. We could not feel that we owed any duty to our country, because we felt that we could no longer respect it. We were no longer tied to it for orders, nor for pay or food or any sentimental considerations. A dimly guessed impulse drove us on. We had a fresh source of strength, of hope and we were freed from the burden of piteous claims which had accompanied us day by day and step by step. Outcasts, exiles, homeless beggars – we held our torches high.

Small wonder that von Salomon titled his Freikorps memoirs, *Die Geächteten* (The Outlaws). Of the enlistinent under Awaloff, Salomon says:

> All kinds of fantastic schemes were simmering under his fur cap. . . we were ready to make an ally of the Devil himself, so long as we could annoy the English and stay. We fastened Russian cockades to our caps, though we cunningly allowed the German ones to show over the top. We cheerfully took the paper money which Awaloff-Bermondt printed – backed by the army supplies we intended to secure as booty. We rather sulkily drank vodka and learned to swear in Russian. So, since we had been discarded by Germany, we became Russians.

The absurd Awaloff alienated any remaining Balt allies by

proclaiming the territory annexed to Imperial Russia. Pending the Czar's restoration, the Baltic would be ruled by 'Prince' Awaloff himself! When his privately printed currency failed, Awaloff proposed to employ slave labour to run sawmills and ship paper pulp to the West.

As Awaloff's army finally took the field in October, the British-equipped Latvian army offered furious resistance, aided by a shore bombardment from the guns of Britain's naval squadron. Awaloff's attempt to re-capture Riga was doomed from the start. Thrown back in confusion, the ragged, embittered, hungry and dysentery-ridden Freikorps took out their rage on the long-suffering Balts: their retreat towards the German border was marked by a long trail of burnt villages, razed farms and murdered bodies. Freikorps apologists are quite unashamed in describing their progress:

> The soldiers of the Iron Division and the German Legion unloaded all their despair and fury in one wild power-blow against the Letts . . . villages in flames, prisoners trampled under foot, chaotic revenge and joyous destruction. The leaders were powerless – or looked on in grim approval. (Heinz)
>
> We saw red: we roared out our songs and threw our grenades after them. We no longer had anything of human decency left in our hearts. The land where we had lived groaned with destruction. Where once peaceful hamlets had stood was now only soot, ashes and burning embers after we had passed. We kindled a funeral pyre – there burned our hopes, longings, bourgeois codes, the laws and values of the civilised world; there burned everything. And so we returned, swaggering, drunken, laden with plunder. (Salomon).

The plight of the Freikorps was parlous indeed: in November the Iron Division was pushed into a pocket of land near Thorensburg. Completely surrounded, it was saved at the last moment by the Rossbach Freikorps which marched to the rescue in an epic twelve-hundred-mile journey from Berlin, averaging forty miles a day. Their leader, Captain Gerhard Rossbach, was one of the most notorious of the Freikorps chiefs: a brutal, sadistic homosexual who was later to play a prominent part in the

Munich Beerhall Putsch and the early days of the Nazis. (He is 'credited' with designing the Nazi stormtroopers' brownshirt uniform and for personally seducing the Chief of the SA, Ernst Röhm, into homosexuality.)

As the battered remnants of the Baltic Freikorps straggled back across the frontier many of them must have felt a renewed sense of defeat and betrayal, recalling the events of November 1918 exactly one year before. There was the same conviction of having been stabbed in the back by those at home whom they had been defending ('It is for you we stay on and fight . . . for you!'). This led the volunteers to vicious and baseless allegations against the Ebert Government: they had closed the border and refused to allow reinforcements across. (False.) They had refused to allow Freikorps recruitment within Germany. (False.) They had kowtowed to the arrogant Allies. (True – but faced with the threat of blockade and/or invasion they had little choice.)

But the Freikorps soldiery were not interested in the facts. They re-doubled their determination to square accounts with the socialists of every stripe – by fair means or foul. With that purpose in mind, Goltz, Bischoff and Rossbach did their best to hold their Freikorps together – often disguising their roles under rather transparent covers. Bischoff, for instance, resolved to stage a march on Berlin to overthrow the Republican regime and broke down his Iron Division into gangs of 'Agricultural workers' who were given shelter and food by the big land-owning Junkers of East Prussia and Pomerania. Rossbach's Corps were disguised as foresters, while other volunteers went off to work in the coal mines of Upper Silesia, where they met the men of other famous Freikorps – those of Naval Commanders Ehrhardt and Löwenfeld. Here in the heathlands and brooding forests of eastern Germany the volunteers, whether working in sawmills, cycle shops or peat-fields, gathered, recuperated, oiled and stacked their weapons and generally licked their wounds while waiting for better times. They would not be long in coming.

The historian von Oertzen says of this hard core: 'They were only a few thousand strong now – but they were anything but broken. They had seen and experienced too much to be able to change over to a safe and comfortable civilian life. They remained Freikorps fighters.'

Von Salomon speaks eloquently for the men themselves: 'We did not belong anywhere, we were strangers in a strange land. We had offered ourselves to fate unconditionally – and Fate had thrown us away like a stone.'

11

THE MUNICH SOVIET

'We Communists are dead men on leave.'
Eugen Leviné, leader of the Second Munich Soviet Republic,
to the judges who condemned him to death, May 1919

With the suppression of the March uprising in Berlin, and the setting-up of the National Assembly in Weimar, the storm centre of political events inside Germany in the Spring of 1919 moved south to Bavaria, to the country's second city, Munich. To explain the background of these events, it is necessary for the narrative to move backwards in time to that climactic month, November 1918.

Bavaria was, after Prussia, the largest and most important of the German states. Indeed, until Bismarck decisively established Prussian hegemony over the rest of Germany in 1871, she had vied with her northern neighbour for the leading role in the nation. The two states were as different as chalk and cheese. Prussia was Protestant, dour, uncultured, militarist and increasingly industrialised. Bavaria was Catholic, traditional, rural, artistic and easy-going. Her ruling Royal dynasty, the

Wittelsbachs, had sat comfortably on their throne for seven hundred and fifty years. In comparison, the Hohenzollern Emperors were mere upstarts. In recognition of these traditions, Bavaria was allowed a large measure of administrative autonomy, known as the 'reserve rights'. With the outbreak of war in 1914, however, Bavaria had gone along with her Prussian overlord and Bavarian armies had equalled the Prussians in valour on the battlefield. The Bavarian Crown Prince, Rupprecht, had proved one of the most able and successful of the German commanders.

With the collapse of the Western Front, Bavaria had suffered a revolutionary spasm just as devastating in its results as the simultaneous events in Kiel and Berlin. On 7 November 1918, the SPD leader in Bavaria, Erhard Auer, called a mass peace demonstration in one of Munich's largest parks, the Theresienweise. The event was progressing in the customary relaxed Munich manner, with brass bands serenading the strolling crowds of workers and a sprinkling of off-duty soldiers, when attention began to focus on a wild-eyed speaker orating on the edge of the main meeting. This figure appeared to be a caricature of the traditional anarchist revolutionary, complete with unkempt beard, floppy-brimmed black hat, long matted hair, and glittering pince-nez. All he lacked was the smoking bomb concealed under his shapeless old overcoat.

The man was in fact Kurt Eisner, for long a familiar feature on the bohemian fringe of Munich's café life. A Jewish journalist and political dabbler, he was a former editor of the SPD newspaper *Vorwärts* but had made his home in Munich since abandoning his wife and children in 1907. He joined the Independent Socialists after their split with the majority SPD in 1917, and fomented anti-war strikes in January 1918, serving a spell in jail for his pains.

Eisner addressed the main thrust of his remarks to the soldiers among his audience, urging them to return to their barracks, win over their comrades, arm themselves and depose their officers.

The man had found his moment. To Eisner's delighted surprise, the crowd followed him out of the park to the Guldien school, which had been commandeered as a munitions depot by the Bavarian army. Brushing aside those officers bold enough to resist, the mob of soldiers and workers seized rifles and swept on to take control of the Maximilian Kaserne and the other main barracks in Munich.

Eisner himself moved on to the Mathaser Brauhaus, one of the city's innumerable beerhalls, where he met members of Munich's workers' and soldiers' council who authorised him to set up a Bavarian Republic. Within a few hours, red flags were flying from Munich's main public buildings and Eisner was master of the city. He formed an ad-hoc emergency cabinet, consisting of three fellow Independent Socialists, three Majority Socialists and one non-aligned radical. Eisner himself was proclaimed as Bavaria's Prime Minister.

The Wittelsbach dynasty collapsed like a house of cards. The palace guards defected to the revolution without attempting resistance and the elderly King Ludwig III fled with his family in a car – which promptly ditched in a muddy field outside the city.

The composition of Eisner's cabinet was conventional enough. Eisner's style of Government, however, was eccentric in the extreme, as this portrait of him at work by a French journalist, Paul Gentizon indicates:

He looks like a frail and seedy old man, [Eisner was fifty-two] a Shylock in a shiny frock coat and greasy skull cap. Diplomatic papers, parchments, revolutionary proclamations and telegrams cover tables and armchairs in a confusion suggesting the backroom of a shop. He hardly tries to conceal the most compromising documents from the indiscretion of journalists who besiege him. On the contrary, in his desire to break entirely from the past, Eisner offers to their curiosity the acts concerning his own politics: Would you like the telegram sent today to the Berlin Government? Here it is . . . the order for today's cabinet meeting? Here . . . A hurried visitor, bored with waiting, bursts unannounced into the office where young men and women secretaries are at work, smoking and eating sandwiches in a chaos of tables and chairs piled high with newspapers. No method and no organization seems to prevail in the working of this strange ministry.

The major achievement of Eisner's brief rule came on 24 November when, in an effort to establish his credentials with the Allies as a man of peace determined to turn Bavaria's back on the old order, he published a series of files 'liberated' from the archives of the Royal regime, which provided damning proof of the German Government's belligerent machinations in the days leading up to the outbreak of war in 1914. This infuriated Ebert's struggling Government in Berlin which saw the revelations as a treacherous stab in the back at a time of tricky negotiations with the Allies. Affronted by this reaction, Eisner promptly cut the diplomatic links with Berlin.

The extreme right marked Eisner down for vengeance. But Eisner's enemies were also at work within his own cabinet: the SPD leader, Auer, who had never forgiven him for stealing his thunder on the Theresienweise, demanded that Eisner should test his popular support by holding elections to the Bavarian state parliament, the Landtag. Despite the Premier's prevarications, the poll was eventually scheduled for 12 January.

These elections did not suit the book of the harder men who stood behind Eisner's comic opera regime: the Spartacists. Communists distrusted Eisner's brand of idealistic Socialism. Despite rightist efforts to portray the gentle poet as a blood-drenched Bolshevik, Eisner himself remarked: 'We have neither used Russian methods nor pursued Russian objectives. There is no Russian Bolshevism in Germany.' Correctly fearing that the coming elections in the backward Bavarian countryside would return the Right to power, Munich's tiny Left wing attempted a putsch on 7 December to oust the majority SPD from the Government. A spearhead of revolutionary sailors, backed by the city's Spartacists, surrounded Auer's office and demanded his resignation at pistol point. Although Eisner swiftly suppressed the outbreak, the incident did nothing to quell the mounting paranoia of the right or to mollify the injured Auer's hostility.

Meanwhile, the condition of the Bavarian economy deteriorated rapidly: the state's coffers were almost empty; its railways had been stripped of rolling stock as reparations by the Allies; vast sums were being paid out to the unemployed and repatriated soldiers as dole money; and discontent against Eisner personally was mounting. Demonstrations against the regime began to take on an anti-Semitic character, with right-wing students gathering to yell slogans such as 'Down with the Israelite devil!' or 'Bavaria for the Bavarians!'. Ever the idealist, Eisner attempted to mute the protests by appeals to sweet reason. He organised a 'Fête of the Revolution' in Munich's ornate Opera House at which the audience were regaled by a revolutionary hymn composed by Eisner himself. The unappreciative gathering responded by roundly booing the diminutive poet-Premier when he dared to appear on stage. For half an hour, Eisner struggled to make himself heard above calls of 'Scoundrel!' 'Slacker!' and 'Swine!'. When quiet at last descended, the theme of Eisner's address was revealed to be: 'Education and Democracy', a typically high-falutin' subject, but hardly calculated to appeal to hungry and angry people.

By the New Year, Eisner's position was impossible: brought to power on a sudden wave of sentiment, which had receded as rapidly as it had arisen, events had revealed him as an idealistic daydreamer rather than a practical politician.

The January elections proved how much his popularity had declined. Eisner managed to cling on to power for five further weeks but on 21 February his time finally ran out. That morning, he set off on the short walk from his office in the Foreign Ministry to the Landtag with his resignation speech in his pocket. He never delivered it. Round the corner from the Ministry, a young

Bavarian aristocrat, Count Anton Arco-Valley, a discharged Army officer of violently nationalist opinions, lay in wait. The Count was smarting at his recent rejection by the Thule society, one of Munich's innumerable right-wing groupings. Research had revealed that Arco-Valley's mother was of Jewish descent and the Count was denied membership. The rebuff had merely reinforced the Count's resolve to do some courageous deed which would redeem his tainted blood in the eyes of his fellow rightists.

At 9.45 a.m. the doomed Premier emerged on to the Promenadestrasse, accompanied by a pair of bodyguards and two secretaries. When the little group drew abreast of him, Arco-Valley pulled out a pistol, aimed and fired. Hit twice in the head at point-blank range, Eisner fell dead to the pavement. His furious guards emptied their guns at the assassin, hitting Arco-Valley in the throat, mouth and chest. An angry crowd of Eisner's supporters gathered at the spot, raining kicks and blows on the wounded Count who lay weltering in his own blood. Eisner's secretary, Felix Fechenbach, singlehandedly saved the murderer from the crowd and dragged his prostrate body into a courtyard of the Foreign Ministry.

Arco-Valley was tried the following year and sentenced to death for his crime. But in the prevailing right-wing atmosphere, the sentence was commuted to life imprisonment by his judges, who commended his deed as 'Springing not from base motives but from the most glowing love of his "Volk" and country'. He was freed completely in 1924 on grounds of ill health, but survived until after the Second World War when he died after being run over by a U.S. Army jeep.

Eisner's assassination started a slaughter that was ultimately to take thousands of lives. The revenge of his infuriated supporters was instant, bloody and brutal. Exactly one hour after Arco-Valley struck, Erhard Auer was at the rostrum of the Landtag delivering a tribute to the murdered Eisner that, considering their rivalry in life, was hypocritical in the extreme. A young apprentice butcher named Alois Lindner calmly walked into the chamber, drew a revolver, took steady aim at Auer and shot him down. Leaving the SPD chief writhing in agony on the floor, Lindner strolled out of the building the way he had come, only pausing to shoot dead an officer, Major von Jahreiss, who unwisely tried to bar his path. Another assassin took the life of Oesel, the leader of Bavaria's conservative People's Party. (Lindner fled to Austria, was extradited, and served fourteen years in prison. Auer was severely wounded, but recovered and later resumed his political career.)

The shootings plunged the city into panic. The extreme Left, believing that Eisner's murder was the signal for a general pogrom, arrested members of Munich's bourgeoisie and flung them into jail as hostages. For their part, the SPD Government ministers feared the attempted assassination of Auer would presage a real Red Terror and fled the city for the small town of Bamburg, where they set up a sort of Government-in-exile under Adolf Hoffmann. The scene of Eisner's murder became a gruesome shrine: workers erected giant pottraits of the fallen leader at the site, which was garlanded in flowers. Red Guards forced passing members of the middle class to doff their hats in homage. Members of the Thule Society reacted by soaking sacks in the sweat of bitches in heat and dumping them on the spot, which was consequently defiled by dogs.

The power vacuum in Munich was occupied by a motley collection of Eisner's left-wing cronies who set up a Government outdoing even their late leader in crazed idealism. The main power brokers in the regime were two writers, Ernst Toller and Erich Mühsam. Mühsam, an anarchist and café intellectual, was one of the first victims of the Nazi concentration camps, where he was to be done to death in atrocious circumstances – beaten so badly that his eardrums were exposed. The young Expressionist playwright, Toller, was author of the influential drama, *The Machine Wreckers*. Both, incidentally, were Jewish, as was the anarchist philosopher Gustav Landauer, who found himself the new Commissar of Public Instruction, and speedily ordered the end of the study of history, 'that enemy of civilisation'. The character of the Government was perhaps most piquantly expressed by the Minister of Finance, Silvio Gesell, who believed in the abolition of money, and the Foreign Minister, Dr Franz Lipp, who had recently been released from a mental institution.

Lipp was the most deranged figure to have been thrown up even in this insane epoch. He despatched a series of telegrams. One to the Pope complained that Hoffmann had stolen the key to his Ministerial toilet. Another, to Lenin, talked of Noske's 'hairy gorilla hands dripping with blood'. A third, to the Minister of Transport, informed his startled colleague: 'I have just declared war on Württemberg and Switzerland because the dogs did not send me sixty locomotives at once. I am certain of victory. I have sent a message to the Pope – a very good friend of mine – begging him to bless our arms.' After this, even Toller was obliged to have Dr Lipp escorted home from his ministry by two male nurses.

Not to be outdone, for his part the Commissar for Housing declared the immediate requisition of private dwellings and decreed that all future houses built in the city should be designed with the living room placed over the kitchen and bedroom. But if this Government of clowns provided a welcome moment of light relief, a grim retribution would not be long delayed.

March 1919 seemed a promising moment for revolution in central and eastern Europe: Berlin was convulsed by the second Spartacist uprising; Russia's Bolshevik regime was successfully consolidating itself against its White enemies; in Bavaria's neighbour, Austria, the infant Socialist Republic appeared to be taking a Marxist course well to the Left of Germany; while further down the Danube, in Hungary, a ruthless Communist minority, led by another Jewish revolutionary, Bela Kun, had just seized power from an ineffectual Social Democratic regime and – with Russian backing – seemed about to set middle Europe ablaze with the fires of revolution. But Bavaria was unpromising soil for revolutionary seeds. The revolutionary writ hardly ran outside Munich's city limits. The Catholic peasantry remained stolidly immune to the temptations of social unrest. The powerful Roman Catholic clergy were fiercely opposed to all leftist manifestations – priests in Munich had to be compelled at gunpoint to ring Church bells during the huge funeral obsequies for the fallen Kurt Eisner. Despite the nominally 'Socialist' nature of Hoffmann's Government in Bamburg, the Left in Bavaria remained a minority, representing just over a third of its eight million citizens. Within this minority, the extremists who held power in Munich were a mere splinter faction. But in the face of the menacing hostility surrounding them, the brave idealists led by Toller went ahead with their bold social experiment. While Munich's population succumbed to famine they busied themselves with irrelevant schemes to transform human life by means of high art.

After several weeks of intrigue and confusion following the blood-letting of 21 February, the twenty-five-year-old Toller proclaimed himself Premier of a new Soviet Republic in a ceremony on 6 April held in the former queen's bedroom in the Wittelsbach palace. His regime was to last for just six days.

Hoffmann and his Minister of War, Schneppenhorst, were consolidating their hold on provincial Bavaria and raising a small army of 8000 men to re-take the capital. The Bavarian SPD were anxious not to surrender local autonomy by appealing to Berlin for military aid. Noske was only too eager to unleash his Freikorps against 'Red' Munich, but Hoffmann and Schneppenhorst persuaded him to hold his hand until they had tried to subdue the city on their own. Their preliminary move was to impose a blockade around the capital, holding back food and coal supplies from the starving and freezing population. In these dire straits, Toller's lofty idealism collapsed – he was replaced by professional revolutionaries rather than play-actors, hard men who had been sent to Munich by the Communist party and Comintern to salvage what they could for Communism from the chaos.

The trio concerned were all Jewish, all committed Communists and experienced Bolsheviks, and all profoundly pessimistic about the outcome of events: Eugene Leviné, Towier Axelrod and Max Levien. Axelrod was born in Moscow and had been Lenin's Press Chief. His Bolshevik masters had sent him to Germany in July 1918 with the express purpose of fomenting revolution. Leviné was last encountered playing a leading role in the January Spartacist uprising in Berlin. Escaping from that fiasco, he had been sent to Munich in March. Levien, also of Russo-German origin, had taken a leading role in the workers' and soldiers' council.

The triumvirate set up a Munich edition of the KPD paper the *Rote Fahne* which they turned into a platform for revolutionary agitation. Unlike Eisner, Toller and the Independents, they had no illusions about the immediate outcome of the struggle. Looking at the situation with the coldly objective eyes of true Communists, they saw clearly what Rosa Luxemburg had seen in Berlin two months before: that Bavaria was not ready for revolution. It would take years of agitation, organisation and propaganda before a disciplined revolutionary party could hope to seize and cling on to power. The present ferment could only have one outcome: defeat for the Left. However, the revolutionary workers, soldiers and sailors were irrevocably committed to the struggle and the Communist party must stand at their side. The triumvirate resolved to go down fighting. Of the three, Leviné was the revolutionary who most nearly possessed the cold steel will of a Trotsky or Lenin. He set himself the task of reining in the impulsive Independents and building up the forces at his disposal.

Upon arrival in Munich in March, Leviné's first move had been to recall all the Communist party cards that had been issued in the city by the thousand since the revolution. After inspection he reissued only three thousand of them – a small nucleus of reliable Communist cadres who could be depended upon in the tight spot that was so evidently approaching.

Leviné's next act was to supplant the already tottering Toller Government. The Communists had already – via Max Levien – secured a commanding influence on Munich's workers' council and they managed to have Toller arrested on 9 April. Although he was freed after a few hours' detention, his position as an idealistic intellectual was precarious among the professional political functionaries of the KPD – who had enormous prestige among the city's proletariat because of their links with Lenin and his revolution. An attempt by the moderate SPD to regain the power they had lost within Munich itself was the cue for Toller's fall.

On 12 April, the Republican Guards, a right-wing Socialist militia, bribed by Hoffmann to the tune of 300 Marks a head, mutinied against the Toller regime. Moving at dawn, the Guards seized the Landtag and the other main government buildings, arresting Erich Mühsam and the mad Dr Lipp and transporting them to Bamburg for trial. The Guards had reckoned, however, without the red-hot militant sentiments of the city's working class. Workers gathered in their thousands on the Theresienweise, where Eisner had first raised the standard of revolution, and resolved to fight the putschists. Joined by the newly-formed Red Guard militia, they moved back into the city centre in force and overwhelmed their opponents by their weight of numbers, re-taking the Landtag and the main railway station. One company of Republican Guards held out in the Luitpold Gymnasium, which was stormed by a force led by Toller in person. But, despite his valiant performance, the victorious workers decided that a stronger hand than Toller's was necessary on the revolutionary tiller. The day after the failed putsch a new revolutionary council was elected: the Communists took all the chief posts and Toller was again arrested on Levien's orders.

The Communists instituted a rule of iron in the wake of the anarchic excesses of Toller's friends. Scores of upper-class and bourgeois hostages were rounded up and jailed in makeshift prisons. Motor cars were confiscated and requisitioned. Red Guards staged punitive raids in search of food and booty on the homes of the wealthy. Up to 12,000 rifles were distributed to the proletariat, while the arms of the bourgeoisie were impounded.

The most impressive achievement of the Soviet's rule was the creation of a Red Army within the space of a fortnight. The command of this scratch force was given to the third sailor to play a leading role in the German revolution after Karl Artelt in Kiel and Heinrich Dorrenbach in Berlin. Rudolf Egelhofer was a twenty-six-year-old former naval aviator and a veteran of the Kiel mutiny. He acted with all the fanatical dynamism of youth in the service of his Communist cause. By the end of April his force numbered an estimated 25,000 men. Although there were good non-ideological inducements for joining the Red Guards – pay was 25 Marks a day for privates, 100 a day for NCO's and 500 for officers, and free food and accommodation were considerable temptations to a starving populace – about half the Guards were genuinely committed Communists who fought with courage and tenacity when events came to a climax.

For all their energy and efficiency, the new 'Russian' rulers could not prevent the general situation in the city from sliding further into chaos and confusion. Sensing that a reckoning with their enemies could not be long put off, many of the revolutionaries gave themselves up to orgies of drunkenness and sexual debauchery. The ancient palace of the Wittelsbachs became the scene of generalised bacchanalia as the champagne flowed and the Munich whores plied a roaring trade.

By the middle of April, with the economic blockade of the city pinching ever tighter, the Hoffmann Government judged the time ripe to attempt its recapture. Cautiously, their little army approached Munich from the northwest. Informed of the advance and freed from jail once again, Toller left Munich to form a defence line. The two forces came face to face on 18 April at the little town of Dachau – later notorious as the site of one of Hitler's earliest concentration camps. After inconclusive bargaining both sides opened fire with artillery. Toller – once again displaying military competence surprising in a writer – led the Red army against the barricades erected by the 'Whites'. Joined by the workers from Dachau's munitions factory, they soon put Hoffmann's small force to flight, capturing five officers and thirty-six men. The women of the town pursued the Whites into the countryside, hurling stones, while the Colonel commanding the beaten force commandeered a railway locomotive to speed his retreat. The triumphant Toller, magnanimous in victory, ignored an order from Egelhofer to shoot his prisoners. Chaired shoulder high by his followers he became the hero of the hour.

The defeat of his little army at Dachau left Hoffmann with no alternative but to appeal to Berlin for military aid. Noske furnished a force consisting of two divisions of Guards commanded by General von Friedburg, a Brigade of cavalry scouts commanded by Colonel Magnis, Ehrhardt's second Marine Brigade Freikorps, the Gorlitz Freikorps under Lieutenant Colonel Faupel, and two Swabian Freikorps from Württemberg under General Haas and Major Hirl. In addition to this 'foreign' force, the Freikorps was to have a stiffening of native Bavarians consisting of the remnants of Hoffmann's little force commanded by General von Mohl, and the largest Freikorps in Bavaria, commanded by Colonel Franz Ritter von Epp.

Epp's Freikorps plays such an important part in the Freikorps story that it is worth considering in detail. Originally set up at Noske's prompting in January 1919, it had quietly been gathering recruits at Ohrdruf in neighbouring Thuringia until it had swollen to one of the strongest forces in the country. Most of the early recruits were regular Bavarian Army officers who enlisted as privates. Von Epp himself was a fire-eating martinet who later became one of the earliest Nazi leaders, and under Hitler's rule 'Statthalter' or Governor of Bavaria. Surviving the Second World War unscathed, a substantial portion of his estate was confiscated by the state on his death as reparations for his war crimes. Epp had been itching for the chance to hit at the Reds for months, but Hoffmann had held him at arms' length until circumstances forced him to accept Epp as part of Noske's relief force. Like other SPD chiefs, Hoffmann would soon learn the bitter lesson that to summon Freikorps aid meant exchanging the frying pan for the fire.

Noske's terms for giving aid were harsh: he, not Hoffmann, would be in political control of the expedition. Military supremacy was vested in the overall Commander, General von Oven, who would only give Hoffmann back his power when he deemed that Munich had been thoroughly subdued. The other chief condition was that after the conquest of the city a re-consti-tuted Bavarian army would form an integral part of the provisional national Army – the Reichswehr – that Noske was in the process of creating. Hoffmann was forced to agree. The 30,000-strong Freikorps army began to cross into Bavaria on 27 April, a week after the 'Battle of Dachau'. The plan was to surround and then throttle the Red city. On 28 April, Epp's men crossed the line of the Glonn. The following day the Freikorps seized Freising, Erding, Wasserburg and Gars, some twenty miles north of Munich. The same day, 29 April, Starnberg, south-west of the city, was taken by the Freikorps from Württemberg, despite a determined defence by 350 Red soldiers. Twenty-one unarmed Red medical orderlies were captured and shot on the spot – an atrocity presaging many similar massacres in the coming days.

News of the approaching army's atrocities threw the Red defenders of Munich into panic: Axelrod left the city by plane in a bid to summon help from the Bolsheviks of Hungary or Russia. But his aircraft failed to get further than Austria, where he sought sanctuary. Levien, too, left Munich for Austria. Of the Red triumvirate, only Leviné remained in hiding in the city. The task of organising Munich's defences fell to the Red army commander, Egelhofer. Scorning the 'rat run' taken by his comrades and thousands of other Red Guards who deserted and disappeared, Egelhofer issued a stream of increasingly hysterical calls to resist:

> Workers! Soldiers of the Red Army! The enemy is at the gates of Munich! The officers, students and sons of the bourgeoisie and White Guard mercenaries are already at Schliessheim. There is not an hour to be lost . . . Protect the revolution! Protect yourselves! Every man to arms! Everything is at stake! At Starnberg the White Guard dogs murdered our hospital attendants . . . Forward into combat for the proletarian cause!

In a last effort to buy the allegiance of the populace, Munich's Finance Commissar, a twenty-five-year-old bank clerk named Emil Männer, had the city's printing presses rolling night and day to churn out worthless banknotes. But paper money could not hold off the inevitable: on 29 April, the Gorlitz Freikorps captured Dachau, scene of Toller's triumph the week before. The next day the ruling revolutionary council had its last meeting. By the evening of that day, 30 April, only Toller and Egelhofer remained to organise the defence from their HQ in the War Ministry. As they talked, a false report came in that the Whites were in the city and had taken the railway station. The rumour was enough to touch off a mass desertion, and within minutes Toller and Egelhofer found themselves almost alone in the huge ministry.

Only Egelhofer's bodyguard, a twenty-year-old sailor, stayed, calmly stuffing grenades into his pocket.

Emboldened by the approach of the Freikorps and the decay of the Red defences, Munich's bourgeoisie rose up to speed their liberation. They seized the Wittelsbach palace, the Rezidenz, and substituted the old blue and white Bavarian national banner for the Red flag. The city's clergy rang the bells in cathedrals and churches to celebrate deliverance from Godless Communism.

On the outskirts of Munich, a Freikorps armoured train rained shells on the city, while aircraft from its air squadron droned overhead dropping leaflets combining threats with promises of liberation. In desperate panic, Egelhofer ordered that the hundred or so bourgeois hostages held in Munich's jails be massacred. Most of the hostages were held at the Luitpold Gymnasium, where they were in the care of a discharged former Bavarian army officer named Seidel. Upon receiving Egelhofer's murderous order, Seidel had his captives pushed in pairs to a wall where they were shot and bludgeoned to death. When Toller heard what was afoot, he rushed to the scene and stopped the slaughter, but not before some twenty of the hostages had been killed in a horrible fashion, probably by Russian former prisoners of war who had carried out the grisly task after German Red Army members refused to take part. Rumours swept the city that the genitals of the male hostages had been hacked off and thrown in a dustbin. Students slipped through the lines to report the massacre to Epp and Ehrhardt who immediately ordered their men into Munich – a day earlier than planned.

Many of the murdered hostages were leading figures in the Thule Society, held responsible by the Reds for the murder of Kurt Eisner. The Reds had only narrowly missed netting two future Nazi leaders who evaded the hostage trawl – Rudolf Hess, who slipped away to join Epp's Freikorps, and Adolf Hitler himself, who, he later claimed, held off the three Red Guards who came to capture him on the morning of 27 April, with a rifle. Other hostages – like the murdered Prince Thurn und Taxis Hohenlohe – were monarchist members of Munich's aristocracy.

On the morning of 1 May, while Socialists and Communists round the world celebrated international Labour day, the Freikorps entered Munich. They encountered almost no organised opposition. Most of the Red Guards had thrown away their weapons, torn off their armbands and melted away. The long columns of Freikorps soldiers arrogantly goose-stepped into the captured city, to be greeted by a joyful middle class and an ecstatic Catholic clergy, who promptly celebrated a Te Deum thanks-giving service and an open-air Mass for their liberators.

A Freikorps squad moved into the Mathaser beerhall where Eisner had proclaimed his government and which had since become the HQ of the Communist workers' council, and gutted it with flame-throwers. Only Egelhofer, with a few Red diehards, put up a last-ditch resistance in the area of the main railway station. After an artillery battle, Egelhofer attempted to flee in a car. He was stopped and immediately shot dead. He was luckier than one of his former Government colleagues, Gustav Landauer. The anarchist philosopher and literary critic was found hiding in his friend Kurt Eisner's former home. He was brought to the Stadelheim prison by Freikorps soldiers who beat in his face with rifle butts and shot him in the head as he lay choking in his own blood. The former Commissar for Public Education continued to breathe, causing the Sergeant in charge of the patrol to jest: 'The putrid thing has two lives', before he pumped another bullet into the body. The boots of the Freikorps finally kicked and trampled the remaining life out of Landauer. His battered body was left lying in the prison yard for two days.

This killing was typical of many perpetrated by the Freikorps army, who made full and liberal use of Noske's licence to do as they pleased in the conquered city. Angry at the loss of sixty-nine comrades during the re-conquest, the Freikorps gave full rein to their murderous instincts, until the White Terror outdid in horror the Red Terror that had preceded it and sickened even the Munich citizenry who had originally welcomed their liberators. The lead for the indiscriminate slaughter was given by the adjutant of the Lutzow Freikorps, Major Schulz, who told his officers: 'Anyone who doesn't understand that there is a lot of hard work to be done here or whose conscience bothers him had better get out. It's a lot better to kill a few innocent people than to let one guilty person escape. You know how to handle it . . . shoot them and report they attacked you or tried to escape.' True to his promise, after his 'pep talk' Schulz sent one of his officers, Lieutenant Georg Pölzing, to the town of Perlach outside Munich to terrorise the population. Pölzing chose a dozen people, apparently at random, brought them back to the Hofbrauhaus – the famous Munich beerhall where Hitler launched his putsch in 1923 – and had them shot out of hand. Brought to trial seven years later in 1926, Pölzing was acquitted of all charges, despite the fact that none of his victims had been Communists.

The worst single atrocity occurred two days later, on 6 May, when a group of Catholic workmen belonging to a religious club, the St Joseph Society, were holding a regular meeting to discuss the innocuous subject of Education and Theatre. This harmless gathering was suddenly disrupted by a Freikorps patrol led by a Captain Alt-Sutterheim who picked out thirty men and had twenty of them shot, beaten and bayoneted to death as 'Communist terrorists'.

So many victims perished during the purge that Munich's harassed undertakers were overwhelmed and bodies were left to decay in the streets. Mass graves were dug and the carcasses were piled in. This makes the calculation of the number of victims difficult. The Freikorps themselves claimed 600 but this figure represents only the number of 'official' executions. 'Unofficial'

'Comrade! Help me!' A Freikorps recruiting poster appeals to old soldiers to recreate the comradeship of the trenches in combating the Bolshevik menace.

General Ritter von Epp,
Freikorps leader.

'I hate the revolution like
sin!' Friedrich Ebert, first
President of the Weimar
Republic. His Faustian pact
with the Freikorps doomed
German democracy.

Street fighting men: revolutionary soldiers, sailors and civilians take to the streets of Berlin, January 1919.

'We are fighting for the gates of Heaven.' Spartacist leader Karl Liebknecht harangues a Berlin crowd, 4 January 1919, but he and his revolution were doomed.

'The bloodhound of the revolution.' Defence Minister Gustav Noske, the Government's strong man, inspects the Marine Brigade Freikorps he formed to neutralise the naval mutiny in Kiel – and later used to crush the Spartacists in Berlin.

Munich's Red Republic drowns in blood: a Freikorps unit moves in to crush the chaotic Soviet Republic in the Bavarian capital, May 1919.

Future uncertain: a Spartacist revolutionary captured by the Freikorps grimly awaits his likely fate.

Tables turned: insurrectionary officers interrogated in front of the Trade Union building in Kiel during the Kapp Putsch, March 1920.

Revolutionary discipline: members of the 'Red Army of the Ruhr' on parade, Spring 1920, before they were crushed by the Freikorps.

Cometh the hour, cometh the man: Hitler (in soft helmet) at the time of the Beerhall Putsch in Munich, November 1923.

Friekorps figurehead: Great War hero General Erich von Ludendorff (in spiked helmet) with Nazis during the Beerhall Putsch.

Our time will come: Nazi demonstration in central Munich during the Beerhall Putsch, November 1923. Temporarily defeated, they would have to wait another decade before their triumphal return.

murders totalled 1200, according to Freikorps propagandist Freidrich von Oertzen, and this figure is almost certainly an underestimate.

The Red leaders who had been unwise enough to remain in Munich shared the fearful fate of their humbler comrades: Leviné was arrested, brought before a military tribunal and condemned to death. Before going to the firing squad he defiantly told his judges: 'We Communists are all dead men on leave.' The blind leader of the Red Bavarian Peasants' League, Gandorfer, was also shot. Mühsam and Toller, the café intellectuals, were, for the moment, luckier. Tried by more lenient Bavarian courts, they were given jail terms. When Hitler came to power, Mühsam was murdered in a concentration camp. Toller fled into exile and eventually committed suicide. Axelrod successfully claimed Soviet nationality and diplomatic immunity when he was arrested. Levien returned to Russia, only to perish in the Stalinist purges of the Thirties.

Finally, by 7 May, General von Oven reported to Noske that the city was 'pacified' and 'cleansed' and the Hoffmann Government could return to Munich. Nevertheless it was a further week before the Bamburg regime returned. They found a greatly changed city. Gone was the easy-going capital. Munich had been thoroughly terrorised by its six months of chaos, revolution and counter revolution. Too much blood had been shed, and from now on the city on the Isar was to be, in von Oertzen's words '. . . the matrix of National Socialism'.

Scared stiff by its brush with red revolution, Bavaria returned to blackest reaction and Munich became a haven for every type of radical rightist: Nazis, nationalists and soon Freikorps fugitives from justice found the city a happy hunting ground, for, as Oertzen points out:

> If we search in the history of the National Socialist movement for its earliest contact with the Freikorps . . . we must conclude that this

contact, with all its direct and indirect consequences, was the liberation of Munich, carried out by the Freikorps from all over Germany – even though at that time Adolf Hitler was still a completely unknown corporal about whom the officers and men of the Freikorps knew nothing.

They were to find out soon enough.

12

VERSAILLES: RESISTANCE OR SUBMISSION?

'May the hand wither that signs the Treaty.'

Chancellor Philipp Scheidemann,
June 1919.

For the last half of 1919, German national politics were obsessed by one theme only: the treaty dictated to the defeated nation by the Allies at Versailles. The consequences of those distant deliberations in the Hall of Mirrors, where Bismarck had proclaimed the German Empire in 1871, were to provide Adolf Hitler with his most potent and persistent grievance; were to saddle the struggling Weimar Republic with crippling and unpayable war debts; and were to cover the politicians who submitted to it with such ignominy and shame that – in many cases – it led to their deaths at the hands of the vengeful Right. But the most immediate and not the least of the consequences of Versailles was the only full-blown attempt by the Freikorps to overthrow the detested Republic and substitute a dictatorial Fascist regime: the Kapp Putsch.

As the Munich Soviet Republic crumbled under the Freikorps guns an official German delegation left Berlin for Paris on 28 April to hear the peace terms decided upon by Woodrow Wilson, Lloyd George and the French Premier Clemenceau after prolonged wrangling. The delegation was headed by the Foreign Minister chosen by Chancellor Philipp Scheidemann in February when he succeeded Ebert, who had been elevated to the office of President. Count Ulrich von Brockdorff-Rantzau was an aristocrat chosen because it was thought his long diplomatic experience would impress the Allies. There could hardly have been a worse choice; haughty, monocled, stiff, Rantzau represented in Allied eyes the worst type of unreconstructed Prussian arrogance. Rantzau took with him German proposals for the treaty, supposing that the Allies would be willing to treat with their former foes as equals. He was to be grieviously disappointed.

As soon as the Germans crossed the border, their reception set the tone: the train was forced to crawl across the war-ravaged fields of northern France at a steady ten miles per hour so that the Germans could feast their eyes on the devastation their armies had wrought. In Versailles they were housed in a hotel surrounded by barbed wire, like quarantine lepers. Here they were forced to kick their heels for a whole week before the Allies deigned to summon them to the Palace to hear their fate. Clemenceau greeted them with the ominous pronouncement: 'The hour has struck for the weighty settlement of our account.' The elaborate German peace proposals never left the attaché cases of the delegation: they were merely called upon to receive and transmit the terms already decided upon.

The terms they heard were stunningly harsh: so harsh that President Wilson himself was heard to mutter: 'If I were a German, I think I should never sign it.' Baldly, Germany was to lose the provinces of Alsace and Lorraine – acquired after the Franco-Prussian war of 1870 – to France. France would also occupy all German territory on the east bank of the Rhine, plus the rich coal and steel producing district of the Saar which was to be administered by the newly formed League of Nations. Poland was to receive the coal-producing province of Upper Silesia in the east, plus most of Posen province and substantial portions of west Prussia – cutting off east Prussia from the rest of the Reich – and incidentally forming the Danzig 'corridor' – creating yet another grievance for Hitler to exploit, and the one which was to provide the immediate 'casus belli' for World War Two. Denmark and Belgium were also to get large chunks of German border territory.

Germany was to be ruthlessly stripped of her African colonies: German East Africa (today's Tanzania) and South West Africa (Namibia). She was to lose her High Seas Fleet, at that time interned by the British Royal Navy at Scapa Flow in the Orkneys. Her Army was to be limited to a professional force of only 100,000 volunteers. Conscription and the General Staff were to be entirely abolished. To ensure that Germany could never again menace the peace and security of her neighbours, she was to be forbidden to possess tanks, planes or even armoured cars. Economically, Germany would be forced to pay huge sums in reparations to the victims of her aggression: the exact amount was to be determined by an Allied Commission, but preliminary estimates ran as high as 120 *billion* dollars. The Kaiser and other high-ranking 'war criminals' held responsible for the outbreak of hostilities were to be handed over for trial and, most humiliatingly of all, the German Government had to make a formal admission of sole responsibility for causing the war and all the ensuing loss and damage: the notorious 'War Guilt' clause.

The Germans were given no time to argue or dispute this 'Diktat': they were merely allowed a fortnight to digest the 75,000-word, 450-page draft before the Treaty was finalised and signed. The delegates stumbled away from the Hall of Mirrors and prepared to telegraph the terrible terms back to Berlin. The

news reached Berlin on 8 May and caused immediate consterna-
tion. On 12 May, the National Assembly convened for the first
time in the capital to debate the draft. To unanimous applause,
Chancellor Scheidemann denounced the bulky document as
unacceptable, declaring: 'What hand would not wither rather than
bind us in these chains?' Recommending rejection of the treaty,
Scheidemann re-affirmed Germany's demand for a 'just peace',
based, as the Armistice had been, on Wilson's Fourteen Points. He
failed to take into account that Wilson himself had been forced to
bargain away many of his points by his angry Allies: Britain and,
even more vindictively, France.

Speakers from all the political parties rejected the Treaty, line
by line and clause by clause. Scorn and anger were heaped on the
heads of the Allied statesmen, with Wilson being singled out for
special condemnation for his 'betrayal' of his originally liberal
peace proposals. After five hours of this unaccustomed unanimity,
the debate concluded with the whole Assembly rising and singing
'Deutschland über Alles'. It was an ominous sign for the future:
the nationalist, world-defying spirit of August 1914 seemed to
have returned in full patriotic fury.

Like the diplomat he was, Rantzau remained in Paris and
attempted to persuade the Allies to modify the Treaty. Already
Allied doubts were surfacing about Germany's ability to pay
mountainous reparations and the morality of French military
occupation of the Rhineland. The famous economist, John
Maynard Keynes, an advisor to the British delegation at
Versailles, and the South African soldier-statesman Jan Christian
Smuts both pointed out that as Germany's Gross National
Product amounted to 75 million dollars she could hardly be
expected to pay reparations of upwards of 100 billion: she would
collapse in ruins and drag the rest of Europe down with her. These
sane arguments had great influence on the British Prime Minister,
Lloyd George, but his last-minute effort to revise the treaty came

up against an exhausted Wilson and the inflexible hostility of 'Tiger' Clemenceau who was already being accused by Marshal Foch of being too soft on the beaten enemy. Rantzau's 20,000 word counter-proposal document was contemptuously rejected: beyond the grudging granting of a plebiscite to determine the future of Upper Silesia and the limiting of French occupation of the Rhineland to fifteen years, the treaty remained unaltered.

On 16 June the Germans were given just five days – later extended to a week – to either accept or reject the Treaty. They were left in no doubt that rejection would mean a renewal of the war and the outright occupation of all Germany. Bitterly, Rantzau led his delegates back to the Fatherland. He recommended rejection of the Treaty at any price. In his view it was 'Unfulfillable' – but the final decision now rested with the Government.

Rantzau returned to confront his Cabinet colleagues in Weimar. He found a Government greatly changed in its attitude to the treaty: Matthias Erzberger, leader of the Catholic Centre party, which held three cabinet seats, had retained high-level contact with the Allies since the days when he had led the German armistice delegation to the Forest of Compiègne. He left his colleagues in no doubt that failure to ratify the iniquitous 'Diktat' would result in instant Allied invasion. On the other hand, the wily Erzberger pointed out, signing the treaty, even at the pistol's point, would buy Germany that most precious commodity: time. With the passage of time, much could change; the Allies would fall out amongst themselves, their war-weary peoples would lose their taste for retribution and Germany would be able to claw back much of the ground she had lost. In addition, Germans were starving and the lifting of the Allied blockade would mean that food would reach the hungry cities and neutralise the still-looming threat of revolution and Bolshevism.

Erzberger's arguments found surprising support from Noske, the strong man of the Cabinet, who reluctantly recommended

signing the treaty, saying, in his customary blunt way: 'It's all very
well for us fifteen heroes to sit here and refuse to sign. But behind
us, the nation is at an end. What is the use of heroics in such a
situation?' Noske, as Defence Minister, was speaking in full
knowledge of the attitude of the Army Chiefs. Although the Army
High Command attacked the treaty with even more venom than
the politicians, the more realistic among them knew full well that
they were in no position to resist. Hindenburg himself admitted:
'We cannot count on successfully repelling a determined attack by
our enemies.' At the same time, in his usual dithering way he
added: 'As a soldier I would rather perish in honour than sign a
humiliating peace.' Once again, as in November 1918,
Hindenburg handed the poisoned chalice of responsibility to the
despised politicians via his Quartermaster-General, Groener.

Groener was once more playing the role he had assumed at Spa
the previous November: the voice of reason among the military
leaders. He asked his chief to tell Ebert clearly that armed
resistance was impossible. Faced with this awesome task,
Hindenburg havered; 'You can give the answer to the President as
well as I', he lamely answered. Having taken the coward's way
out, he told Groener, once he had delivered the news, 'You have
taken a heavy burden on yourself.'

A few among the officer corps were in favour of a general
withdrawal to Prussia's ancient heartland where they could defeat
the Poles and Slavs and re-constitute the Reich, but Groener
favoured the more realistic course advocated by Erzberger. He
didn't like the treaty, but he preferred a slow sentence of death to
instant suicide.

The divided cabinet argued for hours over the agonising choice.
When Ebert finally called for a vote on the evening of 19 June, his
Ministers split down the middle. Chancellor Scheidemann, two of
his SPD colleagues and the four Democratic Party Ministers voted
against signing. Erzberger, his two centre party colleagues plus

Noske and four more SPD Ministers voted in favour. Scheidemann and Rantzau promptly resigned and Ebert cast around for a new Chancellor and Cabinet.

For the whole of the next day, 20 June, Germany was without a Government. Towards the end of 21 June, Ebert finally managed to cobble together a new cabinet, composed only of the SPD and Centre parties. An SPD union leader, Gustav Bauer, became the new Chancellor; the ambitious Erzberger had to content himself as Finance Minister, while Noske – who had rejected a demand by Maercker and other military leaders to take over as dictator – retained the Defence portfolio.

On Sunday 22 June, with just one day left before the expiry of the Allied ultimatum, the Bauer cabinet faced the National Assembly. The devious Erzberger had concocted a plan to get the treaty through the Assembly by deleting the articles – known as the 'Shame Paragraphs' – relating to Germany's war guilt and the extradition of war criminals. After impassioned debate, this motion was passed by 237 votes to 138.

Unfortunately for Germany, the Allies were in no mood for such last-minute changes. Their resolve had been hardened by news just in from Scapa Flow, where the pride of the German Fleet had been scuttled by its own crews in preference to being permanently impounded.

Wilson coldly drafted a reply to the German Assembly's motion saying: 'The time for discussion is past.' The Government was invited to sign – or reject – the Treaty whole, with no further additions or deletions, within twenty-four hours.

On the evening of the 23rd, with thirty Allied divisions massing in the Rhineland ready to move into Germany, and with the Polish and Czech armies ready to march on Berlin from the east in a coordinated campaign, Bauer's cabinet secured the National Assembly's approval for the treaty to be signed. A note was sent to the Allies signalling that the Government was 'Yielding to overpowering force' in submitting to the 'unheard of injustice' of the 'imposed peace'. The note was received just ninety minutes before the allied armies were due to march.

The humiliation was complete. The country's military leadership, supported by the professional middle-class, seethed with contempt and virulent hatred for the young Republic, born, as they saw it, from the shame of revolution, and baptised by the crowning disgrace of the Versailles 'Diktat'.

For the moment, the Army busied itself with the re-organisation demanded by the Versailles Treaty's provisions, limiting the Reichswehr to 100,000 men with a small officers' corps of only 4000, equipped with only light weapons. The Reichswehr's regular strength in early 1919 was estimated at 350,000 but this excluded the hundreds of thousands enlisted in the various Freikorps. It is difficult to give an exact calculation of the fluctuating Freikorps numbers, but at their height they probably fielded up to half a million men – indisputably the most powerful political/military force in the nation.

The new Reichswehr was to be formed by blending the Freikorps system with the remnants of the old army. In some cases, individual Freikorps officers and soldiers joined the Reichswehr with their old ranks. In others whole Freikorps joined en masse: Maercker's Freiwillige Landesjägerkorps became, more prosaically, Reichswehr Brigade No. 16; Reinhard's Freikorps became the 15th Brigade; while von Epp's Bavarian Freikorps became the 21st Bavarian Infantry Brigade.

The fusion of the Freikorps into the Reichswehr itself became a source of friction: neither Freikorps fighters nor Reichswehr soldiers liked the new colours of the detested Republican flag – black, red and gold. They insisted on wearing the black, white and red cockades of the old Imperial Army. Similarly, many officers objected to taking an oath of loyalty to the Republic, as demanded by the Weimar constitution. Noske and the other Republican officials had to tread warily when dealing with the ruffled military sensibilities and in many cases Republican rules were openly flouted and the new army marched under its old colours.

Discontent among the military with the restrictive Versailles regulations twice boiled over into open revolt during 1919. In late June, when it became clear that the Government was about to sign the treaty, the hardline General Otto von Below, Commander of the 17th Army Corps, led his men and assorted Freikorps units in an attempted Putsch that was quickly snuffed out by his more realistic brother officers, fearful of provoking an outright Allied attack. They preferred to bide their time until the opportunities for reaction became riper.

One of the most reactionary of the senior officers was General Walther von Lüttwitz, who had been Military Commander of the 1st (Berlin) Army district since January. In the summer of 1919 he came out openly with a demand that Noske should act even more brutally to suppress the extreme Left:

> If the Government lets the time pass before acting, it will lose its military power through the reduction of the Army and will strengthen Bolshevism. Because the Government depends on the energetic co-operation of the troops, everything must be avoided that is likely to influence the temper of the Army against the Government . . . such as a change in the uniforms, renunciation of the old Imperial flag, or abolition of special military courts. Today the army is the foundation of state power.

When Noske refused to act on his recommendations for fear of alienating the SPD's diminishing support among the working class, Lüttwitz lapsed into a state of brooding insubordination. In this mood, he fell prey to the machinations of that inveterate right-wing intriguer, Captain Waldemar Pabst, still Chief staff officer of the Guards Cavalry Division. Pabst was openly plotting a military overthrow of the Republic, and was busy co-ordinating the actions of various extreme right-wing groups with his own plans for a military putsch. In late July Pabst succeeded in convincing his immediate superior, the Guards Division Commander, General Hermann von Hofmann, to march on Berlin on the pretext of suppressing a fictitious Communist uprising. The troops were already in the suburbs of the capital before other officers, including Maercker, succeeded in getting Hofmann to call off the Putsch. His troops were withdrawn, and subsequently dispersed around the country.

This setback did not deter the indefatigable Pabst: he set to work to weave yet another plot. There was plenty of combustible material for Pabst's incendiary activities: discontent over Versailles, disputes about flags and insignia, distrust of the Government that was preparing to reduce the numbers of men under arms and had 'betrayed' the Freikorps in the Baltic, all fused into a mood of embittered rage and despair among the Freikorps. Now that the left-wing revolts inside Germany had been comprehensively crushed, there seemed little left for the Freikorps to do and the resulting boredom as they kicked their heels in gloomy barracks only stoked their smouldering frustrations. For the wilder elements among them, the prospect of absorption into the grey ranks of the Reichswehr, with its standardised rigidity, discipline, and old Prussian hierarchy, seemed the very antithesis of the freebooting Freikorps spirit. In addition, the choicest plums among the jobs to be allocated in the shrunken General staff – re-christened, in deference to Versailles, the 'Truppenamt' (Troops Office) – were clearly to go to the 'old boy network' among the General Staff, many of whom had held sniffily aloof from the amateur soldiers of the Freikorps.

It all seemed a poor reward for the sacrifices made and dangers run by the Freikorps in the desperate months since January when they had been the only force to stand between the young Republic and 'Bolshevik chaos'. In short, the unemployed Freikorps fighters, frightened, as they had been in 1918, by the imminent prospect of demobilisation and dissolution and with bitter feelings of betrayal against the Government and the new professional Reichswehr, provided a vast reservoir of revolt. This could be used by the reactionary conservatives who had never accepted the November revolution and were actively planning a restoration of the old Imperial order. It was the function of Pabst and his co-conspirators to knit these two strands of nihilism and reaction together in a rope strong enough to strangle the hated Republic.

13

THE KAPP PUTSCH

'What do we care when a Putsch goes wrong?
– We'll make another before too long!'
Rhyme sung by members of Ehrhardt Brigade,
March 1920

The military muscle for the conspiracy was to be provided by the returning Baltic Freikorps veterans who were being frozen out of the Reichswehr by its new Commander, General Hans von Seeckt, who had taken over in the wake of Hindenburg's and Groener's resignations after the ratification of Versailles. Pabst had learned the lesson of the failure of his putsch in July: he would put his reliance on these desperate 'Baltikumer' – hardened fighters with nothing left to lose – rather than on the well-drilled caution of the regular Reichswehr. Pabst was sophisticated enough to realise that an outright military Government would be unacceptable to the Allies and he set about creating a fig-leaf civilian organisation to cover the militarist nature of the regime he intended to establish.

By October, Pabst was putting his plans into action. His chosen cover was a right-wing political group calling itself the National

Union, whose leading figures were two ghosts from the past:
Wolfgang Kapp, founder of the ultra-nationalist wartime
Fatherland Party, who was now Agriculture Minister in East
Prussia, and Ludendorff.

Ludendorff had returned quietly from his exile in Sweden,
where he had ridden out the most turbulent months of revolution
and counter-revolution writing his war memoirs. Germany's
wartime dictator had now come back to Berlin where he had
taken a suite at the city's leading hotel, the Adlon – thoughtfully
provided free by the management – under the transparent
pseudonym Karl Neumann ('New Man'). By coincidence, the
Allied Commission supervising German disarmament was
quartered in the same hotel and, although Ludendorff was
theoretically one of the chief German war criminals due to be
extradited under the terms of the Versailles treaty, the rules of the
international fraternity of military gentlemen apparently allowed
him to mingle freely with the Commission's members. One day,
while chatting with the British representative on the Commission,
General Malcolm, Ludendorff advanced the view that the German
armies had not been defeated in the war, but betrayed by the
cowards and traitors at home.

'Not defeated?' queried the puzzled Malcolm. 'You mean they
were stabbed in the back?'

'Yes, yes!' agreed the excited Ludendorff, 'That's it exactly. We
were stabbed in the back!' One of the most powerful legends of
the German right was born in that phrase.

Pabst's first idea was to install Noske as Germany's new
dictator. He called upon the 'Bloodhound' to put the proposition
to him, urging, with an undertone of menace: 'It would be unfor-
tunate, Herr Minister, if you did not find yourself on the side of
the officers when the national uprising occurs.' Noske replied that
he had long suspected that one day Pabst would arrest him, along
with the rest of the Government. Pabst hotly denied any such

intention, but Noske refused to give a similar guarantee that he would never arrest Pabst for his naked political plotting. True to his word, two days after this exchange Noske ordered Pabst's Horse Guards Division to be disbanded and Pabst himself was dismissed. Freed from his military responsibilities, Pabst turned his full-time attention to perfecting his plot. He appointed himself Secretary of the National Union and recruited several influential comrades and friends to the organisation. In addition to Kapp and Ludendorff, Major Stephani, Commander of the powerful Potsdam Freikorps, was roped in, along with Colonel Max Bauer, Ludendorff's chief wartime aide; General von Lüttwitz, and the industrialists Arnold Rechberg and Hugo Stinnes – the latter one of the rich Captains of Industry who later financed Hitler's rise to power.

Besides this collection of distinguished names the National Union contained a remarkable assortment of misfits and political intriguers of dubious backgrounds and nationalities including two extraordinary characters calling themselves 'Doctor Schnitzler' and Trebitsch-Lincoln. Schnitzler's real name was Handke and, though he claimed to be a political scientist, his 'doctorate' was in dentistry, and had been acquired via a correspondence course. Later he became 'political adviser' to the Kapp regime, and later still, to the Ehrhardt Freikorps, before lapsing into a career as a blackmailer and extortionist.

Trebitsch-Lincoln had an even more peculiar pedigree: born a Hungarian Jew, he went to England where he became an evangelical preacher and a Liberal MP! During the War, he had been unmasked as a German agent and forced to flee to the United States. This chequered past did not prevent Kapp from naming him as his Press Officer.

The Union set up shop in the Fatherland Party's old HQ in Berlin's Schellingstrasse. Throughout the autumn and winter of 1919/1920 meetings went on here, and in Ludendorff's new flat on the Viktoriastrasse, as the conspirators strove to broaden their support. Fearing that Ludendorff would prove too controversial and unpopular to be the military figurehead of the revolt, Kapp and Pabst turned to Lüttwitz, who had the added advantage of still being a serving officer, with an important Command covering Berlin itself.

Lüttwitz was hardly an ideal choice, since his political grasp was nil, and his indiscretion legendary. Ignoring the secrecy essential for the success of a political coup, Lüttwitz made a habit of calling on various Government offices leaving, in Kapp's phrase, 'the calling card of the counter-revolution'. He threatened all kinds of retribution if the Government did not instantly eradicate unemployment, outlaw all strikes and suppress mounting Press attacks on the Army and Freikorps.

Although Ebert and Noske treated Lüttwitz's demands with the derision they deserved, the actions they were independently taking were indeed having the effects that Lüttwitz professed to desire: labour disputes *were* dropping dramatically, unemployment *was* falling, and with the lifting of the economic blockade, even the perennial food shortages were easing. In fact, political and economic stability were the last things that the plotters of the National Union desired. Their best hope of garnering support lay in continued instability and rising discontent. People would only turn to their extremist solutions if all other hope seemed gone.

At the close of 1919, with the clouds that had lain over Germany for a year beginning to lift, and the Republic's institutions looking increasingly secure and permanant, the one issue that the right-wing plotters could use to lever their way into power was the demobilisation and reduction of the Freikorps. Unless the plotters could rally sufficient support among the threatened malcontents of the Freikorps it looked as though the window of opportunity for the right-wing revolt would soon slam shut.

Lüttwitz did his best to muster support among his fellow senior officers, both Regulars and Freikorps chiefs. He called a meeting attended by some of the most prominent names in the counter-revolution: Generals Maercker, von Hulsen, von Hofmann, von Oven and von Lettow-Vorbeck, the legendary wartime Commander of German East Africa who had fought a brilliant campaign of guerilla warfare that had tied down an Allied army commanded by Smuts for the entire course of the war. After the war, von Lettow-Vorbeck, a distinctive figure in his slouch bush hat, had formed a Freikorps which had taken part in the suppression of Left-wing revolts in Berlin and Hamburg. A traditional monarchist rather than a Fascist, von Lettow-Vorbeck was one of the few Freikorps veterans to become an active anti-Nazi plotter. He survived the Second World War and died, in his nineties, during the 1960s.

Led by Maercker, the Generals refused to join Lüttwitz in immediate revolt against the Republic, but did agree to back him if the Government appeared ready to capitulate to the extreme Left, or to undue Allied pressure. Undeterred by this cool response from men he felt should have stood at his side, Lüttwitz forged ahead with his plans for a putsch.

All this activity did not escape the attention of either the Government or the new Reichswehr chief, von Seeckt. Noske had been warned of the budding plot as early as July, and Ebert himself had been directly approached by Lüttwitz with his arrogant demands. As for Seeckt, he was so disturbed by Lüttwitz's meddling in his careful plans to reconstruct Germany's military power that he issued a special order of the day on 18 October warning his Generals against taking part in a Putsch.

'We need peace, order and work', Seeckt declared: 'Everything that now breeds dissension and unrest among the people must be avoided. I warn against toying with revolutionary ideas without consideration of the consequences and against following credulous, irresponsible counsellors in word and writing.' Noske underlined this clear message with a speech to the National Assembly at the end of the month, warning that he would not hesitate to put down a revolt by force.

Lüttwitz plunged on, ignoring the warnings of friend and foe alike. His resolve was strengthened by the arrival in his Berlin command area of the most powerful, fanatical and well-trained Freikorps: the Second Marine Brigade, commanded by Naval Lieutenant-Commander Hermann Ehrhardt. Ehrhardt was a war hero who had taken part in the battle of Jutland as a torpedo corvette Captain.

Horrified by the mutinies in his beloved Service at the war's end, Ehrhardt had been one of the officers who had foregathered in Kiel in the earliest days of the revolution to plot retaliation against the Reds. Occupying the Thousand Man Barracks in Wilhelmshaven, he had formed his own Freikorps, the Second Marine Brigade, in parallel with Wilfried von Löwenfeld's Third Marine Brigade, and Noske's First, or 'Iron' Brigade.

By virtue of his vigorous, uncompromising character, Ehrhardt had built his force into the hardest and most ruthless of all the Freikorps. Despite harsh discipline, the Brigade's members were devoted to their Commander, known to one and all as 'The Captain'. In spite of their sea-going origin, Ehrhardt's men fought all their campaigns on land. They took part in the suppression of the Spartacist uprisings in Berlin, cleared the northern coastline of Reds, played a leading role in the 'liberation' of Munich and had recently put down Polish separatists in Upper Silesia.

Ehrhardt's reputation stood so high among the Freikorps that recruits flooded in and he was able to choose the bravest, hardest and most determined men. Most of his staff, like himself, were former naval officers and many of his foot-soldiers were right-wing students. The Brigade always retained a salty, nautical flavour, greeting each other with cries of 'Shit-Ahoy!' and lustily

belting out their own marching song, the 'Ehrhardt Lied' which
was later adapted, with suitable change of words, to become the
theme song of Adolf Hitler's personal bodyguard:

> 'Hakenkreuz am Stahlhelm,
> Schwarz-Weiss-Rotes band,
> Die Brigade Ehrhardt
> Werden wir genannt'

> ('Swastikas on our helmets,
> Red-white-black armband,
> The Ehrhardt Brigade –
> That is our name.')

Indeed, it was the Ehrhardt Brigade that first brought the evil
symbol of the crooked cross, adopted by Hitler as his emblem, to
the notice of the world. Loathing the Republic and all its works,
simple, brutal and blunt, Ehrhardt was just the man to convert
Kapp's, Pabst's and Lüttwitz's plans into direct action. His five-
thousand-man Brigade of tough troopers would form the strong
arm and spearhead of the Putsch.

Seeckt was aware that Ehrhardt had been brought into the plot:
his counter-plan was to order the dissolution of both Ehrhardt's
and Löwenfeld's Marine Brigades as part of the Government's
general programme of reducing the Reichswehr to one hundred
thousand men announced in February 1920. Lüttwitz violently
opposed the order – just as Seeckt anticipated, since without
Ehrhardt's malcontents behind him, Lüttwitz would lack the
military muscle necessary to transform his Putsch dreams into
reality. The deadline for the dissolution was set for 10 March.

On 1 March, Lüttwitz was guest of honour at a ceremony
marking the first anniversary of the Ehrhardt Brigade's formation.
Behind the parades and festivities, the plotters gathered together
in small groups, perfecting their plans to ensure that there would
be a second anniversary for the Brigade to celebrate.

The plotters decided to forestall the Brigade's dissolution by striking first, thus bringing forward the date for the putsch which had been set for April. Speaking to the Brigade on parade, Lüttwitz ringingly declared that he would never permit the demise of such a perfect unit, 'in these turbulent times'.

As the countdown to the more-or-less openly proclaimed coup ticked away, both sides moved feverishly to strengthen their position. Lüttwitz's own Chief-of-Staff, General von Oldershausen, who opposed his superior's treasonable plans, personally informed the head of Berlin's Security Police, Colonel Arens, of the projected Putsch. Arens, with a policeman's natural sympathy for the authoritarian right, did not attempt to arrest Lüttwitz but put him in touch with leaders of the legitimate right-wing political parties in a bid to moderate his insurrectionary intentions. Two meetings with the chiefs of the Nationalist and German People's parties failed to move the pig-headed General. When the rightist politicians told Lüttwitz to wait for new elections when the right would assuredly sweep the country, he replied with airy arrogance: 'I prefer to rely on my battalions.' In despair, Seeckt tried a last-minute personal appeal, visiting Lüttwitz at his HQ and endeavouring to get him to call off the coup. He was unsuccessful.

Noske tried to defuse the Putsch by transferring command of the Ehrhardt Brigade from Lüttwitz to Admiral von Trotha on 10 March in preparation for its dissolution. Enraged, Lüttwitz stormed into the Chancellery and angrily insisted that Ebert and Noske rescind the order. When they politely declined, he left in a huff.

Noske, having received a full report from the security police on the subversive activities of the plotters at the National Union, belatedly decided to relieve Lüttwitz of his command, at the same time ordering the arrest of the leading lights of the Union – Kapp, Bauer and 'Dr Schnitzler', though excluding the hallowed name of

Ludendorff. But when the police raided the Union's offices they found the building deserted and the birds flown. Hearing news of the raid, and knowing his plans were unmasked, Lüttwitz realised that he would have to launch the Putsch at once or call it off. He decided to go ahead, and ordered his staff car to drive hell-for-leather for the Ehrhardt Brigade's camp at Döberitz, fifteen miles west of Berlin. Ehrhardt, similarly alerted, was driving full tilt in the opposite direction. The two most active plotters met half way and held an emergency council of war at the roadside. Lüttwitz told 'the Captain' that the moment for action had arrived, and asked him to return to camp and prepare his men for a march on Berlin the following day.

Ehrhardt drove back to Döberitz and issued orders for the march, for which his men had been long preparing. The next morning Lüttwitz drove to Döberitz once more and ensured that the military preparations for the putsch were going smoothly. He arranged with Ehrhardt that his Brigade would be at the Brandenburg Gate at 6 a.m. the following day, Saturday 13 March.

When Lüttwitz had gone, Ehrhardt called his officers together and issued orders for the morrow's march. The Brigade would be on the road at 10 p.m. that night, spearheaded by an assault company with orders to ruthlessly crush all resistance.

The Government rapidly got wind that something unusual was in the air at Döberitz and a reluctant Admiral von Trotha was sent to the camp to investigate. When Trotha reached Ehrhardt's HQ, all seemed quiet. (Not surprisingly, since the members of the Brigade were mostly asleep in preparation for the night's exertions). 'The Captain' was thus able to bluff the Admiral that nothing untoward was happening. But perhaps Trotha only saw what he wanted to, since the following day he rapidly went over to the putschists' side. Noske, still suspicious even after receiving Trotha's assurance that all was well, ordered the Berlin garrison

put on a state of alert. Thanks to the equivocal attitude of the
Reichswehr to the Putsch, it appears that these orders were not
put into effect. The only forces immediately at the Government's
disposal around Berlin to combat the putsch were the 3000
members of the 29th Reichswehr regiment, and the 9000-strong
Security Police. Neither force, even if they stayed loyal, could
hope to match the toughness and determination of Ehrhardt's
5000 hardened veterans.

Late in the evening of 12 March, a nervous Noske, receiving
reports from a journalist that Ehrhardt was about to march, sent
a high-ranking delegation to try to dissuade him. These emissaries
were General von Oven, who had commanded the army that had
'liberated' Munich from Red rule, and Lüttwitz's Chief of Staff,
General von Oldershausen. Passing the Brigade already on the
road, the Generals entered the camp at Döberitz and confronted
Ehrhardt.

'The Captain', alone in his quarters, received his two superiors
with a drawn and loaded pistol. Disconcerted, the pair explained
their mission. Ehrhardt replied that things had gone too far to
draw back. He was only obeying the orders of his and their
superior, Lüttwitz, and he advised them to do the same. The
Generals asked Ehrhardt for a list of his political grievances and,
having scribbled Lüttwitz's minimum political manifesto down,
the two men agreed that Ehrhardt should halt his Brigade at the
Siegesallee, on the edge of Berlin's Government quarter, early the
next day, while awaiting the regime's reply to the demands. With
that, the disconsolate duo made their way back to Berlin.

Noske berated his Generals for not having killed the mutinous
Captain on the spot, and then called an emergency council of war.
The meeting was attended by the Defence Minister himself, the
Prussian War Minister, General Reinhardt, and Generals von
Seeckt, von Oven, von Oldershausen, Admiral von Trotha and
Noske's faithful military ADC, Major von Gilsa. Noske demanded

that the Generals lead their men against the right-wing rebels, but this suggestion was only backed by Reinhardt and Gilsa. Seeckt, the Head of the Reichswehr, remained icily aloof. When pressed for an answer, the sphinx-like Commander-in-Chief drew his thin frame up to its commanding height and, his monocle glittering, replied: 'Reichswehr do not fire upon Reichswehr! How can you, Herr Minister, countenance a battle at the Brandenburg Gate between troops who have fought side by side against the enemy?'

In a twinkle of Seeckt's glassy eye, all the illusions that Noske had nourished and cherished for more than a year, vanished like smoke. When he had been confronted by angry fellow Social Democrats, worried by the massacring of the working class by the Freikorps, he had always insisted that this was all for the greater good of creating a new Reichswehr, a democratic Army, shorn of its traditional élitism and loyal to the Republic. Now the scales fell from his eyes. In a single sentence, Seeckt had shown that when it came to the point, the Army would not draw its sword against rebellion – providing, of course, that the revolt came from the political right.

Noske huffed and puffed. He threatened that the Police would be mobilised against the revolt. Seeckt smiled grimly. On the contrary, he replied, his information indicated that the Police were already about to defect to the rebels. Noske was on the point of tears. Brokenly, he bleated: 'Everyone has deserted me. Nothing remains but suicide.' Then, summoning the last shreds of his dignity, he declared the meeting ended.

Noske and Reinhardt hurried away to another meeting with their cabinet colleagues, the 'Bloodhound' still continuing to whine about the 'treachery' of the officer corps. Seeckt, meanwhile, having committed the Reichswehr to a policy of masterly inactivity, retired to his home to sit out events, waiting to see which side came out on top. At the Cabinet conference, Noske was all for leading a detachment of loyal soldiers to the

Brandenburg Gate to meet Ehrhardt's men with machine guns. Reinhardt, the leading General to stay loyal, also advocated a hard line, commenting that a whiff of grapeshot would snuff out the spark of revolt. Their civilian colleagues evidently had less faith in their powers of armed resistance. They elected to call on the working and professional classes to declare a general strike against the military Putsch.

Then, without waiting for the results of such an appeal to the residual loyalty of a proletariat whose patience they had tried so severely, the Cabinet members piled into a collection of cars and fled Berlin as fast as they could, Ebert and Noske in the lead. Vice-Chancellor Schiffer, a Democrat, was left behind in the capital to parley with the insurgents.

As the convoy containing the Cabinet left Berlin for Dresden in the south-east, the leading columns of Ehrhardt's Brigade were marching into the sleeping capital from the west. With the newly-painted Swastika symbol gleaming on their green-grey 'coal scuttle' helmets, freshly-issued leather knapsacks creaking on their shoulders, and jackboots crashing down on the hard road surface, the grim-faced Freikorps troopers made a sight to stir an old nationalist's heart as they swung through the slumbering suburbs, cheerily roaring out their 'Ehrhardt-Lied' with its mixture of threat, bluster and bravado.

On the edge of the city, by the Pichelsdorfer bridge, they paused at 5 a.m. as agreed, to brew up hot soup and coffee and await further orders. When none was forthcoming, Ehrhardt ordered the resumption of the march and the Brigade proudly unfurled the old black-white-red Imperial naval flags as they marched the final mile into the heart of Berlin. They stomped up the Bismarckstrasse and into the Tiergarten where, by prior arrangement, the civilian conspirators were waiting. At 7 a.m., as the Brigade neared the bulk of the Brandenburg Gate, old Ludendorff himself appeared, his rosy face radiating delight at seeing 'real soldiers' again after all the shame and humiliations of 1918. With Ludendorff – who later claimed that he had merely been out on his early morning constitutional and had met Ehrhardt by 'chance' – was Dr Kapp, the new Chancellor, his beefy neck and bullet head freshly razored under a shiny top hat; his porky bulk crammed into morning coat, striped trousers and spats, ready for his installation as head of the new regime. Ludendorff, Ehrhardt and Kapp were swiftly joined by Lüttwitz, who, grinning broadly, told his fellow-plotters that the Berlin garrison and the Security Police had both placed themselves under his command. The city lay defenceless at their mercy.

The triumphant column turned under the Gate, wheeled right towards the deserted Reichs-Chancellery and seized the building without bloodshed. Once in charge of the administrative Headquarters of the Reich, the conspirators set about drawing up a list of their new Cabinet. This task proved more difficult than anticipated: Kapp took the Chancellorship as predicted, while Lüttwitz, the real power behind the throne, became Reichswehr Minister. Two Junker friends of Kapp, Traugott von Jagow and Freiherr von Wangenheim, were named ministers of the Interior and Agriculture, but the putschists' nominee for the Economics Ministry, a Social Democrat named Karl Severing, not unnaturally declined the honour. When the list was finally complete, another problem arose: as it was a weekend, no civil servants were available to carry out the new regime's orders. Even the skeleton staff nominally on duty had deserted their posts, partly in response to the general strike call, partly out of fear. Not even a typist could be found to pound out Kapp's first proclamation, and he had to delegate the job to his own daughter! The delay meant that the proclamation missed the deadlines of the next day's newspapers.

Distracted by the confusion, Kapp paced the Chancellery corridors plaintively calling for his political adviser, 'Dr

Schnitzler', without whom, he complained, he found it impossible to rule. That dubious dentist was nowhere to be found, having been turned away from the Chancellery doors by Ehrhardt's guards in all the chaos.

The administrative confusion was compounded by the legitimate vice-Chancellor, Dr Schiffer, who persuaded the heads of the civil service and provincial administrations to ignore the orders of the putsch leaders. At the Reichswehr Ministry, Lüttwitz's directives were similarly cold-shouldered by a group of officers under Colonel Wilhelm Heye, who, wearing civilian clothes, did their best to keep army administration ticking over, while refusing to carry out the wishes of their nominal new masters. Seeckt, Reinhardt, Schliecher and other high-ranking Reichswehr officers remained at their homes and refused to report for duty, Seeckt actually drafting his resignation.

By noon on Saturday 13 March, the first day of the Putsch, with the coup chiefs apparently in the seats of power, the first moves were under way to undermine, then destroy the Kapp Putsch. The orders for a General Strike, signed – although in their absence and probably without their knowledge or approval – by Ebert and Noske, had gone out. The proclamations echoed the revolutionary language of the Spartacist calls to arms of a year before: 'Workers! Party comrades! The military putsch is here . . . The work of an entire year will fall into ruins. Therefore quit work! Strike! No hand dare move! No proletarian dare help the military dictatorship! General strike all down the line!' The strike calls were immediately, and almost universally, obeyed all across the Reich. The chief architect of the strike in Berlin was Legien, a right-wing SPD Trade Union leader, who speedily united with his mortal left-wing enemies in the USPD to ensure the effectiveness of the stoppage throughout the capital. On Sunday 14 March, Berlin awoke to an eerie quiet that was more than the calm of the Sabbath. No trains or trams ran. There was no electricity, no gas, and water just dribbled from taps. Shops stayed shuttered as even Sunday traders forswore profits to heed the strike call. Because of the lack of stenographers, Kapp was unable to issue his manifesto until Monday, so the rest of the Reich remained in ignorance of the purpose of the Putsch, and vital time was lost.

Meanwhile, the fleeing members of Ebert's Government had reached Dresden and conferred with the military governor of that city, none other than General Maercker. This officer, while disapproving of the methods of the putschists, had some sympathy for their aims. Ebert, Noske and other Cabinet members who had tried to enlist his support to crush the Putsch, felt it safer to go on to Stuttgart, capital of sleepy Swabia, and rally their forces there. Maercker remained to attempt mediation between the two sides.

Back in Berlin, the first forty-eight hours of Kapp's rule were a welter of confusion and chaos. Order was followed by counter-mand; threats to shoot the strikers were followed by wheedling promises and attempted negotiations. The new Government, widely suspected to be of the blackest reactionary and monarchist hue, at first promised 'Peace, order and action', then tried to do a deal with the Socialist extreme left. Its own supporters started to lose heart.

On Monday, the full effects of the General Strike began to bite. The only part of Germany where Kapp's writ ran was the conservative, Junker-ruled, East-Prussian heartland. Growing restive, the ruffianly soldiers of Ehrhardt's Brigade began to make threatening noises about their pay. 'The Captain' carried his men's complaints to the harassed Chancellor. Kapp, forgetting for a moment his ingrained bureaucratic habits, told Ehrhardt to go and break into the Reichsbank – whose keys had been carried away in the pockets of striking civil servants. 'I am not a bank robber', the Freikorps idol stiffly replied.

Desperately, the embattled putschists opened negotiations on a number of fronts to try to prop up their crumbling authority. Lüttwitz deputed the astute Pabst to hold discussions with vice-Chancellor Schiffer in an effort to open a channel of communications with the deposed civilian Government. But the talks ended in failure by Tuesday evening.

Members of the Reichswehr hoped to use the Putsch as a lever to prise some concessions from the Ebert Government which they could already see was going to triumph. Maercker travelled to Berlin to learn the putschist's demands, and then went on to present them to Ebert in Stuttgart, where the legal regime was convening an emergency session of the National Assembly. The Kapp/Lüttwitz programme was contempuously rejected. In a final and desperate throw of the dice, the putschists opened a third front of negotiations with their sworn enemies, the striking Trade Unionists. This too ended in predictable failure, with the Unionists, riding high on a tide of proletarian support, turning down the Kappists' Vision of a new union of soldiers and workers against the middle-class politicians who had betrayed them both.

Already on Sunday night, knowing that the Reichswehr 'Wehrkreis' regional commanders in Munich, Munster, Kassel and Stuttgart were remaining loyal to Ebert, Maercker had told Kapp: 'Germany is divided into two parts. The one the whole of western and southern Germany, the other the north and the east. If this state of affairs is not ended soon, a battle between Reichswehr and Reichswehr is inevitable, and that must be prevented at all costs.' Confronted by the streams of conflicting orders, most officers, knowing their men were not behind the Putsch, sullenly sat on the fence, and this neutrality, implying a refusal to put down the near-universally successful General Strike, worked in favour of the Ebert Government.

Apart from the Ehrhardt Brigade and a scattering of 'rootless' mercenary freebooters left over from the Baltic adventure, the rest of the Freikorps throughout Germany failed to move in any significant way to support their comrades in Berlin. This was partly because of the scattered nature of the Freikorps formations, each owing loyalty to their individual 'Führers', who were, for the most part, unwilling to surrender their authority to a rival chief. But it also reflected the amazing confusion and haste in which Lüttwitz had launched his coup.

The conspirators failed to take any concrete steps to launch a parallel Putsch in Bavaria, which was choc-a-bloc with unemployed Freikorps fighters and awash with right-wing sentiment after the bloody destruction of the Munich Soviet. As a result, the many powerful Bavarian-based Freikorps failed to take any action in support of the Putsch until it was too late. Elsewhere, the members of the Hindenburg Freikorps, a grouping who had taken the name of the fallen Field Marshal for their own, chose the day of the Putsch to receive a visit from the revered Hindenburg himself The celebrations were so strenuous that when the telephone call came through from Berlin announcing the unexpected Putsch, officers and men were too drunk to take part! Only in Silesia, where Löwenfeld's Third Marine Brigade seized the capital, Breslau, in the name of the Putsch, was there a vestige of Freikorps backing. But this was soon dissipated by the atrocious behaviour of the freebooting Löwenfeld Brigade, which left the patriotic population, in the words of a military observer, General von Lequis: 'In a state of indescribable hatred of the military.' Löwenfeld's and three other Freikorps in the region were accused of carrying out a campaign of murder, arbitrary arrests – even of brother officers – assault and anti-semitic propaganda.

North of Berlin, the most powerful Freikorps was probably the 'Iron Host' (Eiserne Schar) commanded by the charismatic Rudolf Berthold. Berthold had been one of Germany's most famed air aces in the war, earning the 'Blue Max', the coveted Pour le Mérite cross, for his fifty-odd enemy 'kills'. He had most of one arm shot away in combat, but he still insisted on taking to the skies – requiring his batman to pick splinters of broken bone out of his open wounds with pincers before taking off. After the war, his 'Schar' had fought in the Baltic and gained a formidable reputation. Although informed of plans for the Putsch by Pabst as early as January, Berthold was not kept abreast of later developments, and was only told that the Putsch was 'on', the morning it actually got under way. He spent most of that day nursing his wounded pride, before calling his 'Host' together and telling them that they might as well support the undertaking – although gloomily predicting its failure. Berthold's belated support – as we shall see – was to cost him his life.

Even the fabled Gerhard Rossbach, hero of the Baltic war and a close comrade of Ehrhardt, indeed almost as renowned a Freikorps hero as the 'Captain' himself, was not told of the Putsch until the night of the march when it was too late for him to take effective supporting action.

But the primary reason for the failure of the Kapp Putsch was the total unity displayed by the working class and civil service in their strike against the uprising. By a mixture of solidarity, sabotage, and sheer defiance, they broke the will of the rebels. One of Captain Ehrhardt's officers, Lieutenant Mann, later reflected ruefully: 'If we had only shot more people, everything would have been all right.' Another right-wing rebel, Lieutenant Friedrich Wilhelm Heinz agreed: 'Blood is the cement of revolution. Whoever shrinks from letting it flow is no revolutionary.' The fearsome 'Captain' heartily concurred and even persuaded the reluctant Kapp to issue an order that strike pickets would be shot. When this order was hastily cancelled, Ehrhardt recommended cutting off water supplies to the working class areas of Berlin.

On the night of Tuesday/Wednesday, the 16/17 March, following the dispiriting news of the breakdown of Pabst's negotiations with vice-Chancellor Schiffer, Lüttwitz and Kapp were told by two separate emissaries, that Britain, the main interested Allied power, utterly refused to accept or deal with their regime. Further blows then rained fast and hard on the discomfited conspirators. News came in that the numerically strong Security Police, who had declared for Kapp on Saturday, were now demanding his resignation. At about the same time, the Guards Engineer Battalion in Berlin mutinied, seized its officers, and declared for Ebert. Reports came in that other troops were coming under the influence of anti-Kapp agitators and more mutinies could shortly be expected. Finally, and most ominous of all, came tidings that Red Soviets had been proclaimed on the Ruhr by striking workers and that sailors in Kiel and Wilhelmshaven – rejecting the authority of their officers, who, reactionary as ever, had gone over wholesale to Kapp – had mutinied and hoisted the Red Flag. Once again, the spirit of November 1918, the spectre of revolution, had returned to terrify the officers.

At that, Kapp capitulated. He resigned in favour of Lüttwitz, and early on Wednesday afternoon, after issuing a final absurd manifesto claiming that he had fulfilled all his aims, a taxi was seen to draw up at the Chancellery and a portly figure muffled in a scarf and felt hat, waddled down the steps and got in. The ex-Chancellor's belongings had been hurriedly slung into a knotted sheet which was secured to the roof of the cab. His weeping daughter followed her father into the car. The taxi drove off to Tempelhof airfield where a plane was waiting to fly Kapp to Sweden and exile. His rule had lasted just five days. Kapp later returned to face charges of treason, but died in jail, in 1922, while awaiting trial.

Lüttwitz, left in sole charge, toyed with the idea of further resistance, urged on by Ehrhardt who was all for arresting Loyalist Reichswehr officers and mowing down the insolent workers who dared to resist the rebels' authority. A bloodbath was prevented by Colonel Heye of the War Ministry who, supported by Seeckt, advised him that a majority of the Army now opposed the regime. Lüttwitz reluctantly joined Pabst, who had already taken refuge with Admiral Horthy's reactionary regency in Hungary. Lüttwitz eventually returned to Germany in 1925 and died in 1942. Pabst went on to organise Freikorps units in Austria, became an ardent Nazi and lived until 1970, unapologetic about his youthful behaviour until the end of his long life.

One of the other chief plotters, Ludendorff, and his chief aide, Bauer, left Berlin by train that evening for Munich. Ludendorff, once more assuming a false name, Herr Lange, told Bauer that they were richer for the 'bitter experience', having witnessed 'the complete unreliability of the officer corps . . . and the fickleness of the public.' Ludendorff concluded that more revolutionary and ruthless leadership was required. As we shall see he was to find what he sought in the smoke-filled beerhalls and hate-laden atmosphere of Munich, where reactionary forces had taken advantage of the past few days' confusion in Berlin to overthrow Hoffmann's SPD-led Government in Bavaria and install an ultra-Conservative regency under a Kapp-like monarchist civil servant named Gustav von Kahr. From now on, Munich was to become the magnet for all right-wing revolutionaries determined to bring down the Republic by fair means or foul. Here Ludendorff, Rossbach and Ehrhardt would gather and come under the influence of a little-known political agitator named Adolf Hitler.

In Berlin, the man whose Freikorps had provided the sword and arm of the Putsch, Hermann Ehrhardt, refused to 'go quietly'. As the price for vacating the Government quarter, Ehrhardt demanded the right to leave Berlin as he had entered: marching in military formation with arms shouldered and

Imperial flags flying. Once more, the squads of the Ehrhardt
Brigade tramped down the broad boulevard of the Unter den
Linden. Gloating crowds of civilians gathered to watch them go.
As the Brigade reached the Brandenburg Gate, the tension was
broken by the laughter of a small boy who dared to mock the
departing warriors. Two Freikorps men broke ranks, beat the
boy to the ground with rifle butts and kicked his prostrate body
until it lay still. Someone in the crowd began to hiss and a chorus
of booing went up. An Ehrhardt officer barked a curt command,
machine guns were levelled at the crowd and a brief volley was
fired directly into the people. Then the Ehrhardt Brigade resumed
their march, leaving the dead and dying behind them.

It was left to Seeckt, who had played a vital role in sapping
support for the putschists in the army, to clear up the mess they
had left. The more 'moderate' members of the Reichswehr,
epitomised by Seeckt and the ubiquitous reptilian Schliecher,
had held aloof from the Putsch for three main reasons: they
were more politically aware than the old Lüttwitz-Ludendorff-
Hindenburg generation of Army commanders and realised that
the Putsch stood no chance of consolidating itself inside
Germany against the united opposition of the progressive
middle class, the SPD and the Trade Unions, let alone securing
the vital external acceptance of the Allies. Secondly, they
distrusted the wild, savage fringe of the Freikorps, represented
by men like Ehrhardt. They preferred a disciplined, professional
army ruled by men like themselves and were only prepared to
admit former Freikorps to the ranks of the new Reichswehr if
they were old regulars like Maercker and Epp. Thirdly,
although they shared the putschists' aim of a return to a strong
authoritarian state, they believed the only chance of achieving
this goal lay in the far future. The best way to work towards
it, in their view, was to build up a modern professional army
within the constraints of the Versailles treaty, that could eventu-

ally become the kernel of later expansion when Germany had grown stronger. Internal political stability must be the first foundation for that longed-for expansion.

14

THE RED ARMY OF THE RUHR

'We even shot some Red Cross nurses. How those little ladies begged and pleaded! Nothing doing!'
Freikorps student volunteer in the Ruhr, Spring 1920

The Kapp Putsch had undermined that stability and led to a resurgence of the extreme left, not in Berlin or Munich, where the brutal repressions of 1919 had knocked the stuffing and heart out of the revolutionary left, but in the industrial heartland of the Ruhr. Suppression of this fullscale revolt now resulted in one of the most bloody and savage episodes of the whole German revolution.

The powerful trade unions based on the vast factories of the Ruhr had responded to news of the Putsch in exactly the same way as their brothers in Berlin: by Monday 15 March, the General Strike had taken full hold. Within hours, under strong Communist influence, this passive opposition to the Putsch was replaced by an upsurge of positive political demands for a disarming of both Freikorps and Army units, and their replacement by a militia of workers' and soldiers' councils. In the south of the Ruhr, even SPD councillors supported this revolutionary programme.

In the town of Hagen, crowds of workers disarmed the police, took over the city centre, and imposed censorship on the local right-wing press, which had come out in support of Kapp. The local Military Commander, General von Watter, based in Münster, reacted by ordering two Freikorps Brigades under a Captain Hasenclaver to move on Hagen and disarm the workers. When Hasenclaver's first battery started to detrain at Wetter-am-Ruhr, they were met by workers' leaders who demanded to know whether they supported the Putsch. Hasenclaver replied frankly that he stood on the side of General von Lüttwitz and a fierce battle commenced around the station. Red snipers opened up from behind bushes and rocks on the surrounding hillside, keeping the Freikorps pinned down. Hasenclaver and three of his officers were killed, along with sixty of their men. A hundred Freikorps soldiers surrendered to the workers, who had lost seven of their own men in the fight. Undeterred, von Watter ordered the Lichtschlag Freikorps to march on Hagen. But by this time the 'Red Ruhr' was in flames.

The workers holding Hagen set up a central military council for the whole region, demonstrating for the first time the sort of discipline that could match their enemies'. The council, under the leadership of Joseph Ernst, rushed trainloads of reinforcements to surround the large city of Dortmund, still held by the military. When Watter tried to reinforce Dortmund's garrison, the railways were sabotaged by the workers, and armed Reds attacked the relief columns at Berhofen and Aplerbeck. The Dortmund garrison, under heavy attack from within the city, decided to evacuate and retreated to their base at Remschied. By Thursday – the day after the Putsch collapsed in Berlin – workers were in undisputed control of the eastern part of the Ruhr.

The important town of Essen was held by units of the green-uniformed security police. But on Friday night, they were attacked by columns of armed workers. A particularly fierce struggle developed, appropriately enough, for control of Essen's slaughter-house, and the police were slowly beaten back towards the city centre, with heavy casualties on both sides. By noon on the following day, the Red flag was flying over Essen's town hall. But savage fighting continued throughout the day. The fighters of the Weissenstein Freikorps held out in a water tower, until forty of them fell, and their leader was shot dead with the white flag of surrender in his hand. Bitter battles continued for a long time around the railway station and the post office. When Essen eventually fell to the Reds, Watter ordered the evacuation of the other chief towns in the western Ruhr: Düsseldorf, Mülheim, Duisburg and Hamborn. The General admitted: 'The present battle in the industrial belt is different from previous struggles to put down disorder, in that on the other side we are faced with well-organised well-armed and well-led troops with a single tactical plan. We are dealing with a purely military operation, the battle of Government troops against the revolutionary Red Army.'

For the first time in western European history, the state's professional armies were in confrontation with a properly organised revolutionary army. Within five days, the Ruhr workers had managed to organise their own force of fifty thousand armed and determined men, fully equipped with modern weapons, including artillery. This scratch force had succeeded in defeating Government militias, police, Freikorps and the regular Reichswehr and were in undisputed command of Germany's main industrial region.

In imitation of the Freikorps, the Ruhr Red Army opened recruitment centres in the main towns where worker volunteers were armed with weapons captured from abandoned police and army depots. They were heartened by support from militant workers elsewhere in Germany, and the more politically ambitious thought of converting their local revolt into a full-blooded revolution. In the words of the Red *Ruhr Echo* newspaper of 20 March: 'The red flag must wave victoriously over the whole of Germany. Germany must become a republic of Soviets and, in union with Russia, the springboard for the coming victory of the World revolution and World Socialism.'

For some days at the end of March this vision looked on the point of fulfilment. In central Germany, the state of Thuringia was alive with revolt: workers and radical police units seized control of Gotha, were driven out by the Army, but returned with reinforcements and took over again after a battle costing fifty lives. In Jena, Weimar and Gera the picture was much the same. Neighbouring Saxony had a radical tradition. In its city of Chemnitz, where the Communists were strong, a centralised workers' council took power. In Dresden, the state capital, fifty workers died when Maercker's troops fired on groups of them storming the post office. In Leipzig, Kappist troops killed fifteen workers when they shot at a demonstration. This touched off a three-day battle until a ceasefire was negotiated.

In northern Germany, after his initial hesitation, Rudolf Berthold decided to support Kapp in Berlin by moving his Freikorps to the capital in a train via Hamburg. His progress was hampered by striking railwaymen, and when the train reached the small town of Harburg, it was completely halted. One of the men who had attached himself to Berthold was our acquaintance from the Baltic, the fire-eating Ernst von Salomon, whose memoirs give us a vivid picture of what followed. As usual, Salomon was not sure of the motives that made him march for Kapp: 'I tried to make the words of the Kapp programme seem real . . . [but] it was not the words of the programme which called us to fight. What was it, then? It was simply that we enjoyed the danger. To march into the unknown was enough for us; for it answered some primal need within us.'

Berthold's men found billets for the night in a Harburg school, but dawn revealed that the building was surrounded by dense crowds of men, women and children armed with machine guns procured from mutinous Reichswehr soldiers and evidently preparing for a siege. Berthold left the school to negotiate with the mob and someone fired a shot. This sparked off a pitched battle, with Salomon cheerfully turning a heavy machine gun on civilians and armed Red snipers alike. A furious hail of fire shook the school, covering the defenders with dust and turning the streams of blood from the dead and wounded, in Salomon's words, into 'a sticky paste'. The suffering of the wounded was heightened because the besiegers had cut off the school's water supply.

Running short of ammunition, Berthold had a school black-board hung out of a window with a chalked demand for a parley. The Reds shot it to smithereens. At nightfall, completely out of ammunition, Berthold was forced to surrender. He and some of his officers suffered a horrible death. The gallant air ace was strangled with the ribbon of his Pour le Mérite medal. His body was then decapitated, one arm torn from its socket, and the furious mob trampled the mangled remains into the gutter. Under the Third Reich, the school where the last stand had taken place was renamed the Berthold school and became an Alamo-like shrine, as did the Essen water tower. Salomon was more fortunate: although he had to run a gauntlet of blows and kicks from the crowd, he managed to escape and survived to play a major role in the final phase of the Freikorps story, before becoming its most articulate apologist and historian.

The end of the Kapp Putsch had placed the Social Democrats in a near-impossible situation. It was the reverse of the problem they had faced a year before: then, they had been forced to rely on the Freikorps – who despised them – to smash their enemies on the left. Now, threatened by the Freikorps in revolt, they had been obliged to summon up in support the demon of workers' power. There was only one way out of the impasse and it was not an honourable one. Once again, they would have to go cap in hand to the defeated Freikorps for help to stuff the genie of revolution safely back into its box. Before the month of March was out, Freikorps fighters, who only a few days before had been in open insurrection against the Ebert regime, were going into action to defeat the striking and rebellious workers who had come out in defence of the very same Government. If the consequences had not been so bloody, the situation would have been laughable.

But the urgency of the situation in the Ruhr did not allow the SPD leadership the luxury of leisured debate. Once more, the very survival of their regime was at stake. The local SPD leader in the Ruhr, Karl Severing, later the last SPD leader nationally before the advent of Hitler, entered into urgent negotiations with General von Watter with the aim of securing a peaceful standdown between the Freikorps and the Red army. On 24 March, the Bielefeld agreement was signed: a compromise which called on both sides to surrender their arms within ten days, and demanded the dissolution of selected Freikorps units and the cessation of Communist activities.

Both sides used the ten-day truce not to disarm, but to build up their forces. Watter, in particular, called on Freikorps support throughout the Reich to help in the coming suppression of the Ruhr. When the period of grace expired at the end of March it was extended to 2 April by the so-called Peace of Münster. On the following day, Severing signed an order formally permitting Watter to re-occupy the Ruhr. Ordering a 'surging attack' Watter launched a full-scale military offensive, moving into the Ruhr from three different directions.

The Wesel division, consisting of Löwenfeld's Marine Brigade, together with the Freikorps Düsseldorf, Freikorps Schulz and Freikorps Liabou moved into the area between Wesel and Münster, supported by the Rossbach Freikorps, the von Aulock Freikorps, the Faupel Freikorps and the Khune and Lutzow Freikorps.

The area east of Münster and Dortmund was assigned to the Münster division consisting of the Von Pfeffer Freikorps – which had supposedly been wound up in the Baltic – the Westphalian Rifles, the Severin Freikorps, the Hindenburg Freikorps, the Gabcke Freikorps and the Haas Division. The Münster division was supported by newly-raised middle-class student volunteer Corps from the Universities of Hanover, Göttingen and Münster, the last consisting of the so-called Academic Defence Corps, a body raised by a former U-Boat Captain who was currently studying to become a Protestant Pastor, Martin Niemoller. Niemoller, at that time a burning nationalist, was embarking on a turbulent career that was eventually to lead him into becoming one of the most courageous and determined opponents of Hitler, a concentration camp prisoner, and finally, after the war, a radical pacifist.

The front south of Remschied and Düsseldorf was held by the Epp Division, consisting of Epp's Bavarian Freikorps, the Leupold Regiment and another big Bavarian Freikorps, the Oberland, later to play a prominent role in Hitler's Beerhall putsch in Munich. They were supported by the von Oven Corps and assorted smaller 'Emergency Volunteer' groups.

On the first day of the offensive, von Aulock's Freikorps took Gelsenkirchen. On the same day, Löwenfeld's Brigade captured Bottrop. Two days later the Wessel division entered Mülheim and the following day, the whole of the Ruhr was under Freikorps control. The atrocities accompanying and following the campaign matched previous patterns of behaviour that had made the Freikorps so feared in Berlin, the Baltic and Bavaria the year before. Hundreds of Red Army captives were 'Shot while attempting to escape'. Scores of civilians who had played no part in the uprising, but were merely Trade Union officials or thought to have leftist affiliations, were rounded up and shot after appearing before illegal Freikorps courts-martial.

The spirit of the campaign is caught in a letter written home by Max Zeller, a student volunteer in the von Epp Freikorps, who told his family after the first day's fighting:

> If I were to tell you everything, you would say I was lying. No pardon is given. We shoot even the wounded. The enthusiasm is tremendous – unbelievable. Our battalion has had two deaths, the Reds two to three hundred. Anyone who falls into our hands first gets the rifle butt and then is finished off with a bullet. We even shot ten Red Cross nurses on sight because they were carrying pistols. We shot those little ladies with pleasure – how they cried and pleaded with us to save their lives. Nothing doing! Anyone with a gun is our enemy . . .

In the Hagen area, the original centre of the revolt, the Reds had laid down their arms before battle even commenced, but that did not save them. According to the local Red Commander, Joseph Ernst, at Hamm the Freikorps first lulled the populace into a false sense of security by staging a musical concert in the market place. The following day, the arrests and shooting began in earnest. At Haltern sixty-five workers peacefully engaged in building a canal bridge were mown down and finished off with grenades. In Pelkum, ninety victims of the Freikorps fury were buried in mass graves, including women and girls in nurses' uniforms.

The total casualties were never counted, but some indication of their scale can be estimated by the fact that Freikorps historian von Oertzen admitted that one thousand 'Reds' were shot in the first two days of the campaign. This, the last and most bloody full-scale military campaign waged by the Freikorps against fellow Germans, left an enduring legacy of hatred, and set the standard for later atrocities by state security forces against their own citizens that was to be followed and multiplied a hundredfold by Adolf Hitler.

The contrast between the savage reprisals meted out to the Reds who had originally risen in defence of the Republic against its right-wing enemies, and the Kapp putschists who had openly intended to overthrow the regime was stark: of the 775 army officers recorded as having participated in the putsch, 13 were lightly punished, 48 suspended and only 6 dismissed. The sum total of their jail terms was five years. Lüttwitz, the putsch leader, was able to retire quietly after his return to Germany on his pension of 18,000 Marks. Ehrhardt was briefly imprisoned in Leipzig, but was 'sprung' from jail in 1921 by his aristocrat wife, and was able to openly continue his subversive activities in Munich unmolested by the Government in Berlin. We shall subsequently discover more about what those activities entailed. The only civilian conspirator actually brought to book for his actions, Traugott von Jagow, was given a derisory two years in jail.

The political consequences for the SPD and particularly for Gustav Noske, were more severe. 'The Bloodhound' came under sustained attack from two sides: from the left and from within his own party for his gullible reliance on the loyalty of the officer corps to the Republic which had been so blatantly exposed during the Putsch; and from the army officers themselves because Noske's name had appeared beneath the 'subversive' General Strike proclamation. Former Chancellor Scheidemann, probably for reasons of personal and political pique, led the pack baying for Noske's blood in the Reichstag debate on the Putsch. Deserted by his allies in the Army, and by his party comrades who had never really forgiven him for his bloody roles in suppressing the Spartacist risings, Noske found himself completely isolated: he resigned on 22 March.

His chief military friends, General Reinhardt, the only leading Army chief to have recommended armed resistance to the Putsch, and his ADC, Major von Gilsa, went with him. Seeckt and Schliecher were left free to fashion the Reichswehr in their own image. The SPD lost control of the important Defence Ministry, with Noske being replaced by a member of the Democrats, Gessler, who lacked the personal authority of the Bloodhound.

Seeckt conducted a highly personal purge of the Army. Under

the guise of punishing the putschists, he forced out a few personal rivals, including General Maercker, but other Freikorps chiefs, like Epp and Löwenfeld, were left unmolested. The Ehrhardt and Löwenfeld Naval Brigades were absorbed into the regular Navy, strengthening its anti-republican and reactionary character, and pro-republican officers like Groener and Reinhardt were frozen out of the Army altogether. Seeckt now set about creating a new 'shadow army' known as the 'Black Reichswehr' which was to be largely composed of former Freikorps. In this way he intended to circumvent the limitations of Versailles and bring the leading Freikorps into the structure of the regular armed forces. Needless to add, those elements were to be implacably hostile to the Weimar Republic and its democratic institutions.

While Seeckt could use disciplined and professional former Freikorps fighters, he had no time for the wilder spirits within the movement. Despite what Seeckt called the 'unperishable services' the Freikorps had given to their Fatherland, the time had now come for them to leave the stage. 'A new building', Seeckt said, 'requires very solid foundations and must be constructed according to a definite plan. The Freikorps had neither the plan nor the construction . . . they were simply not suited for the work of peace.' By 'peace' Seeckt did not mean sweetness, light and universal love. He was sure that the time would come when Germany would have to take to the war-path again to seek revenge on her enemies and re-establish her rightful place in the world. But to do this successfully, a period of internal order and consolidation was essential. Roving bands of anarchic freebooters, with their lack of loyalty to the state, clearly did not fit into this plan. ' "Hands off the Army" is my cry to all parties,' Seeckt declared. 'The Army serves the state and only the state because the Army is the state.'

Seeckt made clear that while he personally disapproved of the

Republic, the penchant of the Freikorps for launching perpetual putsches only created disorder, chaos and bloodshed, and weakened both the state and the Army: 'It cannot be expected that everyone welcomed these changed times in his heart', he wrote, 'nevertheless everyone must be permeated with the fundamental realization that the path to a brighter future is open only when the soldier is loyal to his constitutional duty.'

The Freikorps movement is thus divided into two streams; those like the forces of Maercker and von Epp who – however reluctantly – entered the new Reichswehr, and those like Ehrhardt and Rossbach, who, officially dissolved in the summer of 1920 in the wake of the Kapp Putsch, continued their struggle in new forms: secret, paramilitary groups who conducted a war from the shadows against the republic with the methods of terror and murder.

15

THE POLITICS OF MURDER

'Do what you must – win or die – and leave the decision to God.'
    Inscription on tomb of Kern and Fischer, the killers of Rathenau

The last phase of Freikorps activity before the remnants of the
movement were finally absorbed in Nazism was as important as
the preceding months of open battle and civil war. True, it did not
involve the mass movements of armed men, the savage fights for
control of the great German cities and the brutal repressions that
followed. The civil peace that descended over Germany in the
summer of 1920 was the peace of the graveyard. An estimated
20,000 leftist victims were not around to challenge the Freikorps
power. The extreme Left, so comprehensively crushed after the
battles of Berlin, Bavaria and the Ruhr, lay low, licked their
wounds, and laboriously reconsidered their tactics. They rebuilt
their strength as a mass Communist Party, based on the trade
unions and the urban masses and competing for political power in
elections along with the despised Social Democratic and bourgeois
parties. The experience of 1919–20 had taught the radicals that
they could not hope to challenge the armed might of the state.

Deprived of their main enemy, the Freikorps turned with all the stored-up contempt and bitterness at their command on the 'November criminals' – the moderate Left and Centre Weimar politicians who had called them into existence, and were now ready to consign them to the scrapheap.

The alacrity with which Seeckt was building the Reichswehr as a new professional army showed the recalcitrant Freikorps chiefs that there was no longer a place for their wild freebooting ways in the new order. Many of them retired to the right-wing strongholds of East Prussia and Bavaria to plot their future.

As the Left was split between the Social Democrats who accepted and supported the institutions of the Weimar Republic, and Communist revolutionaries who continued to believe in a dictatorship of the proletariat, so the consequences of the Kapp Putsch led to a split on the Right between those who – albeit reluctantly – accepted the framework of Weimar as the only possible means of reviving Germany as a great power, and those who venomously hated the 'bastard Republic', born, as they saw it, from the unnatural union of defeat and revolution. The former – men like Seeckt, Schleicher, Groener and the leader of the conservative German People's Party, Gustav Stresemann – began to work towards their goals within the existing legal institutions. The latter – Ludendorff, Ehrhardt, Rossbach and their cohorts in Bavaria – continued to dream of a new authoritarian and anti-democratic state. Their bitter experience during the Putsch had not cured them of their penchant for swift and violent solutions to complex political problems. On the contrary, it propelled them further into politics and made them natural bedfellows of the new racist, protofascist ideas that were on the rise in Bavaria. All they lacked was a leader, a 'Trommler' (drummer) or Führer-figure who would bring their disparate forces together and concentrate their aimless energies with the focus of a burning-glass.

In the spring and summer of 1920, the German Government,

under pressure from the Allied disarmament Commissions, began to decree the wholesale dissolution of the Freikorps. Many of the larger and more orthodox Freikorps, as we have seen, were absorbed wholesale into the new Reichswehr. But even these were reluctant to abandon the last vestiges of the old Freikorps spirit. Maercker, for instance, insisted that his men, officially now designated Reichswehr Brigade 16, should bear their old prefix 'Freiwilligen Landesjägerkorps'. In later years, his brigade published their own newspaper which endeavoured to re-kindle the old Freikorps 'geist' and assailed the government for its rank ingratitude to the Freikorps men who had saved their bacon in 1919–20. Maercker also founded a para-military society, the Landesjägerbund, eventually absorbed in the nationalist private army, the Stahlhelm, to keep the spirit of his fighters alive.

Another important early Freikorps, that of Colonel Reinhard, joined the Reichswehr as the 15th Brigade. But their commander retired to his estate in West Prussia and promptly set about recruiting another secret Freikorps, which was so well organised by the spring of 1921 that Reinhard was able to send four companies of trained fighters to quash a Polish attempt to take Upper Silesia.

Bavaria was the most turbulent centre for this illegal Freikorps activity. Colonel Epp's Freikorps joined the Army as the 21st Defence Regiment, but Epp's Chief-of-Staff, the soon-to-be notorious Captain Ernst Röhm, continued to channel Reichswehr funds and recruits to a wide variety of anti-republican para-military outfits. Röhm's memoirs, published in the year of his murder, 1934, were brazenly entitled 'Memoirs of an Arch-Traitor' – referring to his activity as a nominal Reichswehr officer who continued to work heart and soul for the overthrow of the institutions he ostensibly served. When democratic politicians woke up to Röhm's illegal but barely secret activity and demanded his dismissal, his military masters 'punished' him by merely transferring him to another Reichswehr unit where he was able to continue his seditious activities unmolested.

It is very difficult at this distant juncture to follow the fates of all the many nationalist and para-military organisations that sprang up across the Reich in the aftermath of the Kapp Putsch. Their bewildering variety, their secretive and shifting nature, their frequent changes of name, all make precise delineation difficult. But we will endeavour to trace the broad outlines of the most significant groups, in terms both of size and of their later influence on, and development into, the broad swathe of Hitler's Nazi party.

We can divide the rightist and racist groupings broadly into the open, legal, or semi-legal, such as the Organisation Escherich (Orgesch), the Organisation Kanzler (Orka), the Stahlhelm (Steel Helmet), and the Jungdeutscher Orden (Jungdo); and the secret, illegal, underground or outright terrorist, like the Thule Society, the Deutscher Trutz und Schutz Bund (The German Offensive and Defensive League), and the Ehrhardt and Rossbach Freikorps with their myriad offshoots and successor organisations. An added complication is that some of the illegal groups which were banned by the Berlin government were tolerated and even openly encouraged by the Bavarian authorities – particularly by the Police. The open organisations tended to be marginally more moderate in their aims and methods than the terrorist groups. Of the former, the most widespread and numerous was the Organisation Escherich.

Major Dr Forstrat Escherich was an able and ambitious para-military organiser who had succeeded in uniting all the main Bavarian Civil Guards (Einwohnerwehr) under his leadership. The Civil Guards had been set up in 1919 under Noske's sponsorship across the Reich as an adjunct to the Regular and Freikorps forces. Recruited among the local populations of cities conquered by the Freikorps, they had ostensibly been democratic and pro-republican in complexion, but in Bavaria had acquired the prevailing black reactionary hue.

Escherich's reputation spread amongst the nationalists of the north, and in January 1920, Franz Seldte, leader of the ex-servicemen's organisation, the Stahlhelm, wrote to him suggesting that they join forces. The Kapp Putsch interrupted the process and Escherich played a prominent part in the Bavarian equivalent of the Putsch – the bloodless overthrow of the SPD-led Hoffmann Government in Munich.

The unification project was revived after the Putsch and in May 1920, representatives of eighteen different nationalist organisations met in Magdeburg, headquarters of the Stahlhelm, with the aim of forming a single right-wing front under Escherich's leadership. The new group was officially named the Deutscher Hort (German Shield), though it was popularly known as the 'Orgesch'. The organisation set out a political programme calling for the rebuilding of the nation and support of the constitution against putsch attempts from left and right. As military chief-of-staff, the 'Orgesch' chose a former army officer and Prussian junker, Hermann Kriebel, who was later to play a prominent part in Hitler's Beerhall Putsch.

Although ostensibly pledged to a moderate republican programme the 'Orgesch' undertook secret military training and manoeuvres, with Reichswehr officers supervising the drill. Allied disarmament commission officers who called for its disbandment were smoothly reassured that the 'Orgesch' was akin to a volunteer fire brigade! Many of the spurious ranks adopted by the organisation – Gauleiter, and Gruppenführer – were later used by the Nazi party and military units. The 'Orgesch' received their ample armaments directly from the Reichswehr. In Bavaria Epp gave every 'Orgesch' member a rifle and fifty rounds of ammunition; local depots were equipped with machine guns and area organisations had their own artillery batteries. Allied pressure during the autumn of 1920, led to the official dissolution of the organisation and the surrender of 179,000 rifles – itself an indication of its size and importance. But this still left an estimated 220,000 weapons in the hands of the membership. The 'Orgesch' was banned by the SPD-influenced Prussian Government in late 1920, and though it continued to exist in Bavaria until the following year, many of its members moved on to other groupings. In the words of the 'Orgesch's' final statement: 'The form is shattered, but not the movement.'

Another para-military organisation was set up by former Freikorps Führer, Major Stephani, whose Potsdam Freikorps had been dissolved after its participation in the Kapp Putsch. Stephani speedily formed the VNS, or Association of National Soldiers, an anti-republican corps which achieved a membership of 150,000. It was formally banned in 1922 but continued to function under another name.

After the swift suppression of the 'Orgesch', the proponents of authoritarian militarism became even more determined to work against the Republic in para-military formations. Many 'Orgesch' members found their way into two similar organisations – the Stahlhelm, and the Jungdeutscher Orden (Young German Order).

The Stahlhelm had been founded two days after the 1918 armistice by Franz Seldte, a former officer who had lost an arm on the Somme. Originally dedicated to protecting the interests of returning frontline soldiers, the Stahlhelm soon took on a nationalist, authoritarian character, dedicated, as Seldte put it, to 'stopping the "Schweinerei" of revolution.' Swelled by members of the 'Orgesch', the Stahlhelm rose from thirty local groups at the time of the Kapp Putsch to five hundred by June 1922. It gained the allegiance of radical rightist elements, and its newspaper boasted the biting pen of Ernst Jünger himself. It eventually became the private army of the powerful German Nationalist party (DNVP) and by the thirties it rivalled in size the Nazi SA, the SPD Reichsbanner and the Communist Red Front. After the advent of the Third Reich it was forcibly amalgamated with its SA rivals.

The Young German Order (Jungdo) was founded by another ex-officer, Artur Mahraun, at the time of the Kapp Putsch. It appealed to the younger elements on the right, promising a revival of the pre-war Wandervogel spirit. Its growth was spectacular – from its base in Kassel, it mushroomed to a membership of 70,000 early in 1921. It was banned, but continued to function, eventually reaching a membership of around 300,000. Like other paramilitary groupings, it was absorbed by the Nazis after Hitler's seizure of power.

But if these mass and overt nationalist organisations presented a long-term threat to the Republic, a far more insidious danger was posed by the secret underground groups formed by ex-Freikorps members who adopted an extreme policy of violent opposition to Weimar. By far the most effective and notorious of these was the mysterious 'Organisation C' or O.C.

Organisation C grew out of the Ehrhardt Brigade which had been dissolved by decree after the Kapp Putsch. Ehrhardt's officers and men were no more prepared to accept their dissolution after Kapp than they had been before; indeed they expressed their intentions in a ribald couplet which they composed as they left Berlin following the catastrophic collapse of the putsch they had launched:

> What do we care, when a Putsch goes wrong?
> – We'll make another one before too long!

Following their disbanding at the end of May 1920, Ehrhardt and his men immediately founded a successor organisation as a cover for their continuing political activities, called the 'Bund Ehemaliger Ehrhardt Offiziere' (League of Former Ehrhardt

Officers). Its goals, in the words of one of its members, were: 'Patriotic . . . carrying on the spirit of love for the Fatherland and militarism, and leading the battle against the Versailles treaty, the un-German Weimar constitution and Marxism. It fostered the racist (Volkisch) idea.' From the League grew a secret grouping 'O.C.', consisting of the most fanatical and devoted Ehrhardt men, which adopted the politics of terror: assassination and murder of its enemies.

The 'C' in the group's title stood for 'Consul', the cover name adopted by the 'Captain' himself, who was the undisputed Führer of the band. Its general policy was directed by one of Ehrhardt's subordinates, Lieutenant Manfred von Killinger, former Chief of the Ehrhardt Brigade's élite 'Storm Batallion'. The O.C. divided Germany into thirteen areas, or 'Gaus', a division later copied by the Nazis, who also took over Ehrhardt's Swastika emblem and many of his murderous methods. The number of O.C. activists was small, as befitted an élitist secretive force and it was probably roughly the same strength as the old Ehrhardt Brigade – 5,000.

As wanted men in the wake of the Kapp Putsch, Ehrhardt and his followers fled Berlin for the more hospitable climate of Bavaria, where they hid out on the estates of sympathetic landowners, disguising themselves as agricultural labourers. It took about a year for the 'Captain' to pick up the threads of political conspiracy, but by the spring of 1921, O.C. was in being and training men in military camps. The organisation enjoyed the protection and patronage of Munich's towering, coffin-faced Police President, Ernst Pöhner. Pöhner's terrifying personality is illustrated by the story, told with brutal amusement in Ernst Röhm's memoirs, of a democratic politician who went to see him to complain that 'Political murder gangs existed in Bavaria'. 'I know', Pöhner grimly replied, 'but not enough of them!' Pöhner and his Police force stonewalled all attempts by the Berlin Government to halt Ehrhardt's activities and arrest him. As far as he was concerned, O.C. was a group of patriots, and its murder campaign was merely the dispensation of rough justice to the 'November criminals' who richly deserved their fate.

The rationale behind O.C.'s political murders was twofold: they hoped that by killing off the leading lights in the Weimar state they would create such outrage on the Left, as to provoke an attempted revolution which would in turn be put down by a resurgent right. The way could then be cleared for the installation of an outright military/fascist dictatorial state. This 'strategy of tension' has been emulated in our own day by fascist terrorists in Italy, whose campaign of bombings and murders in the sixties and the seventies was deliberately designed to provoke Italy's powerful Communists into anti-democratic revolution.

The other motive advanced by the O.C. was that their killings were righteous justice meted out to traitors. They revived the ancient word 'Feme' (variously spelt Vehm or Fehm) to describe their actions. 'Femegerichts' had existed in mediaeval Germany and were a sort of court or tribunal handing out instant and brutal sentences at a time when no proper judicial system existed. O.C.'s slogan was 'Traitors fall to the Feme!' and the only sentence that the unwitting victims of the Feme could expect was death.

The O.C.'s rules showed the increasing influence of racist ideas on the radical right. Their 'spiritual' (Gestig) aims were said to be: 'The cultivation and dissemination of nationalist thinking; warfare against all anti-nationalists and internationalists; warfare against Jewry, Social Democracy and Left-radicalism; fomenting of internal unrest in order to attain the overthrow of the un-German Weimar constitution.' Its practical or material goals were: 'The organisation of determined, national-minded men, forming local shock troops for breaking up anti-national meetings; maintenance of arms and preservation of military ability; training of youth in the use of weapons.' O.C.'s notice to potential recruits made forbidding reading: 'Only those men who have determination, who obey unconditionally and who are without scruples will be accepted.' Those who were not put off by this swore an oath to enter the secret organisation, pledging blind obedience to the 'Supreme Leader' (Ehrhardt).

What sort of men were attracted to this dangerous and illegal activity? In the proud confessions of a member, Friedrich Wilhelm Heinz, who gloried in O.C.'s campaigns:

> Wherever we conspirators set foot, in every city and village, were found a few trusted men – unconditionally able fanatics. Soldiers of the Great War in whom the fire of battle still burned, freebooters who had fought with Maercker in Saxony, or under Awaloff-Bermondt in the Baltic . . . these were the men who formed the nucleus.

The O.C. began and ended its fourteen-month murder campaign with its two most prominent victims: – Matthias Erzberger and Walther Rathenau. Erzberger was the first to fall to the Feme on 26 August 1921. Between that date and June 1922, when Rathenau was assassinated, according to a conservative estimate by the Reichs Minister of Justice, the Feme accounted for more than 350 'enemies'. The victims were usually prominent political figures, civil servants who obeyed the Weimar government, informers who betrayed Feme members or hidden arms dumps to the authorities, or former Feme comrades who had fallen out with their friends.

Matthias Erzberger was of all the Weimar politicians, the figure most hated by the right wing. This was in some ways surprising because he wasn't even a Social Democrat. A practising Catholic, he was the leading figure of the Centre Party that had gone into coalition with the SPD. The roots of the detestation in which he was held by the nationalists lay in the Great War, when he had suddenly swung from an extreme pro-war position to advocacy of a negotiated peace.

He even had the courage, as early as 1917, to proclaim this belief in the Reichstag. This made him the obvious man to lead the

German Armistice delegation to Compiègne. After this 'treachery' he had compounded his 'sin' by publicly proclaiming the need for Germany to fulfil the treaty, and as Minister of Finance from June 1919, he had set about raising the cash to pay the ruinous reparations levied on Germany. He instituted a tough tax system, taxed war profits and luxuries, thus incurring the mortal enmity of business and the rich, and alienated the army by freezing army promotions. All this roused the right to almost maniacal fury.

Nationalist deputies in the Reichstag accused Erzberger of being in the pay of the Allies. But the pudgy Swabian was a formidable political opponent. Count Harry Kessler observed him in action in the Reichstag:

> I had a full view of his badly-made, flat-soled boots, his comic trousers rising via corkscrew crinkles to his full-moon backside, his broad and thick-set peasant shoulders, of the whole fat, sweaty, unattractive utterly plebian creature. I could see every clumsy move of his clumsy body, every change of colour in his chubby cheeks, every drop of sweat on his greasy forehead. But gradually this clownish, uncouth figure grew into a personality enunciating the most frightful of indictments. The badly framed incoherent sentences piled fact on fact, formed themselves into ranks and battalions of accusation and fell like flails on the members of the right, sitting white, cowering, and ever more isolated in their corner.
>
> [A few days later, Kessler was travelling by train and overheard the conversation of his companions:]
>
> An elderly prosperous-looking man said that he would like to slaughter Erzberger. Someone ought to place a couple of hand-grenades in his car. He spoke quite loudly, with the compartment packed to overflowing. Nobody expressed the slightest objection. [Kessler concluded prophetically] Bitterness against Erzberger is enormous. Muller said that if someone did not get rid of him, he would club him to death himself. No German jury would condemn him for such action. I am very much afraid that Erzberger will share Liebknecht's fate.

The leader of the campaign against Erzberger was Karl Helfferich, former wartime Finance Minister under the Kaiser, and now a leading light in the Nationalist Party. Erzberger had publicly accused him of 'fiscal frivolity', and Helfferich responded with a ferocious assault in the pages of the nationalist newspaper *Kreuzzeitung*. Each article carried the headline 'Erzberger Must Go!' Helfferich charged Erzberger with 'intentional deceit'. 'Not twice or three times but ten and twenty times . . . he dishonestly mixed political activities with personal financial interests.' He challenged the beleagured Minister to sue him, taunting,

> He does not answer all these accusations with legal action, but shirks, like a threatened cuttlefish, and darkens the water in order to escape. This is Herr Erzberger, whose name appears at the bottom of the miserable Armistice agreement, this is Herr Erzberger who, if not finally stopped, will lead the German nation to total destruction.

After that, Erzberger had no choice but to sue. The resulting court hearing was a field day for his right-wing enemies. They packed the galleries of Berlin's first district court, cheering Helfferich and hooting and jeering at Erzberger. After the first week of the trial, a twenty-year-old former Naval cadet, Oltwig von Hirschfeld, followed Erzberger from the courtroom, leaped on the running board of his car, and shot him twice at point-blank range. One bullet entered the Minister's shoulder, the other was deflected by his pocket watch. Hirschfeld, who admitted that his action had been incited by Helfferich's inflammatory articles, got eighteen months' jail for the murderous attack, and the libel trial continued.

After two months of hearings, during which Erzberger's tax returns were stolen and gleefully published by the right, the court handed down its findings. The judgement was delivered on 12 March 1920, coincidentally the day before the Kapp Putsch. Helfferich was found technically guilty of libel and fined a derisory three hundred Marks (£50). But a subsidiary judgement found that Helfferich had proved many of his accusations against Erzberger – specifically, three charges of financial impropriety, six of perjury, and seven of mixing politics and business. The judge praised Erzberger's 'undoubted ability and exemplary industry', but damned him for 'a regrettable lack of judgement.' After this public condemnation, Erzberger was compelled to resign.

Although his Ministerial career was at an end, Erzberger remained in politics and his Swabian constituency loyally returned him in the June 1921 elections. He was not allowed to enjoy the mandate for long. In August 1921, he took his wife Paula on holiday in the Black Forest, where good, fat Germans go for the cure. On August 26, a day of misty drizzle, Erzberger left his wife behind at their hotel in Bad Griesbach while he strolled to the summit of the Kniebis, a nearby hill. His companion on the walk was a fellow Centre Party MP named Diez. Both men were unarmed, but carried umbrellas as protection against thunderstorms.

Deep in political conversation, the two men hardly noticed a pair of hikers who passed them on the track with a muttered greeting. At the top of the hill, Erzberger and Diez paused to catch their breath and take in what they could see of the view through the mist. The two young hikers emerged again from the murk and put down their rucksacks. One of them called out: 'Are you Erzberger?' Surprised, Erzberger answered 'Yes!' The two young men drew pistols from their rucksacks and fired. Pathetically, the politicians tried to defend themselves with their umbrellas. Diez belaboured one of the killers while Erzberger unfurled his umbrella as though the bullets were raindrops. Five shots struck him in the lung, the thigh and the stomach. Emptying their chambers, the gunmen calmly paused to reload. The dying Erzberger took cover behind a fir tree, but his killers were implacable, pumping three more bullets into his head. Erzberger's lifeless corpse rolled ten metres down an embankment and lay still. The gunmen climbed up the slope, picked up their rucksacks and vanished. Diez, bleeding from a chest wound, stumbled back down the hill to raise the alarm. Erzberger's body lay on the forest floor all night. An autopsy found a total of twelve bullets lodged in him. The autopsy also revealed that his heart and liver were greatly enlarged and so he would not have lived for long.

The gunmen were two young members of Organisation Consul named Heinrich Tillessen and Heinrich Schultz. Their short careers had encompassed membership of the Ehrhardt Brigade, the Oberland Freikorps in Bavaria and the Deutscher Schutz-und-Trutz Bund. After the assassination, the murderers returned to Munich where the O.C. was masquerading behind the innocuous name of the 'Bavarian Wood Products Company'. Pöhner's Police issued them with false passports and the pair fled to Hungary where they lay low until the hue and cry had died down. They later returned to Germany to continue their terrorism. Tillessen, the main culprit, became one of the O.C.'s chief organisers and was briefly jailed for his part in plotting subsequent murders. A right-wing politician named Heinrich Bruning pulled strings to secure his freedom. Ironically, Bruning was a leading member of Erzberger's own Centre Party and the last democratic Weimar Chancellor before Hitler, but he said he found Tillessen 'a decent sort of chap'. Tillessen was eventually brought to trial for his crime a quarter of a century later, in November 1946, after the Second World War. He was acquitted, largely because, in the German court's finding, 'The assassination had been motivated by his exalted patriotic desire to lead Germany to a better future'.

Other politicians fell victim to O.C.'s gunmen, including Hugo Haase, leader of the USPD Independent Socialists, shot down on the steps of the Reichstag; and the Bavarian USPD leader Karl Gareis. On 4 June 1922, Tillessen organised an attempt on the life of former Chancellor Philipp Scheidemann, the man who had proclaimed the German Republic from the Reichstag windows on 9 November 1918. Scheidemann had resigned the Chancellorship in protest at Versailles, and retired to be Burgomeister of his native city, Kassel. But a quiet life in this backwater, like Erzberger's retirement to the Swabian Schwarzwald, did not save Scheidemann from attack.

While taking a Sunday afternoon stroll in a Kassel park, the SPD statesman was approached by a would-be O.C. assassin named Hustert, who pulled a rubber bulb from his pocket and squirted prussic acid at Scheidemann's eyes. Unlike Erzberger, Scheidemann always carried a pistol for personal protection and he instantly drew the gun and fired at his attacker, causing Hustert to flee.

A few days after this botched attempt, however, the Organisation claimed its most prominent victim with the assassination of the Republic's distinguished Foreign Minister, Walther Rathenau. The shooting down of Walther Rathenau had such momentous consequences that it led to a vast wave of revulsion against the killers of the right, and temporarily put a halt to their campaign of murder. It led also to the temporary eclipse of the extreme nationalists and cleared the way for the rise to power of Adolf Hitler and his Nazis.

Rathenau was a figure reviled by the right for much the same reasons as Erzberger: he too had believed in and worked for the fulfilment of Versailles, he too had switched from extreme pro-nationalist views during and after the war to support for the Republic. (Indeed, he is thought to have given some £250,000 from his vast fortune to finance the early Freikorps.) But in Rathenau's case, the Right had other and more sinister motives for hating him and encompassing his destruction. In the words of historian Edward Hyams: 'Rathenau died as a human sacrifice to the tutelary spirit of the Teuton Volk. The offering ensured the rise to power of Adolf Hitler, the political Messiah awaited by the Volk'. Rathenau's person embodied the two evils most execrated by the proponents of Volkisch nationalism: the international capitalist, and the Jew.

Rathenau was born to wealth, and increased his fortune when he became director of the great German AEG engineering and electrical enterprise. By 1910 Rathenau was Germany's pre-eminent industrialist and financier. But he was by no means the clichéd hard-nosed businessman. A sensitive soul and lover of music and literature, he had wide cultural interests and was obsessively preoccupied by the effect of industrial life on modern man. He wrote a series of books, some of them best sellers, about the problem of reconciling the boring and alienating nature of the production process with mankind's higher artistic and spiritual aspirations. His ideas were far in advance of their time. He proposed, for example, an outline European Common Market, and a co-operative pooling of the world's natural resources. He also prophesied the coming of the welfare state and, himself a man of vast wealth, advocated punitive taxation of the very rich. Rathenau's internationalism, and the seeming hypocrisy of his advanced egalitarian ideas, made him a figure of suspicion to the Right. Distrust hardened into hatred when, in 1919, he foretold the victory of Bolshevism because of its 'moral superiority' to the West.

When the Great War came, Rathenau, almost alone among Germans, saw that the conflict would be a new kind of war, one that would not be won by military means alone but would require the harnessing of the whole nation's resources, human and material. Although a Jew, Rathenau yielded to none in his German nationalism, and he warned his friend the Kaiser that the country's economy was vulnerable to strangulation by the Allied blockade. As a result he was given the task of setting up a War Raw Materials Department, for husbanding, controlling and rationing.

This selfless act of patriotism, of course, further exacerbated the racist Right, who saw in Rathenau not a saviour of the nation, but a rich Jew cornering the country's must precious commodities. Rathenau's careful economic programme was probably responsible for maintaining Germany's fighting capacity for far longer than it would otherwise have lasted. Some historians have alleged that this, and this alone, prolonged the war for as much as two years. When Ludendorff sought an armistice in October 1918,

Rathenau published an open appeal for continuation of resistance under a new democratic government. This upset Ludendorff, his former friend, and he accused Rathenau in 1920 of secretly plotting Germany's downfall.

Rathenau's technocratic talents could not be ignored by the Weimar Republic's leaders and in 1920 the new Chancellor Joseph Wirth, a politician of the Catholic Centre party, invited him to become Foreign Minister. Rathenau encapsulated the task ahead of him in a single sentence: 'We must discover some means of linking ourselves up with the world again'. Both he and everyone else knew that the Foreign Ministry was a hot seat at a time of frenzied nationalist agitation against Versailles. His much-loved mother asked him why he had accepted the job: 'I had to, Mamma,' he replied, 'because they really couldn't find anyone else.'

In a bold leap of the imagination, Rathenau broke Germany's post-war isolation by negotiating and signing the treaty of Rapallo with the Soviet Union. Backed by Seeckt, who saw the tremendous possibilities of technical military co-operation with the Soviet state, the treaty united the two pariahs of Europe in a mutually beneficial way and showed the West that Germany, for all her debts and defeats, was still a great power with an independent will that could not be ignored.

To the Right, though, Rapallo represented complicity with Bolshevism, Germany's deadly foe. The treaty only stoked their smouldering hatred of Rathenau to boiling point. Inflamed by propaganda that Rathenau was one of the Elders of Zion – the mythical cabal of Jews plotting to take over the world with the twin tools of Communism and Capitalism – the extreme elements decided he must die.

Karl Helfferich led the pack in pillorying Rathenau as a Jew, a neo-Bolshevik, a shameless traitor and slave of the Allies. Open calls were made for the Minister's murder. Gangs of young right-wing thugs roamed the street, chanting their hymns of hate:

> Knallt ab den Walther Rathenau,
> Der Gott-verfluchte Judensau!
>
> (Beat down Walther Rathenau,
> The God-accursed Jewish sow!)

These incitements to murder fell on the willing ears of the O.C. gunmen. One of them was that garrulous and ubiquitous witness to the doings of the extreme right, Ernst von Salomon, whose memoirs give a vivid picture of the ripening conspiracy. Its guiding light was a handsome, twenty-five-year-old ex-Naval Officer named Erwin Kern:

> He always had at least three new plans simmering in his mind and one in his pocket ready to be carried out; he was always on the move and brought fresh air with him; he glowed with an inner fire. This broadly-built man of middle height, with his open face and dark eyes, radiated strength. Unsparing in his demands on himself as well as others, he was always prepared to defend passionately any idea that seemed to him to have value, until he proved it worthless when he lost no time in throwing it overboard. Nothing gave him greater zest than the premonition he had of his early death.

The ideas of these young terrorists were fluid and unformed:

> The country lay open before us like a tilled field ready to take any seed; and we were not prepared to allow any other seed to be sown than the ideas which came to us in our dreams . . . the country was in that condition when anything was possible. It was in a state of cold stagnating flux which needed only the addition of something to make it freeze. If we could not supply that something, all our doing was in vain.

In their search for something to lock their restless beliefs, the young nihilists even considered the leadership potential of their coming victim:

> We looked round to see where we might find a man to speak the word for us. Where might we find a man, apart from the silent Seeckt, with character enough to make a historical figure? Perhaps the shrewd Ebert, or Scheidemann? Wirth, who was honest to the backbone. Or – Rathenau?

The conspirators attended a public meeting addressed by the Foreign Minister to spy out their man and decide whether he was to be their leader – or their prey. Their initial impression was favourable:

> Kern and I managed to squeeze into the meeting and lean up against a pillar, ten feet from the speaker's podium. Among the frock-coated crowd who sat round the table, the Minister stood out by the nobility of his bearing. He stepped to the lectern, with his thin, aristocratic face with its noble brow; the buzz of talk in the hall died at once.

As the Minister made his speech, Salomon decided that he was 'Half God and half Devil', but concluded that 'his heart lay with the coward.'

> When I realized this, my gaze left him and turned to Kern. He was standing almost motionless with his arms folded. Then an extraordinary thing happened. I saw Kern, not three steps away from Rathenau, drawing him under the spell of his eyes. The hall vanished, so that nothing remained in it but one small circle, and in that circle two men. The Minister turned round doubtfully, looked towards our pillar, first vaguely then in surprise. He halted in his speech and tried to regain the lost thread. He found it, but from now on he spoke to Kern alone. Almost imploringly he addresses the man standing by that pillar and grew weary as he did not change his position. As we elbowed our way towards the exit, Kern passed close to the Minister. Rathenau, surrounded by a chattering mob, looked at him questioningly. But Kern pushed past him – unseeing.

The Minister had met his murderer. Kern hesitated between grudging admiration for Rathenau and the need to strike him down:

> Rathenau is our hope – for he is dangerous. ... He indeed is the finest and ripest fruit of his age. I couldn't bear it if again something great were to arise out of the chaotic, insane age in which we live. Let him pursue what fools call a policy of fulfilment [of Versailles] . . . We fight for other things. We are not fighting to make the nation happy – but to force it to tread in the path of its destiny. I will not tolerate that this man should once more raise it up to purposefulness and give to it a national consciousness. For these things belong to an age that was destroyed in the war, that is dead, as dead as mutton. 'In that case,' [concluded Salomon] 'we know who is our enemy.'

The strange love-hate relationship that these nihilists had with their potential target was summed up by Kern:

> On November 9 1918, I blew out my brains. I am dead. Since that day I have lost my ego. I died for the nation. Were it otherwise, I couldn't bear it. I follow my star. I die daily. While my actions are the sole motive force within me, everything I do is the expression of this force. This force is destructive – hence I destroy. I know that I shall perish in the moment when this force no longer has any use for me. Nothing else is open to me than to act as the whole force of my will orders me to act. Nothing is left to me except to reconcile myself to the noble suffering imposed on me by Fate.

Rarely has the philosophy of nihilism received more eloquent expression. But the time for talking was past. It was now time to act.

Kern travelled to Berlin and took over command of a conspiracy that had been hatched against Rathenau by a seventeen-year-old schoolboy, Hans Stubenrauch, son of a General and a member of a rightist secret society, the Bund der Afrechten (League of the Upright). Stubenrauch confided his plans to a friend, Willi Günther, who put him in touch with Kern. Kern approved the idea, but decided that Stubenrauch was too young for the deed; he decided to take over the reins himself and sent for his friend, Hermann Fischer, and the twenty-year-old Salomon.

This trio met on a bench in Berlin's Zoo park. Kern reviewed their terrorist acts to date: 'We are attacking what is material. We have destroyed limbs, but not the head and not the heart. I intend to shoot the man who is greater than all who surround him – Rathenau.' Kern and Fischer attended a Reichstag debate to hear their victim speak. On their way home, they stopped before a photographer's shop on the Unter den Linden and stared at a portrait of Rathenau. After a long silence Fischer remarked: 'He looks a decent sort'.

Kern's original plan was to shoot Rathenau with a heavy British Lewis machine gun from a car. O.C.'s Berlin agent, twenty-year-old Ernst Werner Techow, was sent to Saxony to procure the vehicle and weapons. The Lewis gun proved unsatisfactory when the conspirators test-fired it in Berlin's Grunewald woods, close to Rathenau's home. Kern decided to switch to lighter machine-pistols. The date for the assassination was fixed for Saturday 24 June. The date may have been picked to coincide with the summer solstice, with Rathenau as the chosen sacrificial victim to the sun-gods of ancient Teutonic religion. Certainly, on the evening of that day, young Germans gathered on hilltops throughout the country to celebrate the turning of the year and the destruction of one who, for them, symbolised the powers of darkness.

The plotters lay in wait for Rathenau who was late in leaving his home as he had not got to bed until midnight the day before. There was a slight hitch when the oilfeed in their car broke, but Techow, who was driving, pronounced it fit for a short run. When Rathenau's large, red open-air touring car at last appeared, at 10.45 a.m., with the Minister sitting alone on the back seat, Techow, Kern and Fischer drove in pursuit.

On the Königsallee, Rathenau's chauffeur slowed down to negotiate a double bend and some tram tracks. The conspirators seized their chance. Their six-seater, field-grey car half overtook the Foreign Minister. Absorbed, Rathenau glanced over and came face to face with Kern, in brand new leather coat and helmet, pointing a pistol in his face. Cradling the gun butt in his armpit, Kern fired at close range. A building worker named Krischbin saw what happened next:

> I saw him (Kern) straight in the face. It was a healthy, open sort of face, the sort we call an officer's face. I took cover because the shots might easily have hit us too. They rang out in quick succession like a machine-gun. When he had finished shooting, the other man (Fischer) stood up and threw his weapon – a hand grenade – into the other car which they had driven right up to, alongside. The gentleman (Rathenau) had already sunk down into his seat and lay on his side. At this point the chauffeur stopped his car, just by the Erdenerstrasse and

shouted for help. The big car sprang forward with the engine full out
and tore away down the Wallottstrasse. The other car had come to rest
by the pavement. At the same moment there was a bang as the grenade
exploded. The impact raised the gentleman on the back seat some way
off his seat and even the car gave a slight jerk forward.

A passing nurse, Helene Kaiser, climbed into the back of the car
and attempted to aid the dying Minister. But Rathenau was past
human help. Kern's bullets had smashed his jaw and shattered his
spine and he was fast losing consciousness. The chauffeur drove
the car back to Rathenau's villa and servants gently carried the
dying Minister into his study. By the time a doctor arrived he was
dead.

The oilfeed in the assassins' car finally gave out a few minutes
after the murder so they abandoned the vehicle in a side street and
walked back into the city centre, ditching their weapons and
throwing away their distinctive leather coats as they went. News
of the killing was already spreading through the city, and the
murderers mingled with the menacing crowds of workers who
were streaming out of offices and factories in a spontaneous
demonstration of anger and grief at the deed. At the
Alexanderplatz they listened to street orators addressing the
crowds and calling down curses on the killers' heads. Then they
drifted back to the west of the city, where they took a steamer at
the Wannsee lake and headed north.

The Reichstag convened at three that afternoon. When
Helfferich dared to show his face, the Centre and Left of the
assembly rose as one, shouting 'Murderer!' and the former
Finance Minister slunk from the Chamber. The Chancellor,
Wirth, speaking from beside the slain Minister's usual seat, which
was covered in black crepe and wreathed with white roses, made
a measured and effective condemnation of the killing and
announced draconian measures for the protection of the Republic.

The following day, 700,000 people again filled the streets as the

Reichstag held a memorial service for the murdered Minister. Count Kessler was there: 'Bitterness against the assassins is profound and genuine. So is firm adherence to the Republic.' Pointing dramatically at the nationalist benches, Wirth exclaimed: 'There stands the enemy that is dripping his poison into the wounds of our people. The enemy stands on the right!' The murder seemed to have hit a public nerve and thousands of people felt that the bullets which killed Rathenau had been aimed at all those who served and supported the Republic. As a Berlin newspaper put it in an open letter to the killers: 'Your accursed deed has not only struck the man Rathenau; it has struck Germany as a whole . . . you have slain one man but wounded sixty million.' In death, Rathenau, the rich cosmopolitan who could not have spoken to a worker without embarrassment, became a symbol for all who stood for peace, democracy and justice.

Afterwards, Kessler went to Rathenau's house to view the body of the murdered Minister lying in an open coffin. 'His head was leant slightly back to the right. A very peaceful expression in the deeply lined face over whose shattered lower portion a fine linen cloth was laid. From the dead, wounded face emanated immeasurable tragedy.'

Hunted throughout Germany, the killers roamed aimlessly across the land. Techow fled to the estate of his uncle, a landowner outside Berlin, who turned him over to the authorities; Kern and Fischer, with a price of a million Marks on their heads, arrived by ferry at Warnemünde where a ship was supposed to spirit them across the Baltic to Sweden. But they missed the boat, and turned back to the interior. Travelling by bicycle, they rode through the forests of Mecklenburg, vainly seeking shelter. But the hue and cry had alarmed even their extremist friends, who, while not betraying them, refused to help them. At one point, as a ferryman rowed them across the river Elbe, pursuing police arrived just too late at the bank. Kern and Fischer lived the lives of hunted animals, sleeping rough in the open air and begging food from the houses of peasants. They were reduced to picking berries or digging roots out of fields as the net closed around them. In eastern Hanover they were almost caught when a large posse of police surrounded a wood where they were hiding and then beat their way through it, but somehow they escaped from the trap.

At last the exhausted fugitives found refuge in the twin towers of Saaleck castle near Halle, where they had previously hidden a fellow rightist who had been 'sprung' from jail. Ernst von Salomon had procured fake passports for his friends and hunted high and low to find them. At one point his train passed the castle where they were hiding up – but he did not know they were there.

Villagers near Saaleck, alerted by lights in the deserted castle, called the police and at last the killers were run to ground. Cautiously a pair of policemen ascended the spiral staircase of the eastern tower. Kern emerged at the stairhead and threatened them with a pistol. A siege developed, with a curious crowd gathered outside the castle walls to watch the end of the drama.

On 17 July, a storm arose around the castle, as nature provided a suitable backdrop to the final act of tragedy. Kern and Fischer appeared on the battlements of one of the towers, shouting defiance into the wind: 'We live and die for ideals', they cried out and, prophetically, 'Others will follow us.' Their words were drowned by the rising gale, so they scribbled messages on scraps of paper, wrapped them round stones and flung them down, but they too were whipped away by the wind. Police marksmen, firing from the opposite tower, took pot shots at the pair and a bullet struck Kern in the right temple, killing him instantly.

Fischer gathered up his friend's body and laid it on a bed, bandaging the wound with torn strips of linen. Then, after carefully placing a sheet of brown paper underneath Kern's feet so that his boots would not sully the sheets, he sat on the opposite bed, lifted a revolver to his own temple, and fired.

Exactly eleven years later, after the advent of the Third Reich, a service was held at Saaleck to dedicate a memorial to the 'Martyrs'. The ceremony was attended by Salomon, Ehrhardt and surviving members of the conspiracy, as well as by Ernst Röhm and Heinrich Himmler with the massed cohorts of the SA and SS. Himmler laid a giant wreath on the two men's graves, while Röhm pronounced the funeral oration, telling the dead men's shades that their spirit was that of Hitler's fanatical soldiers. A year after that, Röhm himself was dead, shot down along with many other former Freikorps comrades in the bloody purge known as the Night of the Long Knives. Ehrhardt, warned in time, had fled into the woods on his estate and escape Himmler's SS killers. Such was the Führer's thanks to the men of the Freikorps, on whose backs he had ridden to power, but who found himself unable to tolerate their wild indiscipline, and their failure to recognise him as the sole indisputable embodied spirit of the German national revolution.

The other conspirators suffered a less frightful fate than the actual killers, German justice taking its usual lenient course with rightwing terrorists. Thirteen of the plotters were put on trial. Techow alleged that Rathenau had died because he was one of the three hundred Elders of Zion pledged to deliver Germany over to Bolshevism. He was jailed for fifteen years, but only served four. Resuming his studies, he became a lawyer. Serving on the eastern front in the Second World War he was captured by the Russians and died in a Soviet prison camp.

Salomon served five years in prison for his participation in the plot and other right-wing terrorism. In jail he made friends with a Communist militant and discovered that he had more in common with this revolutionary than with the despised democrats of the Republic or the new Nazis to whom the mantle of the old

Freikorps had passed. Under the Third Reich, Salomon edited histories of the Freikorps, wrote his own remarkable memoirs, and ended up as a film scriptwriter. Unrepentant of his youthful extremism to the last, he died in 1973 in his native Hamburg.

The Rathenau murder represented the high water mark of rightwing terror. The fury it unleashed among the Republic's hitherto largely passive supporters temporarily forced the killers to suspend their murderous activity. But an examination of legal statistics shows that their crimes went largely unpunished. Of almost 400 political murders committed in Germany in the 4 years, 1919–1922, 354 were the work of rightist killers, 22 of left-wing groups. Of the 22 leftist murders, 17 brought heavy sentences, including 10 executions. Of the 354 right-wing murders, 326 went entirely unpunished. The average jail sentence for murder was 15 years for left-wingers, a mere 4 months for rightists. Truly, German justice was blind in the right eye only.

The storm of outrage roused by Rathenau's death soon abated as people's concerns moved on to the economy – worried by rocketing inflation coupled with mounting unemployment. Ehrhardt ordered his gunmen to lie low and himself took refuge on the estate of the Duke of Coburg, a friend of his wife, Princess Margarethe von Hohenlohe-Oehringen. He later hid in a Bavarian monastery, where many of his organisation's weapons were secretly stored in the cellars, and finally resorted to the ultimate indignity of working as a glassblower in the south Tyrol.

Early in July 1922 the thugs of the O.C. carried out their final attack. An ex-Army officer and an accomplice, armed with iron bars, ambushed the well-known republican journalist Maximilien Harden, in the street near his Berlin home. Harden, respected editor of the liberal journal *Zukunft* (Future), was beaten to the sixty-two-year-old man was hit on the head eight times before passers-by stopped the assault. Though critically injured, he managed to survive the attack. Visiting Harden a few days later,

Count Kessler was told by his friend: 'I fought against the Kaiser, but under his regime they didn't kill you for it.'

The extremists of the Right needed new tactics. As one of them said at the time: 'Nothing lasting can be achieved by a handful of conspirators using dagger, poison and pistol. What is needed is a hundred thousand, and again a hundred thousand, fanatical fighters for our view of life. The work must be done, not in secret but in overwhelming mass demonstrations and the conquest of the streets'. The speaker was a street agitator little known outside his Munich 'manor'. His name was Adolf Hitler.

16

ENTER HITLER:
THE BEERHALL PUTSCH

'I am just a drummer.'

Adolf Hitler

On 9 November 1918, the day the Kaiser abdicated, Adolf Hitler was in a hospital, far from the front, in the remote Pomeranian town of Pasewalk. He had been temporarily blinded by poison mustard gas. Hitler had had a 'good war'; indeed the rootless, friendless vagrant from Austria had found in army life the comradeship his early years had so significantly lacked. It had been the most fulfilling phase of his miserable and hitherto futile existence. In many ways Hitler was an untypical soldier. Not only had his military career been marked by outstanding acts of gallantry which had brought him the Iron Cross (Second Class) but this Austrian's devotion to his adopted German Fatherland was second-to-none. Not for him the grumbles and gripes about the war: he had no home to go to for longed-for leave; no sweetheart wrote him loving letters and no family waited for his return. Alone in the world, Hitler placed all his dog-like devotion and ferocious patriotism at the service of Germany.

When the pastor of the Pasewalk hospital called his patients together on the afternoon of 10 November, Hitler was half-aware of what he would say, but even so the news came as a terrible traumatising shock. The pastor, his voice breaking with emotion, told his audience of wounded troops that the Kaiser had gone, and the Fatherland was now a Republic which was suing the triumphant Allies for peace.

> I could stand no more [wrote Hitler later.] Everything went black before my eyes. I groped and tottered my way back to the ward and threw myself on the bed, burying my burning head in the pillow. I hadn't cried since I stood before my mother's grave, but now I could not help it. So it had all been in vain. All the sacrifices and privations . . . did all this happen only so a band of miserable criminals could lay their hands on the Fatherland?

As he absorbed the shock in the days that followed, a new determination and conviction grew in Hitler . . . 'Hate . . . hate for those responsible for this deed . . . hate for the "Lumpen" in the pay of enemy propaganda who stole the weapons from our hands, broke our moral backbone and traded away the crippled Reich for thirty pieces of silver.' There was a reason for the Biblical reference: Hitler's vagabond years in Linz, Vienna and Munich had turned him into a virulent anti-semite, one who blamed the Jews not only for stealing fair Aryan maidens from under his dirty nose, but for all the corruption and decadence at the heart of modern city life: 'Probe the pustulent wound and the maggot Jew emerges, blinking in the sunlight.'

Now, in these 'Terrible days and worse nights' Hitler's earlier ambitions to be an artist or architect were forgotten: 'I resolved to enter politics.' The unknown wounded soldier whom even his army comrades had regarded as a half-cracked joke for his raving diatribes against Marxists and Jews, decided to enter the lists, single handed, against his own 'World of enemies.'

Fortunately for Hitler, the Army could use a dedicated, loyal soldier in the dark days at the end of 1918. He remained on the strength of his unit, the List (Second Bavarian Infantry) Regiment, and when he had fully recovered his sight, was ordered back to Munich where, based at the Regiment's Türken-Strasse barracks, he performed guard duty at a Russian POW camp at Traunstein outside the city. He was well-placed to witness the turbulent political developments in Munich early in 1919, and he came to the notice of his superior officers as a talented extempore speaker, useful for controlling radicals in the regiment or for whipping up nationalist sentiment in the ranks.

What Hitler saw of the successive left-wing regimes of Eisner, Toller and Leviné in Munich, confirmed his passionate prejudice against Jews and Bolsheviks. For their part, his officers rewarded his staunch adherence to the ideas of the radical right. Impressed by the information he gave them after the suppression of the Munich Soviet on the 'Reds' in his regiment – which led many of them to the firing squad – they appointed Hitler as a 'V-Man' ('Vertrauensmann' – or 'Trustie'), in a new army department being set up, the 'Abteilung I b/p'. This was an intelligence outfit charged with weeding out left-wingers in the Reichswehr and also keeping a sharp eye on Munich's myriad mushrooming political groupings. At the same time the Abteilung's propaganda arm would provide a pool of speakers to ensure that the spirit of Germany's new soldiers would remain firmly nationalist, untainted by the political radicalism that had sown the dragon's teeth of November 1918.

As part of his preparatory work for the Abteilung, V-Man Hitler was required to attend a course at Munich University run by the army, at which right-wing professors indoctrinated the potential political agents. One of these, Professor Karl Alexander, had just concluded his history lecture when he noticed a little group who remained behind in the hall. They were gathered round a man who was 'Haranguing them with mounting passion in a strangely gutteral voice.' Alexander noticed that the men seemed 'spellbound' by the speaker. 'I had the peculiar feeling that their excitement derived from him and at the same time, they were inspiring him.'

At his next lecture, Alexander drew the attention of the Abteilung's Commander, Captain Karl Mayr, to the unknown orator. Mayr curtly summoned the awkward soldier for an interview and soon afterwards Hitler was given his first mission 'in the field'. In August 1919 he was sent to give a series of talks at Camp Lechfeld, a transit camp for prisoners of war returning from Russia, many of them still under the influence of Bolshevism. The speeches he delivered convinced Mayr that his thirty-year-old recruit was a 'born demagogue' with a knack for compelling his listeners' attention and converting them, in a near-miraculous way, to his viewpoint.

The following month, September 1919, Hitler was sent to observe a meeting of a tiny political group calling itself the German Workers' Party. The party, despite its 'proletarian' name, was one of the innumerable nationalist right-wing groups that were flourishing in post-Soviet Munich. It was an offshoot of the racist Thule Society, whose leaders had seen the necessity of weaning the working classes away from Marxism and converting them to Volkish nationalism. Their chosen tool was a Munich railway worker named Anton Drexler, noted since the war for his fanatical nationalism. Thus far, the party had miserably failed in its mission to win the workers for nationalism, and when Hitler attended the meeting in the Sternecker beerhall, it consisted of little more than its seven-man steering committee.

The main speaker that night was a Thule Society member named Gottfried Feder, whom Hitler had already heard at his University course. Having listened to Feder's arguments before, Hitler's attention wandered, and he was about to leave the meeting when a Professor named Baumann took the floor and began to advocate the separation of Bavaria from the rest of the

Reich, a popular argument at the time. At once, Hitler's pan-German nationalism was fired, and he interrupted the professor with a spontaneous stream of rhetoric, withering Baumann's intellectual sophistry under a torrent of fiery words. Baumann left the hall under the lash of Hitler's tongue, 'Like a whipped cur'.

Drexler, like Mayr, recognised the power of Hitler's gutter oratory. He hurried after the shabby V-Man and pressed the party's political pamphlet into his hand. That night, as the future Führer lay awake in his spartan barracks room, watching the mice play across the floor, he read through Drexler's manifesto, and saw the potential power of the idea of uniting the basic beliefs of non-Marxist socialism with raucous racist nationalism: National Socialism.

A week later, Hitler was surprised to receive an unsolicited postcard notifying him that he had been enrolled as a member of the German Worker's Party. Half amused, and half curious, he decided to go along to the next meeting of the group at a restaurant called the Altes Rosenbad. Unimpressed by the bureaucratic course of the meeting, which included a treasurer's report that the party's bank balance constituted the princely sum of seven marks and fifty pfennigs, Hitler concluded that the party had no future; it was 'Political club life of the lowest sort; aside from a few broad paragraphs, the party had no full programme, no membership cards, no office, not even a miserable rubber stamp . . .' Nevertheless, after a couple of days, Hitler changed his mind. He saw the possibility of taking over the infant party and moulding it to his own desires. It offered an instrument, and small and amateur as it was, a potential path to power.

He was soon appointed the party's propaganda and publicity man. Using the regimental typewriter at his barracks, Hitler laboriously pounded out invitations to its meetings and dropped them personally in the letter boxes of influential potential supporters. His energetic activity on behalf of his new party began to pay off: membership climbed to twenty-three. Hitler's next idea was to mimeograph his invitations and scatter them in the streets. Membership climbed to thirty-four and the party's next meeting attracted an audience of over one hundred: its best figure yet. Hitler's next move was to take a paid advertisement in the *Volkischer Beobachter,* a racialist newspaper later to become the Nazi party's own organ. His fellow committee members were alarmed, but once again, the bold tactic paid off and Hitler spoke to another packed hall.

Hitler next turned his attention to the party's organisation. Its 'office' consisted of a cigar box containing its meagre funds and a few envelopes. He found a windowless room at the Sterneckerbrau, the beerhall where he had first encountered the party, and rented it for fifty marks a month. To help stump up the cash, he began to charge a fifty-pfennig fee for admission to meetings, an unheard-of innovation. Once more, his timid fellow-members became alarmed, but Hitler's reputation as a rabble-rousing speaker was spreading and the numbers attending meetings continued to climb. By the end of the year membership had reached nearly two hundred, and Hitler had succeeded in deposing his main party rival, the Thule Society journalist Karl Harrer. The newcomer was beginning to pack the party with soldiers from his own regiment, including his wartime Sergeant, Max Amann, whom he appointed business manager, the party's first paid full-time employee.

By February 1920, Hitler thought the party ready for the first plunge into mass politics. He rented Munich's biggest beerhall, the huge Hofbrauhaus, for a meeting and advertised it with flaring, blood-red posters. The colour was chosen by Hitler himself, partly because red is 'The most exciting colour' and partly because he knew it would irritate and provoke his Communist and Socialist opponents who regarded red as 'their' colour. The centrepiece of the meeting was to be Hitler's presentation of a new manifesto, a twenty-five-point programme thrashed out by Drexler and himself, and skilfully combining a heady mixture of racism – hatred of Jews; nationalism – repudiation of Versailles; conservatism – rejection of the Republic; and anti-capitalism – calls to tax big business in favour of the 'little men' and the workers.

Hitler's tactics succeeded beyond his wildest dreams. On the evening of the meeting, 24 February, the Hofbrauhaus was packed with more than two thousand people. After abusing the Jews and the Versailles treaty to much applause, Hitler proceeded to read out his twenty-five points. Despite organised opposition and cat-calling from Left-wingers who had gatecrashed the meeting, Hitler, aided by his own coterie of troops and strong-arm thugs, stayed on top and by the end of the evening had won over even the doubters. He said later: 'When I closed the meeting I was not alone in thinking that a wolf had been born that was destined to break into the herd of deceivers and misleaders of the people.'

Around this time, Hitler made the acquaintance of two figures who were to be of vital importance to him in building up the fortunes of the young party, which had now changed its name officially to the National Socialist German Worker's Party: the NSDAP, or Nazis. The first of these new friends was a certain Captain Ernst Röhm, who had replaced Mayr as commander of the Army Abteilung to which Hitler was still officially attached. Röhm was a formidable figure; short, with a bulky stockyness already running to fat. His face bore the hallmarks of the war in which he had served as a front-line officer on the Western Front. His countenance had been scarred brick-red by an explosion at Verdun, his nose had been reduced to a tiny point by a bullet, and his cheek was slashed across with a bayonet scar. Under this unprepossessing exterior lay a shrewd mind and unmatched skills as a political organiser. Röhm saw himself as a military man pure and simple: 'Since I am a wicked and immature man, war and unrest appeal to me more than the orderly life of your respectable citizen,' he boasted. Röhm was also cut off from 'normal' life by his rampant homosexuality.

Röhm had the post-war task of organising the 'black Reichswehr' in Bavaria. His job was to channel army funds and support to para-military and right-wing groups which could be of use to the army as reserves in times of trouble. As former adjutant to von Epp, the leading Reichswehr and Freikorps man in Bavaria, Röhm was the key link between rightist para-military and Freikorps formations and the regular Army. He decided which groups were to receive the lavish financial support and large caches of arms and ammunition that were busily being stored up in secret hiding places away from the prying eyes of leftists and the roving Allied disarmament commissions. After meeting Hitler at a gathering of a para-military group called the Iron Fist, Röhm decided at once that 'this was the man for Germany' and set about supporting him, both with money and by channelling new recruits into the party from the Army. These war veterans formed the nucleus of the Nazi private army, keeping order at meetings and dealing with hostile hecklers by the rough and ready methods of fist, boot and bludgeon.

Another influential supporter who was of enormous help to Hitler in his early days was the Bavarian poet and dramatist Dietrich Eckart. Like Kurt Eisner, Eckart was a Munich café intellectual, but his politics were of the extreme right and his paper *Auf Gut Deutsch* ('In Good German') was a rabidly racist, Jew-baiting sheet. The middle-aged Eckart, however, already dying of disease and cocaine addiction, was a respected and talented writer and moved easily in Bavarian high society. The Bohemian in Hitler was drawn to this colourful character and Eckart, as well as pouring much of his considerable wealth into the new movement, was invaluable in coaching the gauche Hitler in etiquette, polishing his rough-hewn army manners and introducing him into the moneyed world of Munich's social élite.

During the Kapp Putsch, in March 1920, the new extreme right-wing Government which had seized power in Munich under cover of the prevailing chaos, sent Eckart and Hitler to Berlin on a liasion mission to make contact with Kapp. They travelled in a light plane – it was the Führer's first flight – piloted by a Great War ace, Ritter von Greim, later to be the last head of the Nazi Luftwaffe. The plane made an emergency landing in Red-held territory and the Nazis barely escaped shooting, but they eventually arrived in the capital to find Kapp already fled and the Putsch collapsing. They were horrified to discover the Chancellery occupied only by Kapp's shady PR man, the Hungarian-born Jew Trebitsch-Lincoln. Taking Hitler's arm, Eckart beat a retreat, whispering 'Come on, Adolf, this is no place for us.'

The oddly assorted pair stayed on in Berlin where Eckart introduced Hitler to the strongest nationalist organisation in the north, the Stahlhelm, and to his friend Frau Helene Bechstein, wife of the famous piano manufacturer, who was the first of many wealthy women to fall under the Hitler spell and contribute much-needed financial support to his movement.

Returning to Munich, Hitler took the decisive step of finally resigning from the Army to devote himself heart and soul to the party, and his own mission. He spent the rest of the year, 1920, in organising and building up his party. He provided it with its own sinister and distinctive emblem – the crooked black cross of the Swastika, already used by Ehrhardt's brigade and by other Freikorps and racist groups. The Swastika symbol, on a white circle against a red background, became the official party flag and Eckart provided the party with a slogan: 'Deutschland Erwache!' ('Germany Awake!')

In December, Hitler acquired the *Volkischer Beobachter* newspaper with the help of loans raised by Eckart and von Epp, and soon transformed it into a rabble-rousing propaganda organ.

To edit the paper, Hitler chose a fanatically anti-semitic Baltic German, Alfred Rosenburg, later promoted to be chief 'party philosopher'.

Other leading Nazis who joined the movement at this time included the Strasser brothers, Gregor and Otto, who had run their own Freikorps from their native town of Landshut, and were strongly drawn to the 'Socialist' elements in Nazism. They were both to be disillusioned by Hitler's later collaboration with big business and were drummed out of the party. Gregor paid for his opposition with his life during the Night of the Long Knives. Otto led an anti-Nazi resistance group, the Black Front, from exile in Czechoslovakia.

1921 was the year in which Hitler consolidated his dictatorial hold on the party and transformed it into the leading force on the extreme right of Bavarian politics. Protected by Police President Pöhner, and his deputy, Wilhelm Frick (later the Nazi Interior Minister in Hitler's first Cabinet), the movement went from strength to strength. In January, the NSDAP held its first 'National Congress' in Munich, and twelve days later Hitler spoke at its biggest meeting yet, at the city's largest arena, the Zirkus Krone. More than six thousand people packed the hall to hear Hitler rant for over an hour on the theme 'Germany – Future or Ruin'. The huge audience heard him in silence, but at the end of his oration applause broke over his head in waves like thunder. The rally led to Hitler's first meeting with Gustav von Kahr, the reactionary Bavarian Premier, who wished to use the Nazi movement as a lever to increase his own influence in Berlin and pave the road to a restoration of the Wittelsbach dynasty. Kahr was the first of many conservatives to discover, too late, that none was more adept than Hitler at turning the tables and using the user for his own purposes. Eventually, this discovery was to cost Kahr – and so many others – their lives.

Bolstered by the growing recognition, Hitler felt strong enough in July to stage his own coup for total control of the party. Using a pretext, he resigned from the movement, only to be invited back by his chastened colleagues on his own terms as party chairman and sole arbiter of party policy. Many members of the party's old guard balked at this ruthless arrogation of power and another party congress was called to debate the issue. But Hitler was at his persuasive best, arguing that the party should not merge with other right-wing groups to increase its strength, but that rival parties should be annexed to the NSDAP. He carried the day almost unanimously.

The following month, Hitler was instrumental in setting up a new arm of the party: this was the innocent sounding 'Gymnastic and Sports Division'. Two months later it was re-christened the 'Storm Detachment' (Sturm Abteilung – or SA). The new force was placed under the command of Captain Röhm who intended to use it not only as the party's muscle, a gathering of bruisers and bouncers, but as a full-blown private army with ranks and hierarchy apeing the Army, and with uniforms to match. To officer the new Corps Röhm brought into the party many of his old Army and Freikorps cronies, such as Edmund Heines and Peter von Heydebreck (both destined to perish in the Night of Long Knives) and Manfred von Killinger. Killinger was former Head of Ehrhardt's Storm Company, military chief of the O.C., and destined to be Nazi Gauleiter of Saxony, Consul-General in San Francisco and finally German Ambassador to Rumania, where he committed suicide as the Red Army approached in 1945. Another ex-Freikorps hero who joined was Pfeffer von Salomon, brother of Ernst, former Baltic Freikorps Führer, and later to become Chief-of-Staff to the SA.

While Hitler was building his party in Munich, elsewhere in Germany the remnants of the scattered Freikorps were fighting their final formal campaign. It came in the far-flung south-eastern province of Upper Silesia, which had been part of Prussia since it was annexed by Frederick the Great in the Seven Years' War of the eighteenth century, but had recently been eyed hungrily by Polish nationalists. A plebiscite in March 1921, prescribed under the Versailles treaty, had confirmed the wishes of the majority of the population to stay German, but the Poles had not accepted the result, and an army of Polish nationalist irregulars, tacitly supported by the Polish Government and by French troops on the spot, swept over the border into Silesia. The Berlin Government protested vigorously but, as in the Baltic, it was the men of the Freikorps who took effective action to check the invader.

In the first week of May 1921, a spontaneous gathering of the Freikorps took place in Silesia. Nearly all the hallowed names of the movement were there: Maercker's Landesjägerkorps, the Stahlhelm, the Jungdeutsche Orden, men who had taken part in the Kapp Putsch the month before, and former Baltic fighters who had been lying low, disguising themselves as farm workers and the like on the great estates of eastern Germany, such as the Rossbach Freikorps and Peter von Heydebreck's 'Wehrwolves'. From Bavaria came the Oberland Freikorps to join the fray, and from the north the men of the Reinhard and von Aulock Freikorps. The official commander of the campaign, General Hoefer, ordered a cautious policy, holding defensive positions and waiting for further orders from Berlin, but he was overruled by his deputy, General von Hulsen, who ordered the Freikorps to take the offensive. They needed no prompting.

At dawn on 23 May, the Freikorps stormed the Annaburg hill which, crowned by the convent of St Anna, commanded the east bank of the river Oder. By noon the hill was in their hands and that night the freebooters sat around their camp fires singing their old marching songs. They felt on top of the world once more, but the following day brought a sad awakening. They learned with stunned disbelief that the Ebert Government, bowing to Allied pressure, had once more forbidden the Freikorps, dissolving existing formations and outlawing the foundation of future units. Once again the volunteers tasted defeat in the moment of victory. Once again, it seemed to them, a German Government had stabbed them in the back. The lessons of the Baltic and of Kapp were rubbed like salt into their unhealed wounds all over again.

With savage, smouldering rage, the freebooters went through the familiar process of greasing and burying their weapons and of going underground all over again, taking up their 'cover' as miners, foresters, or agricultural labourers. But some of them went further: Rossbach, Heydebreck, Heines and the Oberland Freikorps, led by Dr Friedrich Weber, moved to Munich where they attached themselves to the one movement that seemed to represent the last, best, chance of overthrowing Weimar and its shameful subservience to Versailles: the Nazi party.

The influx of former Freikorps fighters into the new party led Hitler to adopt an increasingly aggressive and provocative policy. Prompted by the growing strength of the SA strong-arm squads, and influenced by the rising tide of popular resentment against the Versailles reparations, which were biting ever deeper into the already pinched German economy, he sanctioned a series of moves designed, as ever, as much for their propaganda and publicity value as anything else.

Party members assaulted Jews in the street, displayed their Swastika flag where only Republican banners were officially allowed, and openly attacked the meetings of their opponents. Matters came to a sort of head on 14 September1921, when a gang of SA troopers, led by Hitler in person, broke up a meeting of the separatist Bavarian League and beat up its leader. Munich's strong Social Democratic party resolved to respond by breaking up one of Hitler's own meetings in the Hofbrauhaus, but, warned in advance, the Führer briefed the SA to meet violence with violence. When the first heckler interrupted Hitler, he gave the signal and a furious battle, conducted with chair legs and heavy beer mugs, erupted. The brawl continued for half an hour, but, despite being outnumbered, the tough ex-soldiers of the SA eventually prevailed and drove their 'Red' enemies from the hall. Hitler was winning the only war that counted in his book: the primitive struggle for physical control of the streets.

A year later, following the killing of Rathenau, Hitler led the field in a campaign against a new 'Law for the Protection of the Republic', designed to curb right-wing extremism and terror. Resentful after having just served a five-week jail term for incitement to riot, Hitler laid into the new law at a mass meeting in the Bürgerbraukeller beerhall, denouncing it as a 'Law for the Protection of Jewry' designed to stifle all dissent. A few days later, a mass open air meeting on Munich's Königplatz attracted 50,000. Hitler was the star speaker, escorted by an SA honour guard, 600 strong, marching in columns with flags flying and bands playing. It was an impressive public demonstration of Hitler's importance, and he used the occasion to call on the young men in his audience to join the stormtroopers and sacrifice themselves for their ideals.

A man who watched Hitler speak, Kurt Ludecke, later a Nazi who subsequently turned against Hitler, described the effect on the audience:

> Threatening and beseeching with pleading hands and flaming, steel-blue eyes, he had the look of a fanatic. His words were like a scourge. When he spoke of Germany's disgrace I felt ready to spring on an enemy. His appeal to German manhood was like a call to arms, the gospel he preached a sacred truth. He seemed another Luther. I forgot everything but the man. Glancing around, I saw that his magnetism was holding these thousands as one.

Hitler was still modestly describing himself as the 'drummer' – merely the rallying point for the German national revival – but to many others, he himself was looking more and more like the Messiah for whom they had been waiting.

The party's next show of strength came on 14 October, 1922, when Hitler was invited to attend a rally of nationalist groups and volkish societies at Coburg, a small town some 160 miles north of Munich. The meeting was sponsored by the Duke and Duchess of Coburg, patrons and protectors of Hitler's right-wing rival, Captain Hermann Ehrhardt. The Führer chartered a special train to carry his six hundred SA men and his own inner clique to Coburg. With him in his compartment were the brains and brawn of his inner circle: Eckart, Max Amann, an ex-Communist named Hermann Esser, who was the party's new propaganda chief and an orator second only to Hitler; Rosenburg; the freshly recruited Ludecke, and Hitler's personal bodyguards, a huge ex-wrestler named Ulrich Graf and a former bar-room bouncer called Christian Weber. Warned of the Nazis' approach, the workers of Coburg lined the streets from the station to jeer and yell. Insults turned into a hail of cobble stones and then, at a signal from Hitler's rhino-hide whip, the SA squads broke ranks and laid about their tormentors. Another battle with the Socialists and Communists on the following day confirmed that, even when outnumbered, the SA was the most potent fighting machine that Germany's turbulent post-war politics had thrown up.

Later that autumn, the party gained its most prestigious recruit so far: the famous former air ace, Hermann Goering. The last commander of the famed 'Flying Circus' squadron of the Red Baron, Manfred von Richthofen, Goering was just the sort of illustrious name to give the party the glamour and social cachet it so far lacked. With his matchless war record, his contacts with the wealthy aristocracy and his fervent nationalism, Hitler welcomed the young Goering with open arms.

Around this time, Hitler lent the party's backing to an attempted putsch organised by Dr Otto Pittinger, an obscure Kapp-like Bavarian civil servant who headed one of the province's innumerable rightist 'Fatherland Societies' and hoped that a right-wing dictatorship in Munich would trigger a similar movement in Berlin. The plot fizzled out before it even got off the ground. Hitler was enraged by the lack of backbone shown by his fellow right-wingers. 'No more Pittingers, no more Fatherland Societies!' he told Ludecke. 'One single party! These gentlemen, these counts and generals – they won't do anything. If nobody else dares to I shall bring it off alone.' True to his word, Hitler began to plan his own putsch.

His instrument was to be the 'Kampfbund' or 'Fighting League', a coalition of Bavarian Freikorps and para-military groups that had been welded together by Ernst Röhm under the nominal leadership of a former Army Officer, Colonel Hermann Kriebel. The main components of the Kampfbund were the SA itself, now a disciplined force of some 30,000 men; the Oberland Bund headed by Veterinary Surgeon Dr Friedrich Weber, who fielded some 4,000 men; and a smaller force of combat veterans organised by Röhm himself, the Reichskriegsflagge. The leaders of this front began to meet in secret to plan the putsch. As their figurehead and fatherly adviser, they secured the services of General Erich Ludendorff himself, who had been living quietly on the outskirts of Munich since the collapse of the Kapp Putsch three years before. He too had fallen under Hitler's spell.

The SA was growing by leaps and bounds under the energetic leadership of Goering, who had been appointed SA Chief-of-Staff by Hitler soon after he had joined the party. His combination of heroic charisma, military experience and a sort of jovial ruthlessness were perfect for moulding the gangs of street-fighting toughs into a well-oiled military machine.

News coming in from south of the Alps at the end of October 1922 immensely encouraged and fuelled Hitler's putschist plans. In Italy, on 28 October, Benito Mussolini had led his Fascist Squadristi on their much-heralded March on Rome to successfully seize power from a crumbling parliamentary regime. Like Hitler, the Italian Duce was an ex-corporal. Like the Nazis, the Fascist 'squadristi' were organised groups of former servicemen using methods of naked violence to silence and intimidate their enemies. The parallels were so pointed that within days of Mussolini's march propagandist Hermann Esser told a Munich audience: 'What a band of courageous men could do in Italy, we can do in Bavaria also. We too have a Mussolini. His name is Adolf Hitler.'

By the end of 1922, the Nazis were indisputably the strongest force on the extreme right in Bavaria, with Hitler the most powerful political personality in the province. Their gravest weakness lay in the fact that their influence ceased on the Bavarian borders. Outside, in the rest of Germany, Hitler was still virtually unknown or, at best, dismissed as one more street-corner agitator by those who had never heard him speak and felt his magnetic power. Then, at the beginning of 1923, fate presented him with a golden opportunity to relight the boilers of the extreme right and provide a propaganda platform of patriotic righteousness.

The retirement of France's wartime leader, Clemenceau, had left the reins of power in Paris in the hands of President Poincaré, an unreconstructed patriot and a man whose hatred of Germany was so deep that he was to ask to be buried upright – facing towards the enemy in the east. Unappeased by the severity of the Versailles treaty, Poincaré was itching for a chance to strike a mortal blow at the German economy and render her forever weak and helpless. In the first week of January 1923, he seized on a pretext to strike: Germany had defaulted on a promise to hand over 140,000 telegraph poles, as stipulated in the treaty, and Poincaré promptly ordered the French army to occupy the Ruhr, heartland of Germany's heavy industry. A wave of righteous, patriotic anger swept across the nation, and even the unflappable sphinx Seeckt began to prepare for a resumption of war.

As so often in the past, the Weimar Government turned to their sworn enemies on the right in their hour of need. Less than a month after the French occupation, President Ebert, General Seeckt, and the Ruhr SPD leader, Karl Severing, who was also now Interior Minister, thrashed out a secret accord to activate the illegal army reserve – the 'Black Reichswehr'. In practice this meant the recall to the colours of all the old Freikorps who had been disbanded in disgrace after the Kapp Putsch and the Baltic and Silesian campaigns. The 'Labour Associations', 'Sports Societies', 'Gun Clubs' and other groups under which the Freikorps had been masquerading were to dust down their hidden arms and be readied for combat. To disguise its real purpose, this hidden army was to be called 'Labour troops' or 'Labour Commandos' ('Arbeitskommando', or AK). The AK's leader was to be Lieutenant Colonel von Bock – later the General who led Hitler's armies to the gates of Moscow in December 1941. Bock's two chief underlings were a pair of Freikorps veterans, Major Bruno Buchrucker and Lieutenant Paul Schulz. They were joined by other prominent Freikorps Führers like von Heydebreck, Rossbach, Konstantin Hierl and Heinz Hauenstein.

Though Freikorps veterans provided the backbone and officer corps of the 'Black Reichswehr', new and younger recruits flooded in from the middle-class intake in Germany's universities. Students from Berlin, Jena, Leipzig and Halle all joined up for drilling and training. By September, when passive resistance to the French occupation officially ended in the Ruhr, the Black Reichswehr was approaching the numbers of the official Army – up to 80,000 men.

But this revival of the dormant Freikorps took time to mature, and the whole process was too slow for the activists of the extreme right. They saw the situation in the Ruhr as ripe tinder for igniting a fire of resistance against foreign occupation that could then inflame the whole nation in a new war of liberation against

France. The French were trying to detach the territories on the west bank of the Rhine from the Fatherland and set up a puppet buffer state in the Rhineland and Palatinate. The separatist movement was scotched both by lack of popular support, and by the assassination of the separatist leader, Heinz Orbis, who was shot in the back as he sat down to dinner in a hotel in Speyer. The killer was an O.C. member, Gunther Muthmann, who had been sent to the Rhineland by Captain Ehrhardt in response to appeals from patriotic residents.

The resistance in the Ruhr, though spearheaded by the strong local trade union movement, also drew the attention of the extreme right. Freikorps activists organised shock troops who carried out acts of sabotage such as the destruction of bridges and the blowing up of coal transports and French troop trains. It was these groups of armed saboteurs who provided the Freikorps and the Nazis with their most potent martyr: Albert Leo Schlageter.

Schlageter, like so many Freikorps men, was a wartime army officer who had never got used to peace. Decorated with the Iron Cross, first and second class, he had been a comrade of von Salomon in the Baltic. A veteran of both the von Medem and von Löwenfeld Freikorps, he took part in all the major Freikorps campaigns, including the Kapp Putsch and the storming of Annaburg in Silesia. In November 1922 he happened to be in Munich and heard Hitler speak. At once he was mesmerised by the power of the new Messiah and joined Rossbach and Hauenstein in a mission to spread Nazi influence in northern Germany.

News of the French march into the Ruhr sent Schlageter to the area where he became a leader of the secret sabotage squads. On 15 March 1923 he blew up a railway bridge, but was betrayed to the French by two of his comrades and shot dead by firing squad after a court-martial. At once, Schlageter became a martyr to the cause of extreme nationalism. He had joined the NSDAP in the nick of time for Hitler to be able to claim the fallen man as one of his own, and thousands of SA men were despatched to the Ruhr to march in Schlageter's funeral parade. It was the first demonstration of Nazi discipline and the party's power outside Bavaria, and Schlageter's name was shamelessly invoked to whip up patriotic resistance. Despite his sacrifice, the strikes and resistance in the Ruhr were crippling the national economy and the Berlin Government ordered an end on 26 September. The decision was gall and wormwood to the Right. An act of economic common sense seemed to them yet one more stab in the back, another treacherous self-inflicted wound. The campaign of agitation that they mounted against the Government led to changes at the top in both Berlin and Bavaria and resulted in two more putsch attempts.

In Berlin, the current Centrist Chancellor, Cuno, resigned in favour of the conservative though democratic statesman, Gustav Stresemann. At about the same time, one of the organisers of the 'Black Reichswehr', Major Buchrucker, attempted to overthrow the Government in a carbon copy of the Kapp Putsch. Buchrucker's plan was to march his four battalions of troops from their barracks at Kustrine, near Berlin, on the capital and install a rightist regime. He planned to continue the resistance in the Ruhr and mobilise the whole population for a war of liberation and renewal against both France and Poland. Getting wind of the plot, President Ebert invoked Article 48 of the Weimar constitution, which suspended civil liberties, and declared a state of siege throughout the Reich.

Seeckt, as head of the Reichswehr, was given virtual dictatorial power. If the regular Reichswehr had ever been tempted to support Buchrucker's adventure, they had now lost all motive for doing so. Buchrucker himself was all for calling off the putsch, but the more headstrong Freikorps elements would have none of this. Two officers, Captain Walther Stennes, a Freikorps führer who was later to command the SA in Berlin – until he fell out with Hitler – and Major Gunther, a former Ehrhardt Brigade officer, took over command of the Putsch.

Gunther telephoned Captain Ehrhardt in Munich to get his approval for the putsch and then began to prepare for the march on Berlin. Realising that the putsch stood no hope of success without regular Reichswehr support, Buchrucker decided to head it off by staging a fake putsch that would collapse without bloodshed. He ordered five hundred and fifty men belonging to a battalion commanded by a Major Herzen to march – and then tipped off the local Kustrine Reichswehr commander, Colonel Gudowius, that the men were on their way. Gudowius arrested Buchrucker and ordered Herzen to return to barracks. The 'putsch' collapsed without a shot being fired.

Buchrucker was sentenced to ten years' fortress arrest for his plot, of which he served less than four. Herzen and other implicated officers served a few months honorary confinement. The Black Reichswehr soldiers involved in the 'Kustrine Putsch' were officially dissolved and scattered but, as usual, retired to the estates of Prussia to bide their time. Buchrucker, Stennes and Paul Schulz all subsequently joined the Nazis. But both Buchrucker and Stennes later opposed Hitler's autocratic ways and left Germany to join Otto Strasser's Black Front opposition.

If Buchrucker's putsch was a ludicrous fiasco that ended without bloodshed, events in Bavaria followed a very different course. His putsch there was Hitler's one and only attempt to use Freikorps methods and marked his entrance to the national scene – it also signalled the demise of the Freikorps as a significant factor in German politics.

The September events in the Ruhr and Berlin found the Bavarian Right in a state of considerable confusion. There were three main factions competing for power. Captain Hermann Ehrhardt had assembled a small Freikorps army of some 15,000 men under the umbrella of a new organisation, the 'Viking Bund'. His forces were gathered along the border between Bavaria and Thuringia, poised to march north into Saxony where a Red Government had come into power. Then there were the official Bavarian state forces loyal to Gustav von Kahr. Kahr, who had been proclaimed state commissioner with virtual dictatorial powers, was more and more inclined to a monarchist restoration of the Wittelsbachs in Munich. Finally there were the forces loyal to Hitler's Nazis, gathered under the Kampfbund, of which Hitler was the political chief and Ludendorff, Knebel and Röhm the main military figures.

The three power groups, like panthers in a cage, prowled warily round each other throughout the autumn of 1923, nervously waiting for the first leap. Ehrhardt, who had earlier lent his staff officers to Hitler to organise the young SA, had become jealous of the Führer, and withdrew his co-operation in May after Hitler had balked at an attempt to disrupt the traditional May Day parades of the Social Democrats, Communists and Trade Unions. The conservative Kahr had always mistrusted the lawless ways of the Nazis – his ambition was to be Regent or Premier of a reactionary Bavarian monarchy. Hitler himself was torn between his own ambitions and appetite for power, and his nervousness of failing in a premature putsch.

As so often in his career, Hitler withdrew into a self-imposed isolation while he considered his next move: he spent the summer and early autumn at his retreat at Berchtesgaden in the Bavarian Alps, the Berghof, which had been bought for him by moneyed well-wishers. At the beginning of November 1923, events forced his hand.

Word reached the Nazi leaders that Kahr was planning to speak at a mass meeting in one of Munich's biggest beerhalls, the Bürgerbraukeller, on the evening of 8 November. No-one knew what the state commissioner planned to say, but with him on the platform were to be the other two members of his ruling triumvirate: General Otto von Lossow, Commander of the Reichswehr in Bavaria, and Colonel Hans von Seisser, the province's Police chief. It was just possible that Kahr intended to proclaim a putsch of his own and march on Berlin, or declare a separatist Bavaria and a restoration of the monarchy. Either scenario would clearly preempt the Nazi plans and Hitler's cohorts would be put firmly in their place. Obviously the meeting could not go ahead as planned.

Swiftly, the Kampfbund chiefs laid their own plans: SA and Oberland Bund units would be mobilised, brought into the city centre to seal off the Bürgerbraukeller, where Hitler himself would proclaim the start of his own 'National Revolution' and hijack the triumvirate, presenting them with a triumphant fait accompli. At the same time, Röhm's Reichskriegsflagge combat veterans would seize the Bavarian War Ministry to neutralise any possible Reichswehr opposition, and Rossbach's Freikorps would take charge of the city's cadet schools which were stuffed with Nazi sympathisers just waiting for the signal to rise.

Throughout Thursday 8 November, orders went out by telegram, telephone and word of mouth to the militants of the SA, Oberland Bund and Reichskriegflagge to assemble that evening at their section stations, armed, uniformed and ready for action. The Nazi newspaper, the *Volkischer Beobachter* was prepared to print a late special edition proclaiming the putsch.

When Kahr was twenty minutes into his speech, at 8.20 p.m., Hitler, along with his bodyguards, Rosenburg and Drexler, arrived outside the beerhall in his red Benz ear. Wearing a trench-coat over a formal cutaway dinner suit, the Führer stood in the vestibule awaiting his armed 'muscle'. Just before 8.30, the rumble of trucks was heard in the street outside. It was the 'Stosstrupp Hitler', the SA's élite guard, arriving on schedule to block off the street to any further traffic. Spearheaded by a squad of fifteen men, in steel helmets and combat uniform and led by SA Commander Hermann Goering, the Nazi troops stormed the cellar, bursting open the main lobby doors, and covering the perplexed audience with a heavy machine gun. The hall was so packed that no-one could get a clear view, but gradually the figure of Hitler was seen, pushing his way through the dense throng towards the speaker's podium. Kahr stopped his droning oration and stood hesitantly to one side. The Führer, his brow greasy with sweat, reached the platform and stood on a chair. The hubbub in the hall reached fever pitch with some in the crowd cheering, and others jeering and calling out mocking insults. With a flourish, the Führer produced a pistol and fired dramatically into the ceiling.

A sudden hush descended on the hall. 'Ruhe!' (quiet!), Hitler screamed unnecessarily. 'The national revolution has begun! This hall is occupied by six hundred armed men and no-one may leave it!' Hitler then invited Kahr, Lossow and Seisser into a sideroom for a discussion. Menaced by the pointing pistol, the triumvirate filed off stage and a buzz of excited talk erupted in the hall. Many of those present resented being held prisoner and murmurs of discontent began to swell. Goering took charge and brutally called the meeting to order. He concluded his short speech with a typical jest: 'You've all got your beer – what are you worrying about?'

Back in the ante-room, Hitler, with a beer *stein* in one hand and his gun in the other, was exercising all his powers of persuasion on the sullen triumvirs. But, humiliated by their public abduction, the trio remained obdurate, bitterly reproaching Hitler for breaking a promise not to launch a putsch on his own. Exasperated, Hitler broke off the talks and went back to the hall where he launched into a typical tirade which succeeded in turning the hostile mood of his audience inside out, 'like a glove', as one of his listeners put it. He played on the beer-sodden patriotism of the three-thousand strong crowd like a master, told them there would be high office in his new regime for the triumvirate and that the new national army would be commanded by General Ludendorff himself. 'Tomorrow' he concluded, 'will find either a nationalist government in all Germany or us dead.' The hall erupted in a storm of cheers. Buoyed by the support, he returned to his reluctant prisoners.

Fortunately for Hitler, at that opportune moment Ludendorff, clad in an un-military tweed suit, entered the Bürgerbraukeller. Though annoyed that he had been brusquely and suddenly summoned by Hitler's minions, the General was prepared to lend his august name and authority to the putsch. His arrival was decisive in winning over the reluctant triumvirate. The three aristocrats, for whom Hitler was still a vulgar little beerhall revolutionary, bowed to the reputation of Germany's foremost warlord. They agreed with the General that while the putsch might have been launched in a more dignified way, now it was on, the only thing to do was to go along with it. Kahr was the last to agree, but when he shook hands with Hitler, the pact seemed sealed and the leaders filed back into the main hall where they were greeted by another thunderous ovation.

'Beaming with joy and childlike happiness', Hitler made another rhapsodic speech – his third of the evening – moving many in the crowd to tears with his pathetic recall of that day – exactly five years before – when as a blind war cripple he had pledged his life to wiping out the shame of defeat and resurrecting Germany, proud, strong and free. More gruffly, Ludendorff added his considerable weight, describing the putsch as 'a turning point in German and world history'. The meeting concluded with an emotional rendition of 'Deutschland über Alles' before the audience was released into the chill, sleety November night. Elsewhere in Munich, the seeds of the putsch's defeat were already being sown.

At some points the putsch had prevailed: the professional Röhm had done his work well, seizing the War Ministry on the

Schönfelderstrasse, cordoning off the building with barbed wire barricades and stationing machine gun posts at vital strongpoints. One of his stormtroopers in the operation was a bespectacled, weedy-looking Bavarian whose name would one day be synonymous with the most pitiless system of Police state terror the world has seen: Heinrich Himmler, future overlord of the SS. At the Police Presidium, Nazi sympathiser Wilhelm Frick had seen to it that the city's blue-clad police force did nothing to frustrate the putsch.

It was only when the putschists tried to consolidate by winning over the army that things began to go badly wrong. Freikorps leader Gerhard Rossbach had fulfilled his mission by winning over one thousand keen cadets at the Infantry school. Proudly he marched his men over to the Bürgerbraukeller where they were reviewed by Hitler and Ludendorff. But when the putschists tried to seize the barracks of the Engineers, and the HQ of the vital 19th Infantry regiment, loyalist Reichswehr officers rallied their men to thwart the putsch and refuse entry to the stormtroopers. Not willing to fire on the regular Reichswehr, the putschists sullenly withdrew.

Meanwhile, the Nazis were taking energetic measures to neutralise their opponents in the areas they did control. The terror they instituted was a mild foretaste of the mass murders, tortures and intimidation that was to characterise their rule ten years later. At the beerhall itself, a special 'snatch squad' commanded by Rudolf Hess singled out prominent opponents in the audience, including Bavarian Premier von Knilling; Count von Soden, chief adviser to Prince Rupprecht, Pretender to the Bavarian throne; and Frick's non-Nazi superior at the Police Presidium, Karl Mantel. All were placed under arrest. Elsewhere in the city, SA thugs selected Jewish names at random from the telephone book and took several Jewish citizens into 'protective custody'. Bully boys broke into the home of the Munich leader of the SPD, Erhard

Auer, who had been near-fatally wounded on the day of Eisner's assassination, and brutally beat him up along with his elderly wife, Sophie. Shock troops also smashed the presses of the Social Democratic *Munich Post* newspaper and burned out SPD party offices.

Hitler did not remain long in the Bürgerbraukeller to relish his apparent victory. He rushed off to confer with Röhm at the War Ministry. When he returned, the Führer was appalled to learn that Ludendorff had allowed the triumvirs to go free. He remonstrated with the General, but Ludendorff maintained that no German officer and gentleman would break his word. He was forgetting that the promises of support for the putsch had been extracted under duress and the Nazis were now to pay heavily for his mistake. General von Lossow headed back to the 19th Infantry barracks, securely held by loyalist officers under Lossow's deputy, General von Danner, Commander of the Munich garrison. Finding himself surrounded by officers opposed to the putsch, Lossow jettisoned his promise to the putschists and set about transforming the barracks into the nerve centre of moves to counter and crush the coup attempt.

He was soon joined by Kahr and Seisser and a stream of signals went out, disowning the beerhall pledges and summoning loyal troops from outlying areas of Bavaria to mobilise against the putsch. Some of these signals, unknown to Röhm, were transmitted from offices inside the War Ministry still manned by loyal officers. Stiffened by messages from Prince Rupprecht, who ordered the putsch to be crushed at any cost, and by Cardinal Faulhaber, Archbishop of Munich, Kahr decreed the abolition of the NSDAP, the dissolution of the Oberlund Bund and the Reichskriegsflagge and the arrest of the putsch leaders.

By dawn, the Nazi leaders belatedly realised that they had been betrayed. The seal had been set by a message from Berlin in which General von Seeckt and Chancellor Stresemann, with the approval of President Ebert, proclaimed that anyone supporting the 'mad attempt in Munich' would be judged guilty of high treason and punished accordingly. Hitler, Ludendorff and their supporters knew that they stood alone.

Hitler himself, reacting after his hysterical optimism of the night before, told his cronies that he was for throwing in the towel and doing away with himself. Another coup had gone awry when he had told Munich's former Police President, Ernst Pöhner, to assume his old office at the Police Presidium. Pöhner had gone along, only to find himself arrested by his own officers who had reneged on the putsch. Pöhner's underling Frick was also arrested. The news, said Pöhner 'fell like the blow of a club.'

Despite these blows, some things were still going the putschists' way. A squad of putschists, led by Ludendorff's stepson Heinz Pernet, raided the printing works where millions of inflationary Marks had just rolled from the presses. They confiscated the lot to pay their troops, issuing a receipt to the proprietors of the works, the Jewish Parcus brothers.

Troopers acting under Röhm's orders had entered the Franciscan monastery of St Anna, where, to the astonishment of many of them, they found the monks breaking into their own cellars and unearthing thousands of modern rifles, which had been hidden away by Bavarian Freikorps officers against the day of the national revolution. The putschist forces were also boosted by the arrival of SA units from outlying areas, including a strong contingent from Landshut led by Gregor Strasser. If they could only act boldly once again, his supporters told Hitler, all might yet be saved.

At once Hitler's mood swung back to euphoria. Revived by the breaking day and the cheerful sight of lorry loads of his stormtroopers happily collecting their arms, he reflected that he still held the streets of Munich, along with the sympathy of much of its population, who were being whipped up by Nazi orators like Hermann Esser and the party's unsalubrious Nuremberg boss, Julius Streicher. It was Ludendorff who suggested that the situation could be saved if the putschists marched en masse from the Bürgerbraukeller into the city centre. This show of strength would convince the wavering Reichswehr and Police that the national revolution was truly on the march. Faced with such a formidable demonstration, Ludendorff argued, no-one would dare oppose them. For the second time on that fateful night, and not for the first time in his tempestuous career, Ludendorff was to be proved wrong. Flatly ruling out Goering's plan for a strategic retreat to the town of Rosenheim, close to the Austrian frontier, Ludendorff rapped out an order: 'Wir marschieren!' ('We March!').

Between eleven and noon on 9 November – fateful fifth anniversary of the Kaiser's fall and the proclamation of the hated Republic – the Nazi rag, tag and bobtail army formed up in columns outside the beerhall. In the lead were the 'Stosstrupp Hitler', steel helmeted and wearing World War One combat uniforms. Behind them were the massed ranks of the SA in their ski-caps and windcheaters. Somewhere among the mass were Rossbach's one thousand infantry school cadets and the Oberland Bund men in their comic Bavarian lederhosen and green felt hats. Hitler, Ludendorff, Goering, Rosenburg and other top Nazis linked arms at the head of the column. At twelve the little army moved off, marching towards the bridge over the Isar river, hunched against the stinging snow showers and the knifing wind.

When the windswept column reached the Ludwig bridge over the Isar, a small contingent of Seisser's green-uniformed State Police barred their way with levelled carbines. Screaming insults, the Nazi tide swept up to the thin green line and submerged it, disarming and beating the police as they went. Once across the river, the march entered Munich's main square, the Marienplatz, which was filled with cheering people. The square was dominated by the city hall, held by the putschists, and the sight of the swastika and monarchist flags waving side by side heartened the marchers, as did the evidence of their popular support. The press of the crowd was so great that the marchers hesitated, unsure of their route.

Another word from Ludendorff set the columns off again, towards the north where Röhm was still holding the War Ministry for Hitler. The dense throng of men, which had picked up hundreds of civilian supporters en route, now crammed into the Rezidenz-strasse, with the ancient Palace of the Wittelsbachs to their right, and the Odeon-platz in front of them. The mouth of the Odeon-platz was blocked off by another detachment of 'Green Police' commanded by Lieutenant Baron Michael von Godin, a determined young officer who had orders to stop the march in its tracks.

Godin's men levelled their carbines at the marchers. Godin himself bawled out an order to halt. It was 12.30. There was a brief moment of electric tension as the two menacing forces squared up to each other at point blank range. Then someone fired.

The shot signalled a ragged volley that ricocheted along the narrow street. Some marchers died where they stood, the rest dived for cover. The man to whom Hitler was linking arms, Scheubner-Richter, fell dead, dragging the Führer down with him in his death agony and dislocating Hitler's shoulder. A splinter of stone ripped into Goering's groin, disabling him. Only Ludendorff disdained to fall on his face. The Quartermaster General, proudly erect, marched stolidly on, accompanied by his ADC, through the Police ranks and into the open square behind where he was respectfully taken into custody. Hitler, scrambling to his feet, took one look round the scene of death and desolation and stumbled away. Luckily a yellow car, manned by Walther 'Bubi' Schultze, the SA's chief doctor, had been cruising along the length of the march. Recognising his Führer, Schultze ushered Hitler in and the car sped off. The ruins of the Putsch lay behind them.

The mess was quickly cleared up. Ludendorff, from captivity, ordered Röhm to surrender the War Ministry, while Gregor Strasser capitulated with his men who had been holding the Bürgerbraukeller. The Nazi leadership scattered: Goering was patched up by a Jewish doctor and smuggled over the Austrian border, not returning to the Fatherland until 1927. Hitler hid out for a few days at a rural retreat at Uffing, before surrendering to police on 11 November, anniversary of the armistice. It seemed to be all over for the Nazi movement, but it was only the end of the beginning.

EPILOGUE

THE FATE OF THE FREIKORPS

'This is the New Man. The storm soldier, the élite of Middle Europe. A completely new race, cunning, strong, and packed with purpose . . . the axis of the future.'

Ernst Jünger,
Der Kampf als innere Erlebnis
('The Struggle as Inner Experience')

The collapse of the Beerhall Putsch is a convenient and a natural point to conclude the history of the Freikorps. It was the last putsch in which Freikorps fighters participated as armed units and after that watershed its members and leaders were either quiescent, in jail or exile, in the regular Reichswehr or, like pools of water sucked up by the noonday sun, absorbed by the rising might of the Nazi movement. It only remains to finish the story of the Freikorps with a brief consideration of the aftermath of the Putsch and an account of the fates of the remaining leading figures from the five years, November 1918 to November 1923.

Ten of the leading figures in the Putsch, including Hitler, Ludendorff, his stepson Pernet, Weber, Knebel, Röhm, Pöhner and Frick, were tried for their part in the affair. Showing his customary skill at manipulating an audience, Hitler turned the trial into a propaganda triumph. Sympathetic right-wing judges allowed him to denounce the leaders of the State from the dock as the 'real' November criminals. After a hearing lasting a month, nine of the defendents were found guilty of committing, aiding and abetting high treason. Only Ludendorff – to his great disgust – was acquitted.

Hitler, Weber, Knebel and Pöhner were given the minimum of five years 'fortress confinement' – with the opportunity of early parole. They served their time in pleasant conditions in the fortress of Landsberg. Hitler used his eight-and-a-half months 'inside' to good effect, composing and dictating to his faithful amanuensis Hess, his turgid book *Mein Kampf*, a combination of autobiography, convoluted racist philosophy and raving denunciation of the Jews, the Allies, the Weimar republic and his many other hate figures.

Hitler had left the organisation of the banned NSDAP in the palsied hands of his most incompetent aide, Rosenburg, a lacklustre character whose fumbling handling of the party's affairs ensured that no rival Führer – Röhm and Strasser were the men he feared most – assumed Hitler's mantle while he was out of circulation. He emerged from Landsberg in December 1924 and set about rebuilding the party. Eschewing his former revolutionary methods, he methodically built the party into a mass movement bent on subverting the Weimar Republic from within, using the legal methods of propaganda, elections and freedom of speech.

At first, conditions were not propitious: within a week of the Putsch the German Mark was stabilised, thanks to the wise financial policies of Chancellor Stresemann and his fiscal wizard, Hjalmar Schacht, whose aid was later enlisted by Hitler himself to run the finances of the Third Reich. During the middle twenties, unemployment fell sharply, production increased, real wages rose and the Dawes and Young plans drew much of the sting from

Versailles by settling progressively more liberal timescales for the payment of Germany's war reparations. It was a bad time for the violent political extremists who thrived on political chaos and economic misery. As Captain Ehrhardt's former right-hand man, Manfred von Killinger, lamented: 'The good weather for putschists seemed to have finally disappeared. Life wasn't much fun anymore. The Poles did nothing. The Communists did nothing. We were getting soft.' Only with the Wall Street Crash of October 1929 did the 'weather' change again.

The leading figures whose fates have figured in the Freikorps story went to their various ends: the Kaiser continued to live the life of a comfortable country gentleman at the Castle of Doom in the Netherlands. Growing a handsome Imperial beard, he mellowed with the years, and survived to see the Netherlands occupied by Hitler's invading armies in 1940. He died the following year.

Hindenburg was called out of honourable retirement for the second time in 1925 to stand for the post of President. Supported by all parties with the exception of the Nazis and the Communists, he presided over the final years of Weimar with a ponderous dignity. Despising Hitler – 'that Bohemian corporal' – in his last dotage he nevertheless was pressed to name the Führer as Chancellor on 30 January 1933. His final act – though he was by then far gone in senility – was to give the Presidential seal of approval to the bloody Night of the Long Knives Purge in July 1934. On his death the following month, Hitler combined the offices of President and Chancellor in his own person as Führer.

Hindenburg's and Hitler's querulous partner and rival, Ludendorff, was persuaded to stand for President in 1925 on the Nazi party ticket. He secured a derisory 1.1 per cent of the poll and thereafter retired into a psychotic world of his own, scribbling drivelling fantasies of World domination by enemies as varied as the Jews, the Catholics and the Freemasons, and falling increasingly under the sinister occult influence of his second wife. He died in December 1937 and was given a Nazi state funeral by Hitler, whom he had so despised in life.

General Groener, the man who had, with Ebert, saved the tottering democratic regime in 1919, became a politician on leaving the Army. He served the Weimar state loyally as Labour and Defence Minister, in the latter post doing his best to curb the growing influence of the Nazis. He died, a disappointed man, after the Nazi assumption of power. His protégé, Schliecher, the creepy intriguer who had been instrumental in getting the Army to adopt the Freikorps idea, paid the price of his incorrigible propensity for political plotting. After pulling the strings behind many of the last Governments of the Weimar years, he too became Defence Minister and finally, the last Weimar Chancellor before Hitler. A little over a year later, he was shot down, with his wife, in his study by SS gunmen – one of the most prominent victims of the Night of the Long Knives.

Von Seeckt, architect of the new Reichswehr, lived to see his brainchild pass into Nazi hands and become the instrument for military expansion for which he had so efficiently laid the foundation. He too was hated by the extreme right for his failure to support the Kapp Putsch. Surviving an assassination attempt by right-wing killers, he was briefly a nationalist member of the Reichstag before becoming chief military adviser to the Chinese Government of Chiang Kai-Shek at the time of Hitler's takeover. He died in 1936.

The SPD leaders did not ultimately profit from their craven appeasement of the right in the early years of Weimar. Deserted in droves by their working class supporters, the party progressively lost power and influence to the Communists, the Centre parties, and finally to the Nazis themselves.

Ebert, virulently hated by the right, became the target, like Erzberger before him, of abusive hate campaigns in the right-wing press. Worn out by the struggle to clear his name through the prejudices of the courts, he died, in early 1925, of peritonitis following an undiagnosed burst appendix. Ironically the son of this great anti-Communist, also called Fritz, became one of the founders of Communist East Germany.

Gustav Noske, the 'Bloodhound', who more than any other man can be called the father of the Freikorps, never regained the power and influence to which he felt so clearly entitled. Hated by left and right alike – but more by the left to which he nominally belonged – he retired to his native Hanover. Suspected of complicity in the July plot to kill Hitler, he was twice briefly imprisoned by the Nazis in 1944–5. Freed by the advancing Americans, he died in 1946 while preparing for a lecture tour of the United States.

Philipp Scheidemann, the man who proclaimed the Republic from the balcony of the Reichstag and served Weimar as its first Chancellor, lived quietly as Mayor of his native city, Kassel, after surviving the bizarre attempt by O.C. murderers to kill him with acid, in 1922. Forced into exile by the Nazis, he died in 1937.

Joseph Wirth, the Centrist Chancellor who had so eloquently denounced the murder of Rathenau, served as Minister in many Weimar cabinets. In exile during the Third Reich, he became a partisan of a neutralist Germany after 1945 and won the Stalin prize for his pains. He died in 1953.

Erhard Auer, the SPD leader in Bavaria, who came so close to death on the day of Kurt Eisner's murder, survived until 1945 – the same year that saw the death of Eisner's assassin, Count Anton Arco-Valley. Ernst Pöhner, the murderous Bavarian Police chief who did so much to cover up the activities of Freikorps killers in the years when Munich was incubating the Nazi movement died in 1925, like Arco-Valley, in a car crash. His deputy, Wilhelm Frick, served as Nazi Interior Minister and was condemned to death as a war criminal by the Nuremberg tribunal in 1946. He was hanged, the same fate suffered by the inept Nazi 'philosopher' Alfred Rosenburg.

Hermann Ehrhardt and Gerhard Rossbach, those terrible twins of the Freikorps movement, suffered curiously parallel fates. Both fell out with Hitler on his path to power and went into eclipse. Both narrowly escaped death during the Night of the Long Knives, both were jailed by the Nazis and both survived the Second World War to repent of their earlier misdeeds. Rossbach wrote his memoirs in 1950, operated an import-export business near Frankfurt and died in 1967. In his last years he took a prominent part in organising the Bayreuth festivals of Wagner's music. Ehrhardt lived to a ripe old age in an Austrian castle belonging to his wife's family.

Ernst Röhm and Gregor Strasser, Hitler's most able early lieutenants and to some extent his personal and ideological rivals in the party, suffered the penalty for refusing to bow the knee to the 'psychopathic God'. Violent men in life, they suffered appropriately violent deaths.

Strasser was the first to go. Despite Rosenburg's official leadership, the active Strasser played a major role in re-organising the Nazi party while Hitler was in jail and in spreading its influence in northern Germany. Along with his younger brother Otto, he led the radical 'Socialist' wing of the Nazis and, partially seduced by the crafty Schliecher, made an open challenge to Hitler's leadership when the party was on the brink of power in 1932. He lost, was expelled from the party's ranks and was shot on the Night of the Long Knives.

Röhm, too, was active during Hitler's imprisonment, reconstituting the para-military Kampfbund as the 'Frontbann'. Quarrelling with Hitler on the latter's release from Landsberg, Röhm left Germany to become military adviser to the Bolivian Government. He was recalled by Hitler in 1930 when the Führer needed a strong man to rebuild and discipline the fractious SA.

Röhm succeeded in this task only too well, building the Brownshirts into a gigantic private army some three million strong, which did much to pave the Nazi path to power. After Hitler took power, this turbulent force became an extreme embarrassment. Röhm, like Strasser, pressed for a 'second revolution', a radical programme that would mean the merging of the SA and the Reichswehr into a new 'People's Army'. With Reichswehr compliance Hitler turned on his old friend and mentor on 30 June 1934, arresting him and the other leaders of the SA on the pretext that they were planning a putsch.

Röhm was incarcerated in the same cell at Munich's Stadelheim prison that had previously held Kurt Eisner, Anton Arco-Valley and Hitler himself. After refusing an invitation to kill himself, Röhm was shot dead by the SS. The same fate was meted out simultaneously to other SA leaders who had been prominent Freikorps fighters – including Karl Ernst, Edmund Heines and Peter Heydebreck. Another victim of the purge was Gustav von Kahr. Aged seventy-two and retired from politics, he did not escape Hitler's memory and hatred. He was dragged from his house, and his body was found hacked to pieces in a swamp near Dachau a few days later.

Captain Mayr, the army intelligence officer who had first plucked Hitler from obscurity, turned against his former protégé and became a military adviser to the Social Democrats' militia, the Reichsbanner. Imprisoned by the Nazis, he died in Buchenwald concentration camp. Baron von Godin, the Police captain whose volley broke the beerhall putsch, was pursued by Nazi hatred. Driven into exile in Austria, he was arrested and tortured, but somehow survived the war to become Munich's post-war Police chief.

The two bards of the Freikorps, Ernst von Salomon and Ernst Jünger, both survived into old age. Jünger, the more considerable figure of the two, refused to join the Nazis, although they revered his writings. He lived as a writer and entymologist, became one of the first authors to describe the effects of the hallucinogenic drug LSD, and served in the Second World War as a staff officer in Paris, in touch with the ill-fated conspirators of the July plot. He dared to write an anti-Hitler allegory, the remarkable novel *On the Marble Cliffs* which was a best-seller before it was banned by the Nazis. Jünger died in 1998, aged 102, writing vigorously to the last. He crowned his remarkable literary career in 1983 by winning Germany's premier literary award, the Goethe prize. In an interview with the author in 1983, Jünger gave the secret of his survival: 'Always an observer – never a participant.' The grand old man of German nationalism was also philosophical about the new Europe of the EU: 'What does a nation mean when you can fly across it in ten minutes?'

Jünger's comment reveals how far we have travelled since the days when the Freikorps warriors set out, in their leather coats and steel helmets, as the self-appointed saviours of Germany. They seem almost as remote, with their fierce cruelties and political passions, as the legendary Arthurian knights of the Holy Grail. What have their deeds to do with our Hi-tech, politically pragmatic age?

To assess the historical significance of the Freikorps, one must see them in the world that gave them such a bloody birth. They arose from a defeated Germany. (Despite the 'Stab in the Back' legend beloved of the German Right, the armies of Germany *had* been roundly vanquished in the field before the first revolutionary stirrings convulsed the country.) Tempered by four years of war, the Freikorps could not realistically have been expected to behave other than as Hitler described them: 'Swift as greyhounds, tough as leather, hard as Krupp steel'. And – he might have added – as ferociously cruel as the mercenary bands of 'Landsknechte' who roamed devastated Germany during the sixteenth century.

The immediate political legacy of the Freikorps was the militarisation of German politics. Their penchant for what a Spanish Fascist leader described as: 'The dialectic of the pistol and the hand grenade', over the commonly accepted rules of civilised political debate, left an unhealthy inheritance of violence to the Weimar Republic.

The death of Gustav Stresemann, the last 'civilised' German conservative statesman, at the end of the twenties coincided with the Wall Street Crash, the immediate pauperisation of the German bourgeoisie and the spectacular revival of the Nazi movement. During the early thirties Germany, with six million desperate unemployed people haunting the streets, became a battleground with four huge paramilitary private armies struggling for control of the dying republic. The Nazi SA, the Communist Red Front, the Nationalist Stahlhelm and the SPD Reichsbanner, were all the progeny of the Freikorps ideal of marrying military with political life. They all saw themselves as 'political soldiers' and all in their different ways were the antithesis of liberal parliamentary democracy.

The Freikorps themselves were the children of the trenches, spawned by war out of revolution. Owing something to the dark, non-Christian roots of German history, something to the prevailing fashion for anti-rationalist mysticism, but much more to the savage habits of mind bred by four years of war, the Freikorps fighters were above all, the natural representatives of a time of social chaos, confusion, revolution and reaction. As such they were the natural humus for the growth of Hitlerism.

The Freikorps believed they were saving their country from the machinations of the Bolsheviks, the subversion of the Spartacists and the depredations of the Allies; the atrocities committed by Freikorps fighters in a time of savage civil war cannot be condoned but they can be understood. Many of them believed in action for its own sake; it was not the goal of the battle that mattered, it was the exultant experience of battle itself. This failure to decide whether they were fighting to prop up the liberal democratic state which had recruited them or whether they were struggling – like their nominal enemies the Communists – to destroy it, made the Freikorps easy meat for that consummate politician, Adolf Hitler.

Denouncing the SA leaders whom he had just had murdered, in his Reichstag speech justifying the Night of Long Knives purge, Hitler wrote his own epitaph to the Freikorps movement:

> They were permanent revolutionaries who, in 1918, had been shaken in their former relation to the state and uprooted, and had thereby lost all inner contact with the human social order. Men who have no respect for any authority . . . men who found their faith in nihilism . . . moral degenerates constant conspirators incapable of real co-operation, ready to oppose any order, hating all authority, their restless and excited minds found satisfaction only in incessant intellectual and conspiratorial activity aimed at the destruction of all existing institutions . . . These pathological enemies of the state are the enemies of all authority.

Here is Hitler the conservative, pleasing his new friends in the Reichswehr by spitting on the memory of his own 'Old Fighters' – the men of the Freikorps and the SA who had done so much to beat down opposition to his movement, and undermine the Weimar Republic. Ten years later, when the Officer corps had failed to win his war and had indeed tried to kill him, Hitler turned on them with the same fury and proclaimed that the old revolutionary way had been, after all, the right one. In truth, Hitler was the 'postman of chaos', the personification of the dark forces which the Freikorps had so fatally worshipped.

AFTERWORD

The first edition of this book appeared in August 1987. In the very week of its publication the shocking news broke that one of the two major figures to survive from the Freikorps era, Adolf Hitler's former deputy, Rudolf Hess, had died in captivity. What was shocking was not the death itself – Hess was a very old, frail man – but the strange circumstances that surrounded the demise of this, the most faithful of Hitler's heralds, and the reminder it brought to contemporary, sleek, squeaky-clean Europe that a dirtier and darker past was not really so far away after all.

In many ways Rudolf Hess was the archetypal Freikorps man, embodying their most characteristic and typical traits. An idealistic German nationalist, a hero of the Great War both on the ground and in his chosen element of the air, a religious mystic, a 'hard' man, but, above all, a convinced and apparently selfless worshipper at the Hitler shrine from an early date.

Hess was Hitler's chosen instrument, his John the Baptist, who paved the way for the Nazi Messiah by proclaiming his doctrines to a waiting world. Imprisoned with his idol in Landsberg fortress after the abysmal failure of their 1923 Munich Beerhall Putsch, Hess had taken Hitler's dictation in writing down *Mein Kampf*, the turgid tome which is at once the Nazi leader's apologia, autobiography and the manifesto of his movement.

Indeed, so laboured is the prose, so convoluted and downright dotty the philosophy of *Mein Kampf*, that many believe that Hess himself, a university student, was the actual author – or at least, co-author. Certainly he edited the book which, although appearing under Hitler's name, bears all the hallmarks of Hess's own weird and secretive personality. The autodidact Hitler himself was no scholar. His personality was that of an idle Austrian café artist, and even as Germany's master he continued to keep the Bohemian hours of his youth. More than happy to hold forth to a captive audience until the wee hours; he was incapable of the steady, disciplined work of authorship.

Hess remained close to his master after their release from Landsberg. His role in the Third Reich was that of cheerleader and warm-up man to Hitler. Lacking apparent ambition, he steered clear of the cabals and factions ostensibly 'working towards the Führer' but actually more concerned with advancing their own agendas. If the competing egos and empires of Goering, Goebbels, Himmler, Bormann, Speer and Ribbentrop resembled nothing so much as a bagful of fighting cats, then Hess was the cat who walked alone. As such he was both useful and expendable.

With the outbreak of the Second World War, Hess's isolation and vulnerability became clear. As Deputy Führer, an impressive-sounding but hollow title, he had no Ministry or obvious function to fall back upon. But he was still close to Hitler – still the Führer's trusted and loyal confidante. As such, and as one of the few top Nazis to hold a pilot's license (Goering and Heydrich were the others), he was entrusted with the delicate and secret role of a peace envoy to Britain in May 1941. His mission was to parley with a British 'peace party' and secure Britain's withdrawal from the war – thus clearing the way for Hitler's onslaught on the Soviet Union the following month.

Thanks to the patient researches of historians Peter Padfield and Martin Allen, we now know that Hess and Hitler himself had been duped by British Intelligence: the anti-Churchill 'peace party' who Hess flew to Scotland to meet were a blind, a ruse to buy precious time for the embattled islands. Publicly denounced as a lone and mad wolf by Hitler after the evident public failure of his mission, Hess spent the rest of his long life behind bars in Britain, in Nuremberg, and finally back in Berlin. His lips remained loyally sealed, his behaviour in the dock at Nuremberg perfectly fitted the public picture of the lone 'Nazi nutter' it suited all parties to pretend he was, and he was shunned or mocked by his co-defendants and former party comrades. But his play-acting paid off. The assumption that he was a lunatic, plus the convenient fact that Hess had been languishing in British custody since 1941, and had thus been unavoidably absent during the worst excesses of the Holocaust and genocide in Poland and Russia – though he was at least an ardent anti-Semite as the other Nazi leaders – served to save him from the gallows.

Nevertheless, however, the man knew far too many untold secrets of the war to be released, and this embarrassing and apparently mad relic of a painful past stubbornly stayed alive. He was the last prisoner in Spandau jail, still walking the exercise yard long after the release of his fellow lags Speer and von Schirach, until it was given out that he had strangled himself with a light flex in August 1987 during the British watch at Spandau – their Buggins' turn in guarding him. The official story of Hess's suicide was widely disbelieved, and after an unsatisfactory autopsy and the conveniently speedy demolition of Spandau, Hess's family tomb at Wunsiedel in Bavaria became a shrine to Germany's persistent neo-Nazi fringe, and Hess himself a martyr to the cause.

Very different from the long and lonely incarceration of Rudolf Hess was the post-war fate of Ernst Jünger: another Great War hero and certainly the final major surviving figure from the Freikorps zeit. Like Hess, Jünger was a man of extreme politics, yet shrewd enough to steer clear of the vulgar violence of Nazism and even, though ambiguously, to dabble in the anti-Nazi resistance. Jünger died in his bed – after a very late conversion to Catholicism – eleven years after Hess in 1998 at the great age of 102.

Jünger was in at the sharp end of Germany's catastrophic twentieth century, participating in or witnessing all the major events from the outbreak of the Great War in 1914 to the re-unification of his country in 1989 after the self-inflicted wounds of the two world wars and the Cold War. Not for nothing did his biographer Thomas Nevin title his Life: '*Ernst Jünger & Germany: into the Abyss 1914–1945*' (Constable, 1997), while Jünger himself drew attention to his durable lifespan in one of the last of his many books '*Zweimal Halley*' (1987) ('Two-times Halley'). This referred to the fact that he had twice witnessed the passing of Halley's Comet, that traditional omen of cosmic disaster: once in 1910 as a teenager from his father's roof in Hanover, and then again in 1986 as an elderly globe trotter in Kuala Lumpur.

Jünger marched with the German century twice into the abyss and twice out again. He shared the unslaked thirst for adventure of his generation, born into the stuffy repressions of the late Wilhelmine empire. Unlike most of his contemporaries, however, he did something to quench that thirst while still in his teens: running away from his comfortable middle class home to join the

French Foreign Legion in the deserts of North Africa in 1913. Hauled out of the ranks only with some difficulty by his anxious father, Jünger again plunged into military adventure the following year with the outbreak of the Great War.

Four years as a front-line infantry officer in the trenches followed. Wounded fourteen times, decorated with the highest honour that the Kaiser's Germany could bestow, the Pour le Mérite medal, the coveted 'Blue Max', Jünger survived Langemarck, the Somme and countless other bloodlettings until, in his own estimation he became one of the élite of the élite. A 'stormtrooper', refined through constant meltings in the pitiless crucible of war until the residue that remained was the purest gold: the warrior in all his noble, pared-down essence.

In his first and most famous book, *Storm of Steel* (1920), drawn from his diaries and memories of front-line combat, Jünger, explicitly as well as implicitly, advanced the doctrine which was the seedbed of the Freikorps ideology, and in a cruder and more twisted form, that of National Socialism too. He believed that war, far from being the mass aberration or monstrous mistake seen by British writers such as Siegfried Sassoon or Wilfred Owen, or Jünger's own compatriot, the celebrated but untypical Erich Maria Remarque, was in fact a blessing for him and his genera-tion. After decades of stultifying, corrupting peace, war had burst upon Europe with all the destructive yet cleansing power of a thunderstorm.

'Now God be thanked who has matched us with his hour/ And caught our youth, and wakened us from sleeping' exalted Rupert Brooke, comparing Europe's youth streaming to the colours with 'Swimmers into cleanness leaping' while even Wilfred Owen looked forward to the war effecting 'A little useful weeding'. But Brooke and Owen were writing in 1914, *before* the 'cleanness' had become the slime-filled shellholes of Passchendaele. Brooke died in 1915, and long before he followed in the final week of the war, Owen had famously become the 'poet of pity'. But Jünger, who had seen and felt and tasted the slime, was still singing from Brooke's song-sheet in 1918, *after* the war had done its worst for four long years.

To be sure the war had been a test to destruction, but to Jünger those who survived this hardest of hard schools and knocks had become a caste of warrior-priests; charged by their dead comrades with the holy duty of transmitting the message of the blood sacrifice to future generations of Germans.

Yet Jünger is no tub-thumping Brookeian patriot disguising the stark reality of combat in clouds of windbagging rhetoric. He fully acknowledges and memorably describes the sheer horror of modern industrialised warfare: the shredded, eviscerated corpses, the stunning, mind-numbing pounding of high explosive shells, the stench, mud, blood and barbarism of the trenches. But – and here is the essential difference between his work and that of his British contemporaries – he welcomes it with a lover's ardent embrace. His unforgettable prose is informed, indeed saturated, with the overwhelming idea that war is the natural element of mankind. And that the war of the trenches, by virtue of its sheer harshness, had bred an entirely 'New Man', one destined to forge a new world.

Jünger elaborated his doctrines of war-worship and militarist nationalism in other books of the early 1920s and thanks to his writings and courageous combat record, became the intellectual Guru of the Freikorps, although he never participated in their violent activities, preferring to write, travel and study science at university. Unlike Hess, with his naïve and somewhat doglike idolisation of Hitler, there was always something of the aloof aristocrat about Jünger – as if he was holding the noxious riff-raff at bay with a knightly gauntlet.

Although he was courted by individual Nazis such as Goebbels, who could see the propaganda value of rallying this patriotic prince of the trenches to the party; and although he flirted with National Bolshevism, – a leftist variant of National Socialism which wanted to cement the Freikorps soldierly spirit to the cult of the worker emerging in Communist Russia, – Jünger was careful never to commit to the cause. 'I have chosen a high place' he told the National Bolshevik leader Ernst Niekisch at the time of Hitler's Night of the Long Knives purge 'from where I can watch people eating each other up like bugs'.

Jünger always regarded Hitler personally as an absurd, almost obscene clown, contemptuously dubbing him with the omnatopaeic nickname 'Kniebolo' in his private journals. It was fortunate for Jünger that the Führer did not know of this, since he held the author in high regard, even protecting him from those Nazis who wished to persecute him, in the same way that Stalin intervened to save the critical genius Mikhail Bulgakov from the Gulag which devoured so many other intellectuals.

The splinter of ice which Graham Greene said should be at the heart of every writer was certainly present in Jünger, yet this cold, vain man did not lack moral courage – as well as bravery of the physical variety. In 1939 on the eve of the Second World War he published a remarkable allegorical novel – allegory being one of the few avenues open to writers struggling to breathe in stifling totalitarian societies, witness Bulgakov's contemporaneous masterpiece *The Master and Margarita*. Like Bulgakov's novel, Jünger's *Auf den Marmorklippen* (On the Marble Cliffs) was an early example of the style we have come to know as magic realism, describing a dream-like world in which the artist plunges into the vast interior spaces of the imagination to describe an unbearable outer reality.

Jünger's book describes the slow overturning of an ordered, calm, contemplative society by the rampant forces of evil and barbarism. The two brothers at the centre of the story (a self-portrait of Jünger and his poet brother Friedrich-Georg) watch with the fascination of rabbits trapped in a juggernaut's headlights as the anarchic forces of the barbaric followers of the 'Chief Ranger' – a Hitlerian figure – bear down upon them. At the end, in a 1945 apocalypse, all is consumed in fire and storm, but not before the brothers have been afforded a glimpse of the Nazi heart of darkness – the extermination camp system. Jünger's slim novel is, among many other things, a work of prophecy: the war and Holocaust are clearly prefigured in its pages. It is a lament for religion and civilisation consumed in the torrential nihilism of National Socialism.

That is presumably why Goebbels had the book banned after it sold an unprecedented 50,000 copies. By then, just as the brothers in the book slip away from a final climactic battle with the Chief Ranger's savage hounds, Jünger himself had gone into internal exile: joining his old home, the army. Too late, he had seen where his wild calls for the overthrow of democracy could lead. He spent the war years in occupied Paris: rubbing shoulders with the likes of Celine, Cocteau, Braque and Picasso in fashionable salons, describing the ironies and privations of wartime in his diaries with his usual sense of distance, and discreetly mixing with his fellow officers plotting Hitler's destruction. His own eldest son, Ernstl, more seriously implicated than Jünger himself, was sent to a suicide squad in Italy and duly died. Jünger was merely sent home.

Jünger ended his second war with *The Peace*, a call for reconciliation and the construction of a new Europe by a new élite of civilised cosmopolitans. The young Teuton barbarian of 1920 had become one of Europe's Grand Old Men and, in extreme old age, more concerned with ecology than nationalism, a favoured guru of François Mitterrand and Helmut Kohl as they sought to build a new, and impeccably grey-suited Europe in which guns very definitely came behind butter.

The parallel lives but diverging fates of Hess and Jünger symbolise the Freikorps story and the two Germanies which gave them birth. The first edition of this book was written at a time when the Freikorps seemed to come from an incomparably remote era, an age apart from the present. Frozen into the ice age of the Cold War in which 1945 borders seemed sealed in permafrost, it was easy to imagine their world buried forever.

But time takes its whirligigs and its revenges. Since 1987 Europe has seen German re-unification – carried out, perhaps inevitably, on 9 November (1989), the day that saw the Kaiser's abdication (1918), the Beerhall Putsch (1923), and the *Kristallnacht* state-sponsored pogrom of the Jews (1938). Since then it has also seen, in Yugoslavia, its first ethnic war for half a century in which casualties and enforced mass migrations began to resemble 1945 levels.

Simultaneously the fires of ethnic civil strife even began to flicker in Germany itself – with the emergence from under their stones of a plethora of neo-Nazi groups, arson attacks on foreign 'asylum seekers' and (in the week in which I write) a first open assault on the Jews as a 'race of perpetrators' by an MP from the impeccably respectable Christian Democrats.

A symbolic figure of the new Germany is Horst Mahler, once the lawyer representing members of the Baader-Meinhof group, self-styled revolutionary Communists whose cop-killing, department-store burning, anti-American antics grabbed the headlines in the 1970s and 1980s. After serving time inside with his clients, Mahler re-emerged in his new guise: that of a born-again neo-Nazi, railing against Western materialism, Jewish capitalism and hailing the cleansing fires of 11 September 2001. The Freikorps would have recognised him as one of their own. Suddenly the past does not seem so distant or buried after all. And the future looks too grim to contemplate with equanimity.

THE MAIN FREIKORPS, THEIR LEADERS, DATES, FATE, SIZE AND INSIGNIA

This list gives the major Freikorps active in Germany between December 1918 and the summer of 1920. It should be noted that the formal dates of dissolution often did not mean the end of particular Freikorps' activity. Some were only dissolved in name to comply with Allied Disarmament Commission or German Government requests and were immediately reformed under alternate names or transparent 'covers' (sports associations, labour battalions, etc.). Others, like the Ehrhardt and Rossbach Freikorps, continued their activity as part of the political/criminal underground for several years, into the mid-1920s. Even the more official Generals' Freikorps that were absorbed into the Reichswehr wholesale continued to hanker after their freebooting days and to run memorial associations, journals, etc.

CATEGORY I – GENERALS' FREIKORPS

NAME & LEADER	DATES	FATE	SIZE & INSIGNIA
Badischen Volksheer Gen v. Pfeil & Gen v. Friedeburg	Jan 1919–	Became Reichswehr Brigade 13	Brigade strength
Deutsche Schutz Division Gen v. Wissel & Gen v.d. Lippe	Dec 1918– Apr 1919	Became Reichswehr Brigade 25	1,900 Stag's skull with antlers
Freiwillige Abteilung Haas Gen Haas	Feb 1919– Aug 1919	Became Reichswehr Brigade 13	2,300 Acorn & oakleaves
Freikorps Held Gen v. Held	Dec 1918–		
Freikorps Hulsen Gen v. Hulsen	Dec 1918– May 1919	Became Reichswehr Brigade 3	11,000 Acorn & oakleaves
Freiwillige Landesjägerkorps Gen Maercker	Dec 1918- Apr 1919	Became Reichswehr Brigade 16	Brigade strength Acorn & oakleaves
Landesschützenkorps Gen v. Raeder	Dec 1918– Apr 1919	Became Reichswehr Brigade 4	Brigade strength Circular wreath
Garde-Kavallerie Schützen-Division Gen v. Hofmann (Chief-of-Staff: Major Pabst)	Jan 1919– Apr 1919	Broken up. Absorbed into various Reichswehr units	Division strength Wreathed helmet on star over oakleaves
Freikorps Severin Gen Severin	Mar 1919– June 1920	Became Reichswehr Inf Regt 14/II	Battalion strength Oakleaves
2 Garde Infanterie Division Gen v. Friedeburg		Entered Reichswehr	Brigade strength
1 Sachsische Grenzjägerbrigade Gen v. Oldershausen		Became Reichswehr Inf Reg 10	Bugle in wreath

CATEGORY 2 – BORDERGUARD FREIKORPS

NAME & LEADER	DATES	FATE	SIZE & INSIGNIA
Freiwillige Inf Regt Courbiere Maj v. Oertzen & Maj Hartmann	Jan 1919– Jul 1919		Regimental strength 'Courbiere' on armband
Freikorps v. Aulock 1st Lt v. Auluck	Dec 1918– May 1919		305 Coloured 'V' chevron
Freikurps v. Brause Capt v. Brause	Apr 1919– June 1919	Became Reichswehr Inf Regt 40/I	310
Freiwillige Feld-Artillerie Regt No. 6	Jan 1919–		
Freikorps Brüssow Lt Hans Brüssow	Jan 1919– Apr 1919	Became Reichswehr Inf Regt 4	1,200 Totenkopf (death's head)
Freikorps Gerth 1st Lt Gerth	Apr 1919– June 1919	Became Reichswehr Inf Regt 40	625 Totenkopf on oval shield
Freikorps v. Diebitsch Lt v. Diebitsch	Apr1919– Dcc 1919	Became Reichswehr Inf Regt 102/II	948 Star on garter
Freikorps Dohna Capt Dohna	Mar1919– Aug 1919	Became Reichswehr Grenadier Regt 53/II	3,010
Freikorps Himburg/Iyck Capt Himburg	Jan 1919– Jul 1919	Became Reichswehr Inf Regt 39/III	Rampant stag on oval shield
Freikorps Hindenburg (Cunio) Capt Cunio	Jan 1919–	Became Reichswehr Inf Regt 39/II	'H' over oakleaves and acorn

CATEGORY 3 – NAVAL/MARINE FREIKORPS

NAME & LEADER	DATES	FATE	SIZE & INSIGNIA
1 Marine Brigade von Roden (Kiel) 'Iron Brigade' Col v. Roden	Nov 1918– May 1919	Members entered Navy, Labour groups, Ehrhardt Brigade & Shutztruppen Regt I	1,550 Anchor
2 Marine Brigade Ehrhardt (Wilhelmshaven) Lt Cmdr Hermann Ehrhardt	Feb 1919– May 1920	Members went into Navy, the Reichswehr or illegal political groups	5–6,000 Longship on waves over 'EHRHARDT' & oakleaves in oval rope wreath
3 Marine Brigade Löwenfeld (Kiel) Lt Cmdr Löwenfeld	Dec 1918– Jun 1920	Most members entered Navy, Reichswehr, security police or border/labour associations	Anchor on ribboned wreath

CATEGORY 4 – LOCAL & REGIONAL FREIKORPS

NAME & LEADER	DATES	FATE	SIZE & INSIGNIA
Freikorps Kuehme Capt Kuehme	Jan 1919–	Became Reichswehr Jäger Battalion 6	Eagle on star
Freikorps Lierau Capt Lierau	Jan 1919–		
Freikorps Negenborn Capt Negenborn		Became Reichswehr Inf Regt 40/IV	Battalion strength
Oberschliesen Freiwilligen Jägerkorps Lt Col v. Velsen & Maj v. Alt-Stutterheim	Nov 1918– Apr 1919		Regimental strength
Freikorps Paulssen 1st Lt Paulssen	Dec 1918– Jan 1920	Became Reichswehr mountain m/g battalion 201	935

NAME & LEADER	DATES	FATE	SIZE & INSIGNIA
Freikorps Petsch Capt Petsch	Jan 1919– Aug 1919	Amalgamated with Freikorps Hindenburg	
Festung Freikorps Thorn	Mar 1919–		
Freiwilliges Jägerkorps Graf Yorck v. Wartenburg	Jan 1919– Oct 1919	Became Reichswehr Jägerbattalion 20	Battalion strength Stag's skull & antlers crowned by cross
2 Freiwilligen Grenz Brigade			600
Saechs. Grenz- Jägerbattalion 7 & 12 Maj Graf Vitzthum v. Eckstaedt	Early 1919–	Became Reichswehr Inf Regts 37 & 38	Battalion strength
Freiwilligen Battalion 41 Ober Lt Weckmann	Jan 1919– May 1920	Became Reichswehr Inf Regts 2 & 39	560 Cross on shield with crooked arrows
Freikorps Aibling Capt Schaefer	May 1919 –		700
Wachtabteilung Bahrenfeld (Hamburg) Maj Fromm	Mar 1919– June 1919	Became Reichswehr Jaeger Battalion, Gross-Hamburg	Battalion strength
Freikorps Bamberg	Apr 1919– May 1919	Men joined Reichswehr Inf Regts 46 & 5	65
Freikorps Bayreuth	Apr 1919– June 1919	Became Reichswehr Inf Regt 46/III	525 Blue & white Bavarian chevron
Freikorps Bodensee	Apr 1919– June 1919	Became Reichswehr Inf Regt 43/III	151
Detachment Bogendorfer 1st Lt Ritter v. Bogendorfer	Apr 1919–	Amalgamated with Freikorps Epp to form Reichswehr Brigade 21	1,500 Acorn & oakleaves

NAME & LEADER	DATES	FATE	SIZE & INSIGNIA
Freikorps Chiemgau Capt Guertler	May 1919		Eagle's head
Freikorps Düsseldorf Capt Bentivegni	Apr 1919– Sept 1919	Part became Reichswehr Inf Regt 61/III, part entered Niederrhein Freikorps	848 Two four-leafed clovers
Freikorps Ebersberg- Grafing Capt Leeb	Apr 1919–	1,000	
Freikorps von Epp (Bayerischen Schutzenkorps) Col v. Epp (Chief-of-Staff: Capt Ernst Röhm)	Feb 1919– May 1919	Became Reichswehr Brigade 21 with several smaller Bavarian Freikorps	700 Lion's head
Freikorps Erlangen	Apr 1919– June 1919	Became Reichswehr Inf Regt 47 & Art Reg 42	Battalion strength Totenkopf
Abteilung Glasser Maj Glasser	Apr 1919–		1,500
Freikorps Gorlitz/Faupel Maj v. Unruh/Lt Col Faupel	Jan 1919–	Became Reichswehr Grenadier Regt 10	1,500 Chevron on oakleaves twined with 'Freikorps Faupel'
Freikorps Halle	Mar 1919– Jul 1919		1,200 Acorn and oakleaves over Halle coat of arms
Freikorps Göttingen		Became part of Reichswehr Inf Regt No 110	
Freikorps Hessen	Jan 1919–	Entered Reichswehr Inf Regt 15	'HFK' over oakleaves
Freikorps Hessen-Nassau	Mar 1919– May 1919	Became Reichswehr Inf Regt 22/III	'FKHN' over oaklcaves

NAME & LEADER	DATES	FATE	SIZE & INSIGNIA
Freikorps Hessische-Thüringisch-Waldeckisches Col v. Kornatzki	Jan 1919–Oct 1919	Joined Reichswehr Inf Regts II, 20, 21, 72, 90	1,323 Fernleaves
Freikorps Hilger (Freikorps Amsberg)	Apr 1919–Jul 1919	Became Reichswehr Inf Regt 47/III	408 Steel helmet surrounded by leaves
Abteilung Hutschenreuther Capt Hutschenreuther	Apr 1919		
Freikorps Landsberg Maj Mack	Apr 1919–May 1919	Became Reichswehr Rifle Regt 42/III	720 Bavarian arms on branch
Freikorps Münsterland		Joined Reichswehr Rifle Regt 13	
Freikorps Niederrhein		Amalgamated with Freikorps Düsseldorf	Decorative 'N' in leafed wreath
Freikorps Oberland Maj Ritter v. Beckh & Dr Friedrich Weber	Apr 1919–Oct 1919	Part joined Reichswehr Brigade 21 with other Bavarian Freikorps, part allied with SA and other paramilitary groups. (Reactivated & finally dissolved after Beerhall Putsch, Nov 1923)	4000
Freikorps Oldenburg		Became part of Reichswehr Inf Regt No 110	
Freikorps Passau Capt Gaul	Apr 1919–		
Freikorps Regensburg Maj Hendschel	Apr 1919–June 1919	Joined Reichswehr Inf Regt 48/I & Art Regt 24/II	Battalion strength City arms on shield

NAME & LEADER	DATES	FATE	SIZE & INSIGNIA

Abteilung Schaaf
  Maj Franz & Lt Col
  M. Schaaf
	Apr 1919–		

Abteilung Schad Maj Schad	Apr 1919-		600
Freikorps Schwaben Maj v. Pitrov	Apr 1919–	Became part of Reichswehr Inf Regt 43/II	650
Freikorps Thüringen	Feb 1919– May 1919	Became part of Reichswehr Inf Regt 21/II	700
Unteroffizier-Bereitschaft- Battalion Sachsens Sgt Hermann Voigt	Mar 1919–		Battalion strength
Walder Battalion Capts Jolas & Kreuzer	Apr 1919–		Battalion strength
Freikorps Wasserburg 1st Lt Schneider	Apr 1919–		650
Freikorps Werdenfels Maj v. Reiss	Apr 1919–		250 Lion's head
Freikorps Wesel		Became part of Reichswehr Regt 62	Regimental strength Crossed rifles in wreath
Westfaelisches Jäger Freikorps Maj Goetze		Became part of Reichswehr Jäger Battalion 7	
Freiwillige Battalion Wildermuth (Stuttgart) Lt Wildermuth			
Freikorps Wolf Lt Col Wolf	Apr 1919– Aug 1919	Joined Reichswehr Inf Regt 43	607 Wolf's head
Freikorps Würzburg	Apr 1919– June 1919	Some members joined Reichswehr Brigade 21	1,716 City Arms on leaves

NAME & LEADER	DATES	FATE	SIZE & INSIGNIA
Freikorps Schleswig-Holstein Naval Capt Roehr	Feb 1919– Aug 1919	Became Reichswehr Rifle Regt 18/IV	Province Arms on shield

CATEGORY 5 – OLD ARMY UNIT FREIKORPS

NAME & LEADER	DATES	FATE	SIZE & INSIGNIA
Freiwilligen Eskadron d. Braunschwig. Hussar Regt 17 Capt Krossa		(Entered Marine Brigade v. Roden shortly after formation.) Members became part of Reichswehr Cav Regt 40	
Freikorps Caspari (Old Imperial Inf Regt 17) Maj Caspari	Jan 1919–	Became part of Reichswehr Brigade No. 10	3,000
Freikorps Goslarer Jäger			
Freikorps Hacketau (Imperial Regt 16) 1st Lt Carl Menz		Became part of Reichswehr Inf Regt 14/I	Regimental strength 'H' on star
Freiwilligen Batterie d.2 Hannoverische Art Regt 1st Lt Pauli	Feb 1919	Entered Reichswehr Art Regt No.10	
Freikorps Hasse (Imperial Regts 99 & 129) Col. Ernst Hasse	Dec 1918– May 1919	Most members joined Reichswehr Inf Regt 108	1,400
Freiwilligen Battalion, Inf Regt 77	Jan 1919–	Entered Reichswehr Inf Regt 110 (Later I.R. 17)	Battalion strength
Freikorps Heydebreck Capt Heydebreck	Dec 1918–	Entered labour/forestry groups, or political underground	Battalion strength Crown
Detachment Kuentzel (Imperial Grenadier Regt 12 & Inf Regt 52)	Dec 1918	Entered Garde Kavallrie Schutzen Division (qv.)	

NAME & LEADER	DATES	FATE	SIZE & INSIGNIA
Freikorps Majer Capt Majer	Jan 1919– Autumn 1919	Became Heavy Artillery Bn 24 in provisional Reichswehr	550
Freikorps Potsdam (Imperial Guards Regts) Maj v. Stephani	Jan 1919– Mar 1919	Amalgamated with Freikorps Hülsen	Regimental strength Crossed swords behind steel helmet
Freikorps Reinhard (Also Freiwilligen Regt R) (2 & 4 Guards Regts) Col Reinhard	Jan 1919– May 1919	Became Inf Regt 29 & part of Reichswehr Brigade 15	Regimental strength rising to Brigade strength 'R' on shield over '1919' with leaf surround
Freikorps Schulz (8 Lothr Inf Regt 159) Maj Schulz	Feb 1919–	Became Westfälische Inf Regt Schulz, later a battalion of Reichswehr Regt 16	Reinforced Battalion strength Eagle

Schutztruppe Regt v.
Lettow-Vorbeck
  Gen v. Lettow-Vorbeck &
  Maj v. Menges
	May 1919–	Entered
		Reichswehr Inf
		Regt 79 & other
		Reichswehr units
			Regimental strength
			Lion's head on oval
			shield

Schwarze Jaeger or Schwarze Brigade (Formed of old Marine units)	?–Mar 1919	United with Reichswehr battalion Gross- Hamburg (Wachabteilung Barrenfeld) to become part of Reichswehr Inf Regt 18	Reinforced battalion strength

Detachment Stillfried
(Fusilier Regt 35)
  Lt Col Graf v. Stillfried
  und Rattonitz
	Jan 1919–	Became part of
		Reichswehr Inf
		Regt 5	

Battalion Suppe (2 Garde Regt) Sgt Suppe	Dec 1918–	Entered Reichswehr as part of Reinhard Brigade (qv)	Battalion strength

Freiwilligen Batterie Kochs (I Rhein Feld-Art Regt) Capt Kochs	Jan 1919– summer 1919	Became 5th Battery, 5th Art Regt	Battery strength

CATEGORY 6 – REPUBLICAN FREIKORPS

NAME & LEADER	DATES	FATE	SIZE & INSIGNIA
Abteilung Graeter Maj Graeter	Apr 1919–		1,600
Abteilung Denk Maj Denk	Apr 1919–		400
Freikorps Duena 1st Lt Kuhn & Maj v. Rochow	Nov 29 1918–Jan 1919		
Abteilung Heinzmann Maj Heinzmann	Apr 1919–		600
Inf. Geschutz Batterie Leder Lt Julius Leder			Battery strength
'Maikaefer' (Guards Fusiliers) Sgt Lt Schulze	Dec 1918–	Entered Reichswehr	
Freischutzenkorps Meyn Maj Meyn	Dec 1918– Jun 1919	Some members entered Reichswehr Jaeger Regt 32/I. Some entered Security Police	873
Abteilung Probstmayr (Freiwilligen Detachment Probstmayr) Maj Probstmayr	Apr 1919–	Joined Reichswehr Brigade 21	500 Acorn & oakleaves
Reichstag Regt	Jan 1919–	Entered Deutsche Schutz Div and thus into Reichswehr Brigade 15, Inf Regt 29	
Republikanische Schutztruppe München (Bayr. Repub. Schutztrupp) Volunteer Seyffertitz	Apr 1919–	100	

NAME & LEADER	DATES	FATE	SIZE & INSIGNIA
Württembergische Sicherheits Kompanie Lt d. R. Hahn	Feb 1919–		10 battalions, 3 squadrons, 8 batteries
Regiment Liebe Sgt d. R. Liebe			

CATEGORY 7 – BALTIC FREIKORPS
(Some of these units entered Reichswehr, but were expelled for refusing to leave Baltic.)

NAME & LEADER	DATES	FATE	SIZE & INSIGNIA
Badense. Assault Battalion Courland Maj Bockelmann			Battalion strength Coat of arms on oak branch
Schutzen Regt Baltenland			
Eiserne Schar Berthold Capt Rudolf Berthold	Apr 1919– spring 1920	Dissolved for part in Kapp Putsch	800 'B' in acorn wreath
Freikorps v. Brandis Capt Cordt v. Brandis	Jan 1919–	Stag's antler	
Eiserne Division Maj Bischoff	Nov 1918– Mar 1920	Dissolved for part in Kapp Putsch	Brigade strength Totenkopf
Freikorps Eulenberg Maj Graf v. Eulenberg	Feb 1919– Jul 1920	Entered various Reichswehr units	1,800 Eagle
Freiwilligen Jägercorps Goldingen Capt Berding	Nov 1918– Mar 1920	Dissolved for part in Kapp Putsch	Reinforced battalion strength oakleaves & acorns
Detachment Knie (Battalion Sudetenland)			
Detachment Jena			
Freikorps von Medem Capt v. Medem			Edelweiss

NAME & LEADER	DATES	FATE	SIZE & INSIGNIA
Freikorps v. Plehwe Capt v. Plehwe			
Freikorps Rieckhoff			
Freikorps Rossbach Capt Gerhard Rossbach	Nov 1918– Jan 1920	After formal dissolution, many members entered work battalions, forestry settlements, etc. Eventually allied with Nazi stormtroops & political paramilitary underground	992 Stag's skull surmounted by cross over chevron
Freikorps Stever Lt Cmdr Stever	Feb 1919– Jan 1920		923
Freikorps v. Wildemann (Baltische Landeswehr)			

CATEGORY 8 – MISCELLANEOUS

NAME & LEADER	DATES	FATE	SIZE & INSIGNIA
Kompanie Busch		Entered Reichswehr Rifle Regt 13	
Freiwilligen Offiziere Battalion			13 companies
Freikorps Gabcke Gen Maj Gabcke	Feb 1919– Sep 1920	Became part of Reichswehr Inf Regt 14/Ill	1,730 Acorn & oakleaves
Freiwilligen Abteilung Gené Capt Gené			'ZN' in wreath
Freikorps Feldmarshall v. Hindenburg Capt Otto & Maj v. Schleinitz	Mar1919– Oct 1919	Scattered through various Reichswehr units	765 'H' over acorn & oakleaves

NAME & LEADER	DATES	FATE	SIZE & INSIGNIA
Freikorps Hunicken or Freiwilligen Regt Hunicken Maj Hunicken	Mar 1919– Jul 1919	Became part of Reichswehr Rifle Regt 72	1,380 Sword on Maltese Cross over 'H'
Freikorps v. Klewitz Capt v. Klewitz	Apr 1919– Oct 1919	Became part of Reichswehr Inf Regt 6 (60) iv	872
Freikorps Lichtschlag Capt Lichtschlag	Dec 1918– Sep 1919	Became part of Reichswehr Rifle Regt 107	Regimental strength Horse on shield in wreath
Freikorps Löschebrand Capt Löschebrand	Jan 1919– Apr 1919		441 'L' in wreath with oakleaf background
Freikorps Lützow Maj v. Lützow	Jan 1919– Dec 1919	Became part of Reichswehr Jägar Battalion 30	1,376 Bugle
Freikorps Neufville (Garde-Landeschutzen-Abteilung-Neufville) Capt Freiherr v. Neufville	Jan 1919–		Initials in wreath
Freikorps Osterroht Capt Osterroht	Feb 1919– May 1919	Became Third Company of Reichswehr Jäger Battalion 3	635
Freikorps v. Oven Col v. Oven	Jan 1919–	Became part of Reichswehr Inf Regt 91	Decorative 'O'
Freikorps Pfeffer Capt Pfeffer v. Salomon	Jan 1919– Nov 1919	Entered Reichswehr Inf Regts 62 & 16	3,176 Rearing horse
Freikorps Thummel (Freischar Thummel) Lt Col Thummel	Mar 1919– May 1919	Entered Reichswehr Brigade 25	887 Ice hammer between two stars
Freiwilligen Regt Tuellmann Capt Tuellmann			Regimental strength
Abteilung Voigthenleitner Capt Voigthenleitner	Apr 1919–		350

NAME & LEADER	DATES	FATE	SIZE & INSIGNIA
Freikorps Liftl Capt Liftl		Became Inf Gun Battery 44 in Reichswehr	300
Sturmbattalion Schmidt Capt Schmidt		Joined Reichswehr Grenadier Regts	Battalion strength Steel helmet over crossed rifles & grenades
Ost-Preussische Freiwilligen Jägerkorps			Antler on oval crest
Ostpreussische Jäegerkorps Gieseler Capt Gieseler			Stag's head on oakleaves
Friekorps Königsberg			Crossed swords behind steel helmet in oval wreath
Freischar Lautenbacher Capt Lautenbacher			'L'
Freikorps Hübner Capt Hübner			Mailed fist holding sword in circular wreath
Freiwilligen Detachment Doithenleitner Lt Doithenleitner			Lion's head in oakleaves
Freiwilligen Battalion Bulow Capt v. Bulow			Battalion strength Upraised dagger in wreath over 'B'
Freiwilligen Detachment v. Tschirdewitz Capt v. Tschirdewitz			'T' in oval wreath over crossed swords
Freikorps v. Liebermann Capt v. Liebermann			'L' under crown
Freiwilligen Battalion v. Waltzen Capt v. Waltzen			Battalion strength Horn with star on leafed background
Freiwilligen Detachment v. Schauroth Maj v. Schauroth			Totenkopf

NAME & LEADER	DATES	FATE	SIZE & INSIGNIA
Freiwilligen Detachment Michael			Stag's head
Freiwilligen Battalion Poensgen Capt Poensgen			Battalion strength 'P' in wreath surmounted by crown
Freiwilligen Battalion Henke 1st Lt Henke			Battalion strength 'H 'in wreath
Badische Sturm Battalion		Joined Reichswehr Grenadier and local Baden regiments	Battalion strength Shield on leaves
Freikorps v. Petersdorff Col v. Petersdorff			'P' on oval wreath
Minenwerfer Detachment Heuschkel Sgt Heuschkel			Totenkopf over initials in oakleaves
Freikorps Anhalt			Bear
Freiwilligen Sturm Lehr-regiment			Regimental strength Steel helmet over star in decorative garter
Maschinengewehr Scharfschutzen Korps Pren Capt Pren			Shield and three arrows
Freiwilligen Division Gerstenberg Lt Col Gerstenberg			Brigade strength Iron Cross
Freiwilligen Regt Klüfer Sgt Klüfer	1919		Regimental strength Bear or lion's paw
Sturmbattalion Heinz Capt Heinz	1919–1920	Many members entered labour groups and/or political underground	Battalion strength Anchor in wreath over ribbon

NB: This list does not include the various fully-fledged Freikorps air squadrons which fought in the Baltic, Berlin, Silesia and other locations. Some of these units later entered the Reichswehr air arm.

APPENDIX B

FREIKORPS MEMBERS PROMINENT IN NAZI GERMANY

This list of Freikorps fighters who went on to find fame in the Third Reich is not comprehensive; but it does show the large numbers of volunteers and Freebooters who 'graduated' into the NSDAP. Another remarkable feature of the list is the high number of ex-Freikorps men who later, for various reasons, found themselves in opposition to the Führer and his policy.

BORMANN, MARTIN (1900–45?): Head of the Nazi party Chancellery, Private Secretary to Hitler, and effectively the Führer's deputy after he had frozen out his rivals – Goering and Himmler – by controlling their access to their chief. He joined the Rossbach Freikorps in Mecklenburg as a Section leader and quartermaster. He had some hand in the 'Feme' murder campaign and was jailed for a year in March 1924 for his part in the brutal murder of Walther Kadow, his own former schoolteacher, who had allegedly betrayed the Nazi martyr on the Ruhr, Albert Leo Schlageter. Bormann's accomplice in the killing was Rudolf Hoess (qv).

CANARIS, WILHELM (1887–1945): Admiral, and Chief of German Military Intelligence, the Abwehr, until his eclipse by his friend and rival the ruthless Heydrich (qv). Always an ambiguous figure, Canaris combined staunch reactionary nationalism with nervous opposition activity against the Nazis. He may have been a double agent working for Britain. For his Freikorps involvement, see pp. 80–2.

CONTI, LEONARDO (1900–45): Reich Health Leader and a proponent of 'racist medicine', euthanasia and the extermination of the Jews, Conti hung himself while awaiting trial for crimes against humanity at Nuremberg. His Freikorps career compassed membership ofthe Horse Guards Division (the killers of Liebknecht and Luxemburg); the Deutscher Schutz-und-Trutz Bund, and the Berlin branch of the O.C. murder organisation.

DALUEGE, KURT (1897–1946): Daluege was C in C of Police in the German Reich and after Heydrich (qv) was murdered, he became Deputy Protector of Bohemia and Moravia, responsible for the reprisal massacre of Lidice village. Second only to Himmler (qv) in the Police, he played the main part in undermining the independence of the force, and centralising it under Nazi control. A World War One stormtrooper, Daluege, like Bormann, was a section leader of the Rossbach Freikorps, joining the party in 1922 and becoming Berlin founder of the SA. He was executed by the Czechs for his atrocities against their countrymen.

DARRE, RICHARD-WALTHER (1895–1953): Reich Farmers' Leader and Minister of Food and Agriculture in the Third Reich. An artillery officer on the Western Front in the Great War, Darre joined the Berlin Freikorps. He was the main advocate of the Nazi 'Blood and Soil' ideology, recommending a return to the land and praising the peasantry as the core of the German race. His theories became discredited as the war squeezed the German economy and he fell into disfavour. He was jailed for five years by the Nuremberg tribunals.

DIETRIECH, SEPP (1892–1966): The brutal, jovial, ruthless Bavarian peasant who was one of Hitler's earliest bodyguards and went on to successfully command an SS Panzer Army in Normandy and Belgium. He was responsible for many wartime atrocities including the Malmedy massacre of American soldiers during the Battle of the Bulge in December 1944. He was sentenced to life imprisonment for his role in that crime but was freed in 1955. Re-arrested by a German court the following year, he was given 19 months jail for his part in the murder of Röhm and the SA leadership in 1934. He was freed again in 1959 and died seven years later. Dietrich was a member of the Oberland Freikorps and one of the earliest recruits to the Nazis.

DÜSTERBERG, THEODOR (1875–1950): Co-founder with Seldte (qv) of the 'Stahlhelm' in December 1918, Düsterberg had been a Lieutenant-Colonel in World War One. Düsterberg ran as Nationalist candidate against Hitler in the 1932 Presidential elections when the Nazis revealed he was of part-Jewish descent. He withdrew from the race and subsequently refused Hitler's offer of a Cabinet post. Sent to a concentration camp in 1934 for criticising the Night of Long Knives purge, he nonetheless managed to survive the Third Reich.

EPP, FRANZ XAVER, RITTER VON, (1868–1947): Formally joined the Nazi party in 1928 becoming Governor of Bavaria and

Head of the Colonial Policy office. He fell out with Himmler and Heydrich and lost most of his power, dying in a U.S. internment camp. For his Freikorps involvement see pp. 151–58.

FALKENHORST, NIKOLAUS VON (1885–1968): A Freikorps member in 1919 after Great War Service, Falkenhorst rose in the ranks of the Reichswehr and commanded German forces occupying Norway from 1940–44. A British military tribunal condemned him to death in 1946 for ordering the execution of British commandos, but the sentence was commuted to 20 years' jail. He was released in 1953.

FRANK, HANS (1900–46): A member of the von Epp Freikorps, he became an SA stormtrooper and took part in the Beerhall putsch. He became the leading Nazi lawyer, defending Hitler in numerous court cases before 1933, and was appointed head of the party's legal office. After the Nazi seizure of power he became Minister of Justice. In 1939, he was appointed Governor-General of conquered Poland and was responsible for the ruthless genocide of Poles and Jews alike. In 1942, he questioned the party's misuse of justice and was stripped of all power. Tried at Nuremberg, he confessed his guilt and expressed contrition for his crimes before his execution.

FRICK, WILHELM (1877–1946): As head of Munich's political police after 1919, the colourless bureaucrat Frick covered up the crimes of Freikorps murder gangs. He took a major part in the Beerhall putsch. He became head of the Nazi party in the Reichstag, and was appointed Minister of the Interior in Hitler's 1933 Cabinet. In this post he suppressed all political opposition to the regime before his power was superseded by that of Himmler (qv). He was hanged by the Nuremberg tribunal.

GREISER, ARTUR (1897–1946): A Naval officer in the Great War, Greiser joined a Baltic Freikorps, and set up the Stahlhelm in Danzig in 1924. He joined the party and both the SA and SS in 1929, becoming an SS General and party leader in the Danzig district. As local Gauleiter after 1939, he was responsible for expelling and murdering Poles, Balts and Jews. Fleeing to the Bavarian Alps at the end of the war, he was sent back to Poland by the Americans, tried, and executed near his former palace in Poznan, after being paraded round the town in a cage.

GROENER, GEN. WILHELM (1867–1939): With his right-hand man, General Schliecher (qv), Groener presided over the creation of the Freikorps, and provided them with army funds, weapons, uniforms and training. Nevertheless, he was that rare bird, a high ranking officer who was totally loyal to the democratic state. Groener served the Weimar Republic in a number of Ministerial posts, including the Interior and Defence. An opponent of the Nazis, Groener banned the SA in 1932, but was forced to rescind the measure and resign. See pp 24–45, 164.

HELLDORF, WOLF HEINRICH, GRAF VON (1896–1944): Police Chief of Berlin and a member of the anti-Nazi resistance, Helldorf served on the Western Front in the Great War, winning the Iron Cross (First and Second Class.). A member of the Rossbach Freikorps, he took part in the Kapp Putsch, after which he fled to exile in Italy for four years. He joined the party in 1926, and subsequently both the SA and SS, becoming a General in the latter organisation. In July 1935, he became Berlin's Police President. He was notorious for racketeering, including extorting large sums from Jews in return for providing them with passports. Late in the day he joined the anti-Hitler resistance, and suffered torture and execution following the failure of the July Plot in 1944.

HESS, RUDOLF (1894–1987): Along with Ernst Jünger the sole major figure from the Freikorps period to survive into the late 1980s (see pp. 154, 271–74). Never exactly a towering intellect, Hess was given the titular post of deputy Party leader, where his main role was acting as Hitler's cheerleader and warm-up man. Superseded in the war years by his more ruthless rivals.

HEYDRICH, REINHARD (1904–42): The most feared, brutal, intelligent and unscrupulous Nazi of them all (even Hitler called him 'The man with the Iron Heart'), Heydrich was attached to Maercker's Freikorps as a teenage auxiliary messenger in his native Halle. He began a Naval career, was disgraced, and took a job in the SS organisation, where he formed close links with both Himmler and Canaris. He organised many of the Night of Long Knives killings in 1934. Head of the Berlin Gestapo, and then head of the Nazi intelligence service, the SD. Initiated the 'Final Solution' against the Jews by first isolating them in ghettoes, then by exterminating them outright. Assassinated by Czechs.

HIMMLER, HEINRICH (1900–45): Heydrich's rival in sheer evil, the mediocre former poultry farmer rose to become overlord of the SS Gestapo, the most hated network of repression of all time. Missing the Great War, Himmler joined a para-military group, and carried a flag in the Beerhall putsch. In January 1929, he became chief of Hitler's bodyguard, the SS, which he speedily built into an élite corps of fanatical Nazi zealots.

HOEPNER, ERICH (1886–1944): General and leading anti-Nazi resistant, Hoepner took part in the Kapp Putsch and Freikorps activity as a young officer. By the outbreak of World War Two he was a convinced anti-Nazi. A successful tank commander, he was nevertheless dismissed for his failure to take Moscow in December 1941. Stripped of the right to wear uniform by a furious Führer,

Hoepner turned to full-time conspiracy. After the July plot he was arrested, put on trial, tortured and eventually hanged.

HOESS, RUDOLF (1900–47): Notorious commander of Auschwitz extermination camp, Hoess had a valiant Great War record, becoming the youngest NCO in the German army at age 17, and winning the Iron Cross (First and Second Class.) In 1919 he joined the East Prussian Volunteer Freikorps for the defence of Germany's eastern borders, and then attached himself to Rossbach's Freikorps. With Bormann (qv) he took part in a brutal revenge killing of an alleged Freikorps 'traitor', which earned him a ten-year jail term, although he was amnestied after five years. He joined the SS in 1934.

JÜNGER, ERNST (1895–1998): One of the greatest and most original German writers of his time, Jünger was also a renaissance man: scientist, soldier, traveller, adventurer, pioneer of hallucinogenic drugs, and a political, military and social theorist of the first rank. As one of the most highly-decorated of officers in the Great War (Pour le Mérite, Iron Cross First and Second Class, wounded fourteen times) Jünger emerged from the carnage of the trenches with a theory of total war as the natural element for modern man. A prophet of technological society, Jünger combined hard nihilism with a lush romanticism in a uniquely disturbing way. His war memoirs became the Bible of the Freikorps generation, and his calls to action, violence and energy the raw materials of proto-fascism. He dabbled in extremist politics throughout the twenties. At one time he was close to Rossbach and Goebbels, at another, he tried to marry Prussian militarism to Bolshevik modernism. Perceiving the truly bestial nature of Nazism, he held aloof from the party, spurning invitations to become an NSDAP MP. He wrote a remarkable allegory of the destruction of Hitlerism before rejoining the Army in 1940 and being posted to Paris. He joined the anti-Hitler officers' circles, and was dismissed from military service after the July plot. His eldest son was sent to a suicide squad. Jünger continued to write prolifically, and won the coveted Goethe prize in 1983.

KAUFMANN, KARL (1900–?): Gauleiter of Hamburg, Kaufmann was an inner member of the Ehrhardt Brigade, taking part in the Feme murder campaign as an O.C. gunman. He also served as an anti-French saboteur in the Ruhr. Gauleiter of the Rhineland in the early thirties, he was stripped of party offices after accusations of embezzlement. Restored to rank as an SS General, Kaufmann became a Hamburg businessman after the war until his murky past was uncovered in 1948. A derisory 18-month jail sentence followed. Arrested twice more in the early fifties, he was finally freed in 1953.

KEITEL, WILHELM (1882–1946): The most subservient of all the Generals to Hitler, Keitel's supine obedience to the Führer's craziest edicts earned him the derisory nicknames 'Nickesel' (Nodding donkey), or 'Lakeitel' (Lackey). His crawling also won him the position of Chief of Staff of the High Command throughout the war. Severely wounded as a Great War artillery officer, Keitel was a Freikorps member in 1919 before rejoining the Reichswehr. Hanged for war crimes at Nuremberg.

KILLINGER, MANFRED, VON (?–1944): Storm leader of the inner circle of the Ehrhardt brigade, Killinger took part in the liberation of Munich, the Kapp Putsch, and was chief planner of the O.C. murder campaign, including the killings of Erzberger and Rathenau. Later leader of the Viking Bund secret society. Under the Third Reich, he became an SS General, a Judge of the People's Court, and German ambassador to Slovakia and finally Rumania. Committed suicide in Bucharest as the Red army approached.

LIST, WILHELM (1880–1971): A General Staff officer in the Great War, List was an active Freikorps fighter in 1919. As a Wehrmacht General he took part in the Austrian anschluss, and the invasion of Poland. After the attack on Russia, in which he commanded an Army Group, List was sacked by Hitler for failing to break through in the Caucasus. Tried at Nuremberg. List received a life jail term, but was freed in 1963.

LORENZ, WERNER (1891–1974): Head of the SS department dealing with Germans abroad, the Volksdeutsche Mittelstelle, Lorenz was a cadet officer and pilot in World War One. Active in the Freikorps, he joined the NSDAP in the early days. As head of the Mittelstelle, Lorenz used fifth-column techniques to destroy and undermine anti-Nazi resistance. Sentenced to 20 years jail as a war criminal in 1948, Lorenz was amnestied in 1955.

MILCH, ERHARD (1892–1972): Munitions Chief of the Luftwaffe, Milch served as a pilot in the Great War before joining the Freikorps, and commanding an air squadron in East Prussia. The Luftwaffe's main technocratic innovator, Milch was mainly responsible for moulding and modernising the force into a formidable weapon of war. Tried as a war criminal, he was jailed for life, but amnestied, and resumed a successful career as an industrialist.

NIEMOLLER, MARTIN (1892–1984): One of the leading figures of the anti-Nazi resistance, Niemoller began his career as a staunch nationalist, serving as a U-Boat commander in World War One, and winning the Pour le Mérite for his bravery. As theological student at Münster, he organised his own volunteer Freikorps, and took part in the suppression of the Red Ruhr rising. Sympathetic to Nazism in its early days, as an influential Protestant Pastor in Berlin Niemoller took an early stand against

Hitlerism after the seizure of power. Eventually sent to a concentration camp where he remained for seven years, his nationalism probably saving him from death. After he was freed in 1945, he resumed his career as Germany's leading churchman, crowning his work with the Presidency of the World Council of Churches in the sixties.

OBERG, KARL (1897–1965): Head of the SS in occupied France, Oberg had an outstanding Great War record, receiving the Iron Cross (First and Second Class). He took part in the Kapp Putsch in 1920, and the next year became business manager of the ORGESCH para-military group in Flensburg, and a link-man between the para-militaries and Reichswehr. Bankrupted as a businessman, he started a second career in the SS and rose to be one of Heydrich's right-hand men. Sentenced to death and extradited to France, he was eventually tried in 1954, and the death sentence was commuted to life imprisonment.

RENN, LUDWIG (1889–1979): He served in World War One as an infantry commander, and recorded his vivid experiences in his book *Krieg*. He was a Freikorps man in 1919, but gave up a Reichswehr commission in 1920 to devote himself to writing. By the end of the 1930s, Renn was a committed Communist. Arrested and jailed after the Reichstag fire, Renn fled to Swiss exile two years later and became chief of staff of the Eleventh International Brigade in the Spanish Civil War. After 1945, he settled in East Germany where he became a leading cultural guru of the socialist state.

RÖHM, ERNST (1887–1934): A Great War officer disfigured by wounds, Röhm was a swaggering, ugly buccaneer who combined physical toughness with effeminate homosexuality, thinking himself a pure military man, and despising communists and bourgeoisie alike. As ADC to Epp, responsible for nurturing Bavaria's myriad Freikorps and paramilitary groups and channelling them arms and cash. He was chiefly responsible for militarising the Nazi party, welding the SA into a massive street army of more than three million men. Began to advocate a 'Second Revolution' which would amalgamate SA and Army under the former's control. The Army and SS united to thwart the threat; Röhm died in the subsequent Night of the Long Knives.

SALOMON, ERNST VON (1902–72): Apostle and bard of the Freikorps spirit. A ruthless activist who did not stop at murder, Salomon was also a writer of undeniable power. For his early Freikorps career see pp. 122–37, 195–96, 200–28. The advent of National Socialism disappointed him, and he concentrated on a successful career as a film script-writer. Arrested by the Americans after the war, he wrote a sarcastic attack on the Allied occupation, which revealed him as an unrepentant anti-democrat and neo-fascist.

SCHLIECHER, KURT VON (1882–1934): Along with Röhm and Strasser, one of the most prominent victims of the Night of Long Knives, Schliecher was also one of the founders of the Freikorps system, which he helped his superior Groener to organise. Throughout the Weimar years, Schliecher perfected the arts of backstairs intrigue and Cabinet-breaking. Utterly amoral, Schliecher was never a Nazi, but over-estimated his ability to control and manipulate the movement.

SCHULTZE, WALTHER ('BUBI') (1894–1979): Head of the Association of University Lecturers under the Third Reich, Schultze was an aviator in the Great War and, after being wounded and discharged, joined the Epp Freikorps. He was a party member from the outset, and organised Hitler's temporary escape after the Beerhall Putsch. At this time he was head physician to the SA. As a doctor and don, he drove Jews from higher education in Germany, and approved euthanasia experiments, for which he was jailed for four years in 1960. Completely unrepentant, he died in 1979.

SELDTE, FRANZ (1882–1947): A chemical manufacturer and wartime officer who lost an arm on the Somme, Seldte founded the Stahlhelm society of war veterans in December 1918. Next to the Nazi SA, the Stahlhelm was the most powerful of the right-wing para-military organisations, tending to attract older and better disciplined recruits and espousing a marginally milder nationalism. The organisation was eventually forcibly amalgamated with the SA, and Seldte became Minister of Labour in 1933, a position he maintained to the end of the Third Reich.

SPERRLE, HUGO (1885–1953): Air Force Marshal, Sperrle joined the air force in the Great War, and commanded a Freikorps air detachment. He led the German Condor Legion that intervened on Franco's side in the Spanish Civil War and was responsible for the razing of Guernica, the first mass terror air raid in history. In charge of air operations against Britain in the Battle of Britain and the Blitz, he also commanded the air arm of the Afrika Korps in the Desert War. He went on to command the aerial opposition to the D-Day landings, with dwindling success. Tried at Nuremberg, the Marshal was acquitted of war crimes and released.

STRASSER, GREGOR (1892–1934), and OTTO (1897–1974): With Röhm, the Strasser brothers represented the 'Trotskyist' strain in the Nazi movement – revolutionary purists, who believed in a third way between Capitalism and Communism and who took the Socialist aspects of the party programme seriously. The Strassers set up their own Freikorps in their native Bavaria before joining the party under Hitler's influence. They never fell wholly under the Führer's spell, however, and like Röhm they were too popular as potential rivals to let live. Gregor was killed in the Night of Long Knives, Otto fled into impotent exile.

STUCKART, WILHELM (1902–53): Fought with the Epp Freikorps and was jailed by the French as a Ruhr saboteur. An early party member and legal adviser, as State Secretary in the Interior Ministry from 1935 Stuckart drew up the Nuremberg laws, codifying persecution of the Jews. A fanatic racial purist, he approved sterilisation and then extermination of 'inferiors'. Detained for four years after the war, on his release Stuckart died in a car 'accident' near Hanover, the probable victim of an anti-Nazi revenge team.

WAGNER, GERHARDT (1878–1938): Leader of National Socialist Doctors, a Freikorps fighter, he was a protégé of Hess, who encouraged his racial manias. He initiated euthanasia schemes against Jews and the physically and mentally handicapped.

WINNIG, AUGUST (1878–1956): A rare example of a Social Democrat turned Nazi, Winnig headed the pre-Great War Mason's union. As SPD Minister-plenipotentiary in the Baltic after 1918, Winnig thoroughly approved the private Freikorps war there, and was expelled from the SPD for supporting the Kapp Putsch. He turned to literary work, extolling the virtues of the 'volk' and hailing the advent of Hitler. A convinced Christian, he opposed the party's anti-Church activities and lapsed into disillusioned silence.

WOLFF, KARL (1900–84): Chief of SS and Police in occupied Italy. From 1918–20 he was a Lieutenant in the Hessian Freikorps. Adjutant to von Epp and Himmler's Chief of Staff,

Wolff rose rapidly in the SS ranks. Unwisely published his memoirs during the Eichmann trial, thus drawing attention to himself. Despite a respectable front as a wealthy businessman, he was accused of sending 300,000 Jews to their deaths at Treblinka, and of war crimes on the Eastern Front. Sentenced to fifteen years' penal servitude in 1964, he was released in 1971. Shortly before his death, he played a prominent part in the forging and marketing of the fake 'Hitler Diaries' to *Stern* Magazine.

SELECTIVE BIBLIOGRAPHY

For an English readership I have confined myself mainly to works by British or American authors, except where translations exist of German texts.

The best overall survey of the period is Harold Gordon's *The Reichswehr and the Genman Repuhlic 1919–26* (Princeton, 1957), a scholarly and exhaustive work whose only fault is a tendency to see events through the eyes of the regular Reichswehr and, thus, to underrate both the irregular Freikorps and the political Left. The same criticism can be directed at F. L. Carsten's *The Reichswehr and Politics 1918–33* (Oxford, 1966), which covers similar ground. Far and away the best survey of the Freikorps proper – indeed the only extant account of the movement in English – is Robert G. L. Waite's *Vanguard of Nazism: The Free Corps Moment in Post-War Germany* (Harvard, 1952). Professor Waite's invaluable book gives a short narrative account of the Freikorps campaigns and admirably explains their place in

German politics. Apart from one or two errors such as killing off Gerhard Rossbach in 1934 (he survived until 1967), I found it faultless. As one would expect from an author who later served as a minor minister in the collaborationist Vichy Government, Robert Benoist-Mechin's *History of the German Army since the Armistice* (Zurich, 1939) suffers from a strong right-wing bias. The book is however invaluable in its detailed account of Freikorps military operations. A left-wing counterblast is Chris Harman's *The Lost Revolution: Germany 1918–23* (London, 1982), which offers a revolutionary Socialist perspective, but is good on the Spartacus risings and the Red Army of the Ruhr. Richard M. Watt's *The Kings Depart: The Tragedy of Germany: Versailles and the German Revolution* (London, 1969) offers a compelling and sweeping account of the story from the Armistice to the Kapp Putsch: a marvellous book. James M. Diehl's *Paramilitary Politics in Weimar Germany* (Bloomington, Indiana, 1977) is particularly illuminating on the groupings outside the Freikorps such as the Stahlhelm, the Orgesch and the Republican Wehr. Sebastian Haffner's *Failure of a Revolution: Germany 1918/19* (London, 1973) offers a brisk account from a radical left-wing viewpoint. It is particularly notable for its vitriolic condemnation of Ebert, Noske and the SPD's 'betrayal' of the revolution. A. J. Ryder's *The German Revolution of 1918–19* (Cambridge, 1967) offers much the same perspective from a more academic angle.

The Armistice negotiations and the collapse of the Kaiser are well covered in three recent books which go over much the same ground: *No Man's Land* by John Toland (London, 1982), *November 1918* by Gordon Brook-Shepherd (London, 1983), and *A Stillness Heard Around the World* by Stanley Weintraub (London, 1986).

The mutiny in the Imperial Fleet which sparked the Revolution is excellently recounted in *Mutiny on the High Seas* by Daniel

Horn (London, 1973) and *The Collapse of Power: Mutiny in the High Seas Fleet* by David Woodward (London, 1973). The revolutionary events in Berlin are memorably told by a participant and eye-witness, the balanced, cool and civilised Count Harry Kessler in his *Diaries of a Cosmopolitan* (London, 1971). There is much valuable eye-witness material, too, in *Before the Deluge* by Otto Friedrich (London, 1972).

The story of the Munich Soviet is told in a number of accounts, most authoritatively by Allan Mitchell in *Revolution in Bavaria* (Princeton, 1969) and by Richard Grunberger's *Red Rising in Bavaria* (London, 1973). An account of events from the point of view of official Communism can be found in Ruth Fischer's *Stalin and German Communism* (Cambridge, Mass., 1948).

Of biographies and autobiographies of participants, I have found useful: *Hindenburg: The Wooden Titan* by Sir John Wheeler-Bennett (London, 1936) and D. J. Goodspeed's *Ludendorff* (Boston, 1966). Peter Nettl's *Rosa Luxemburg* (London, 1966) is probably the clearest account of the charismatic Spartacist leader. (Margarethe von Trotha's recent film *Rosa Luxemburg* is powerful, if over-sympathetic and tending towards sentimentality.) Noske's short memoir *Von Kiel Bis Kapp* (Berlin, 1920), is indispensable, if tendentious. Ernst Röhm's *Die Geschichte eines Hochverräters* (Munich, 1933) is guilelessly revealing. Klaus Epstein's *Matthias Erzberger and the Dilemma of German Democracy* (New York, 1959) is an excellent biography of that ambiguous but strangely sympathetic figure. General Groener wrote his memoirs in *Lebenserinnerungen* (Gottingen, 1957) and his daughter Dorothea Groener-Geyer wrote a biography *General Groener – Soldat und Staatsmann* (Frankfurt, 1955). Karl Meyer's *Karl Liebknecht: Man Without a Country* (Washington, 1957) is a sympathetic study.

Of books openly sympathetic to the Freikorps, Maercker's memoirs *Vom Kaiserheer zur Reichswehr* (Leipzig, 1921) is the most moderate. The three 'official' histories of the Freikorps, published under the Third Reich, are: Ernst von Salomon's *Das Buch vom Deutschen Freikorps-Kämpfer* (Berlin, 1938), a massive tome, lavishly illustrated, comprising detailed histories of all the Freikorps campaigns, often grandiosely over-written by the participants, illustrated with the insignia of almost all the individual Freikorps, and portraits of their Führers. More manageable, but no less bombastic and propagandist in tone, are Edgar von Schmidt-Pauli's *Geschichte der Freikorps* (Stuttgart, 1936) and Friedrich von Oertzen's similar *Die Deutschen Freikorps* (Munich, 1939). More revealing and illustrating are Salomon's autobiographical *Die Geächteten* ('The Outlaws') (London, 1931), a work of real literary merit, and his post-war *Die Fragebogen* ('The Questions') (NewYork, 1954) in which his undimmed nationalist faith is re-stated. Other revealing works by men associated with the movement include F. W. Heinz's *Sprengstoff* ('Explosives') (Berlin, 1930), Manfred von Killinger's *Das Waren Kerle!* ('These were Men!') (Munich, 1944), Ferdinand Freiherr von Ledebur's *Geschichte des Deutschen Unteroffiziere* ('History of the German Junior Officers') (Berlin, 1939), Curt Hozel's *Deutscher Aufstand* ('German Uprising') (Stuttgart, 1934), and Franz Schauwecker's *Im Todesrachen* ('Revenge for Death') (Halle, 1919). Valuable works on the 'Front Line spirit' which informed the Freikorps ideology include almost all the early writings of Ernst Jünger, especially his *In Stahlgewittern* ('Storm of Steel') (tr. London 1929), *Das Waldchen 125* ('Copse 125') (tr. London 1930), *Der Kampf Als Innere Erlebnis* ('The Conflict as Inner Experience') (Berlin, 1933) and *Krieg und Krieger* ('War and Warriors') (Berlin, 1930), an anthology edited jointly by Jünger and von Salomon. A modern work of scholarship which is also intensely readable is Robert Wohl's *The Generation of 1914* (London, 1977). It is most informative and interesting on the mixture of militarism and idealism that motivated the front-line generation in all European countries.

There is little on the Kapp Putsch in English, but Gabriele Kruger's *Die Brigade Ehrhardt* (Hamburg, 1971) probes the most notorious of all the Freikorps, and casts light on its shadowy role in the murder gangs that took the lives of Erzberger, Rathenau and others. Count Kessler's biography of his friend *Rathenau* (Berlin, 1928) is an elegant elegy. There is almost too much on the early days of the Nazi party, but mention must be made of the three basic biographies of Hitler in English: those of John Toland (London, 1978), Joachim Fest (London, 1982) and Alan Bullock (London, 1969). Heinz Hohne's *The Order of the Death's Head* (London, 1969) is an exhaustively documented account of the birth of the SA and SS and the same author's *Canaris* (London, 1979) is an enormously detailed portrait of one of the pivotal figures of the epoch. John Dornberg's *The Putsch that Failed* (London, 1979) and Harold Gordon's *The Beerhall Putsch* (Princeton, 1972) give penetrating and authoritative accounts of Hitler's abortive bid for power in November 1923. Finally, Hans-Joachim W. Koch's *Der Deutsche Bürgerkrieg* (Berlin, 1978) gives the best contemporary summing-up of the Freikorps story from a German source.

Literary works spawned by the period 1918–23 include Erich Maria Remarque's *The Road Back* (London, 1979), his sequel to *All Quiet on the Western Front*, which presents a vivid picture of the demoralisation and collapse of the German Army. Bertolt Brecht's play *Trommeln in Der Nacht* ('Drums in the Night') (London, 1980) is set against the background of the Spartacus rising. R. C. Hutchinson's *Unforgotten Prisoner* (London, 1939) gives a stark picture of the ruin of post-war Germany, while Richard Hughes' *The Fox in the Attic* (London, 1961) and *The Wooden Shepherdess* (London, 1973) give incisive imaginative insight into the nihilist Freikorps spirit and the early days of the Nazi movement in Bavaria. Thomas Keneally's *Gossip from the*

Forest (London, 1975) uses literary licence to reconstruct the Armistice negotiations and presents a convincing portrayal of Matthias Erzberger as the central tragic figure.

The last two decades of the twentieth century added hundreds more titles to the already immense existing mountain of literature on Nazi Germany in particular and Fascism in general, perhaps reflecting fears of a revival of fascism and racism in modern Europe. Although little appeared in English on the Freikorps period specifically, the following added substantively to our knowledge of the background to the era and can be unhesitatingly recommended:

Thomas Nevin's *Ernst Jünger and Germany: Into the Abyss 1914–45* (1997). The first full biography of Jünger in English published a year before the old warrior's death. It pays him the compliment of taking his ideas seriously, and while critical, intelligently and fairly engages with the man and his thought. The first volume of Ian Kershaw's huge two-volume biography of *Hitler: Hubris* (1998) covers the Führer's life up to 1936. Massively magisterial. Michael Burleigh's *The Third Reich: A New History* (2000) achieves the near impossible by contributing new knowledge and original interpretations to what we thought was a familiar story. Burleigh attacks the phenomenon of Nazism from fresh angles, essentially portraying the movement as a quasi-religious cult in a Godless but God-seeking age, with Hitler as its presiding psychopathic deity. An excellent new translation by Michael Hoffmann of Jünger's *Storm of Steel* (2003), the first since its original appearance in English, is now available from Penguin/Allen Lane. Let us hope that it leads to further translations from the voluminous work of this remarkable man.

INDEX

Action Française 112–13
Adlon Hotel (Berlin) 171
AEG 217
Alexander and Augusta Regiment 98
Alexander, Lt. Col. Harold (later Earl) 130
Alexander, Prof. Karl 232–3
Alexanderplatz (Berlin) 49, 56, 58, 67, 97, 98–9, 224
Alsace 160
Alt-Sutterheim, Capt. 156
Altes Rosenbad restaurant (Munich) 234
Altona 20, 89
Amann, Max 235, 244
Amiens 12
Annaburg, the 241, 248
Aplerdeck 193
Arbeitskommando (AK) 247
Arco-Valley, Count Anton auf 144, 265, 267

'Arditi', the xii, 109
Arens, Col. 177
Arnauld de la Periere, Lt. Lothar von 35
Artelt, Karl 19–20, 150
Auer, Erhard 140, 142–3, 255–6, 265
Auer, Sophie 256
Auf Gut Deutsch 237
Aulock, Gen. von (also von Aulock Freikorps) 197–8, 241
Austria 153, 189
Avanti! 111
Awaloff-Bermondt, Count 131–5, 212
Axelrod, Towier 148, 153, 157

Balla, Erich 126
Baltic, the xiii, 7, 123, 137, 170, 186, 187, 195, 212, 225, 240, 241, 242, 248
Bamburg 145, 147

Barth, Emil 37–8, 43, 44, 59
Bauer, Col. Max 172, 177, 189
Bauer, Gustav 165
Baumann, Prof. 233
Bavaria 138–58, 166, 186, 198, 203, 204, 207–8, 210, 216, 228–9, 230–60
Bavarian League, the 242
Bayreuth 266
Bechstein, Helene 238
'Beerhall Putsch', the xiv, 198, 207, 251–60, 272, 279
Belgium 161
Below, Gen. Otto von 167
Berchtesgaden 251
Berhofen 193
Berlin 5, 16, 20, 22, 23, 24, 28–30, 35–50, 55–7, 59, 60–9, 70–83, 84–5, 86, 87, 94–105, 160, 161, 167–8, 170–91, 198, 203, 209, 210, 214, 222–5, 228, 238, 249–50
Berliner Post 66
Berliner Tageblatt 101
Berliner Zeitung 101
Bernstein, Eduard 5, 114
Berthold, Rudolf 186–7, 195–6
Bethmann Hollweg, Theobald von 4
Bielefeld 197
Bischoff, Major Joseph 127, 129, 132, 136
Bismarck, Otto von 2, 159
Bismarckstrasse (Berlin) 181
'Black Front' 239, 250
'Black Reichswehr' 237, 247, 249
Black Sea 124
'Black and Tans' 113–14
Bloc National, the 113
Blücher, Gen. xi, 2, 11

Bock, Lt. Col. von 247
Bolshevism 7, 27, 30–1, 38, 40, 42, 51, 59, 71–3, 108, 114–15, 123–5, 133, 134, 142, 146, 148, 153, 163, 168, 218, 219, 227, 232, 233, 269
Bormann, Martin 272, 297–8
Brandenburg Gate, the (Berlin) 40, 59, 67, 180, 181, 182, 190
Brandis, Maj. Cordt von (also von Brandis Freikorps) 128–9
Bremen 23, 88–90, 96
Bremerhaven 88
Breslau 186
Brest-Litovsk, treaty of xiii, 7, 27, 124
Brockdorff-Rantzau, Ulrich von 160, 162, 163, 165
Bronnen, Arnolt 119
Brooke, Rupert 275–6
Bruning, Heinrich 216
Brunswick (Braunschweig) 5, 93, 102
Buchenwald 267
Buchner, Franz 126
Buchrucker, Maj. Bruno 247, 249–50
Buckow (Berlin) 67
Bulgakov, Mikhail 277
Bulow, Gen. von 124
Bund der Afrechten 222
Bund Ehemaliger Ehrhardt Offiziere 209–10
Bürgerbraukeller (Munich) 243, 251–5, 256, 257
Busch Circus (Berlin) 35, 36, 37

Canaris, Lt. Wilhelm 80–2, 298

Caspari, Maj. (Caspari Freikorps) 88
Centre Party, the 7, 16, 25, 84, 163–4, 212, 216
Charlottenburg (Berlin) 68
Chauseestrasse (Berlin) 39, 40
Chemnitz 195
Chinag Kai-Shek 264
Clemenceau, Georges 160, 163, 246
Coburg 228, 244
Cologne 29
Communism see Bolshevism and Spartacus League
Communist Party of Germany (KPD) 49, 50, 56–8, 61, 66, 74, 76, 85, 86, 87, 95, 148, 149, 150, 203, 204
see also Spartacus League
Compiègne 26, 212
Conti, Leonardo 298
Cork 114
Councils, Workers', Sailors' and Soldiers' 20–3, 27, 35, 39, 40, 41, 51, 85, 88, 89, 90, 91, 92, 102, 141, 149
Croix de Feu 113
Cuno, Wilhelm 249
Cuxhaven 23, 42, 88, 96

Dachau 151, 152, 153, 267
Dahlem (Berlin) 59, 68
Daluege, Kurt 298
Danner, Gen. von 256
D'Annunzio, Gabriele 108–11
Danzig 161
Darre, Richard-Walther 298–9
Daudet, Leon 113
Dawes Plan, the 262
Democratic Party, the 41, 84, 164, 181, 200
Denmark 161

'Deutscher Hort' 207
'Deutscher Trutz and Schutz Band' 206, 216
Dietrich, Sepp 299
Diez (Centre Party MP) 215
Döberitz 178, 179
Dorrenbach, Lt. Heinrich 43, 57, 61, 102–3, 150
Dortmund 193, 198
Douaumont, Fort 128
Dresden 93–4, 181, 184, 195
Drexler, Anton 233, 236, 252
Duisberg 194
Dusseldorf 194
Dusseldorf Freikorps 197
Düsterderg, Theodor 299

Ebert, Friedrich xii, 24, 27, 28, 31, 32–9, 37, 38, 40, 41, 42, 43–4, 50, 53, 55–7, 58, 59, 61, 62, 64, 65, 69, 85, 86, 96, 115, 121, 126, 129, 131, 132, 133, 136, 142, 164–5, 173, 174, 177, 181, 183–5, 197, 220, 241, 247, 249, 257, 264–5
Eckart, Dietrich 237–8, 244
Eden Hotel (Berlin) 68, 75, 76, 77, 78
Egelhofer, Rudolf 150–1, 153–5
Ehrhardt, Lt. Cmdr. Hermann (also Ehrhardt Brigade Freikorps) 87, 94, 102, 136, 173, 175–9, 181–2, 184–90, 200, 204, 206, 209, 210, 212, 216, 227, 228, 238, 244, 248, 250–1, 263, 266
Eichhorn, Emil 49–50, 56, 57, 67, 114
Einnig, August 309
'Einwohnerwehr' (Civil Guards) 74, 93, 100, 206

Eisenach 103
Eisner, Kurt 115, 140–5, 147, 148, 149, 154, 155, 232, 237, 256, 265, 267
Eitel, Prince Friedrich 28, 29
Elbe, River 94, 225
Epp, Lt. Col. Franz Ritter von (also von Epp Freikorps) 151–2, 166, 190, 198, 199, 200, 202, 205, 207, 238, 299–300
Erdenerstrasse (Berlin) 223
Erding 152
Erfurt 96
Ernst, Joseph 193, 199
Ernst, Karl 267
Erzberger, Matthias xiv, 25–7, 36, 121, 163–5, 212–17, 264
Erzberger, Paula 215
Escherich, Maj. D. Forstrat 206–7
Essen 193–4, 196
Esser, Hermann 244, 246, 258
Expressionism 118–19, 145

Falkenhayn, Gen. Erich von 3
Falkenhorst, Nikolaus von 300
Fascism 108–14, 245
Fatherland Party 6, 172
Faulhaber, Cardinal 256
Faupel, Col. (also Faupel Freikorps) 94, 151, 197
Fechenbach, Felix 144
Feder, Gottfried 233
'Feme', the 211
Ferchlandt, Lt. 91
Fischer, Anton 72
Fischer, Hermann 222–7
Fiume 110–11
Flanders 11, 82
Fletcher, Maj. Alfred 126, 130

Foch, Marshal Ferdinand 11, 12, 25, 26, 27
Frank, Hans 300
Frankfurt 24, 47, 266
Franzer Regiment 39
Franzosischestrasse (Berlin) 103
Frederick the Great 2, 241
Freiheit 56
Freikorps
  and stormtroop spirit 8–11
  Schleicher's plan for 34, 45
  Maercker's unit 50–1
  advertisements for 56
  at Luisenstift 63
  methods of recruitment and formation 63–4
  attack on Spartacists in Berlin 64–9
  and murders of Liebknecht and Luxemburg 70–83
  disenchantment with Republic 85–6
  campaign against Bremen and northern ports 88
  in Ruhr 89–90
  in middle Germany 90–4
  and subjugation of Berlin General Strike 96–106
  comparable European movements 107–15
  and anti-Semitism 114–15
  philosophical roots of 115–19
  and Great War 119–22
  and Baltic campaign 123–37
  and Nihilism 126–7
  'liberation' of Munich and first contact with Nazism 157–8
  numbers of 166
  and Reichswehr 166–7
  and putsch plots 167–9
  and Kapp Putsch 170–91

Freikorps *(cont.)*
  and Ruhr uprising 192–200
  and 'Black Reichswehr' 201,
    247
  and political murder campaign
    203–29
  and 'Black Reichswehr' in
    Bavaria 237
  and swastika symbol 238
  members enter Nazi party
    240
  campaign in Silesia 241
  and resistance to French
    occupation of Ruhr 247–8
  involvement in Kustrine Putsch
    249–50
  and Hitler's Beerhall Putsch
    251–60
  and rise of Nazis 261
  fate of leaders and summing up
    261–70
Freising 152
Frick, Wilhelm 239, 255, 257,
  261, 265, 300
Friedburg, Gen. von 151
Friedrichstrasse (Berlin) 100
'Frontbahn', the 266
Furmann, Fritz 88
Futurism 109–10

Gabcke Freikorps 198
Gandorfer, Barvarian Peasant
  leader 157
Gareis, Karl 216
Gars 152
Gelsenkirchen 198
Geothe, Johann Wolfgang von
  268
German Legion, the 132, 135
German Workers' Party 233–6
  see also National Socialist
    German Workers' Party

Gerstenburg, Col. (*also*
  Gerstenburg Freikorps) 88
Gesell, Silvio 146
Gessler, Minister 200
Gilsa, Maj. von 179–80, 200
Glonn, river 152
Godin, Baron Michael von 259,
  267
Goebbels, Joseph 272, 276, 278
Goering, Hermann 14, 122, 244,
  245, 253, 258, 259, 260, 272
Goldingen 127
Goltz, Gen. Rudiger von der 124,
  127, 128, 129, 130, 131,
  132, 133, 136
Görlitz Freikorps (von Faupel
  Freikorps) 94, 151, 153
Gotha 90, 96, 195
Göttingen 198
Graf, Ulrich 244
Greene, Graham 277
Greim, Ritter von 238
Greisier, Artur 301
Groener, Gen. Wilhelm 24–5, 29,
  31, 33, 40, 41, 45, 47, 164,
  170, 201, 204, 264, 301
Grosser Kurfurst, the 18
Grosz, George 99
Grunewald (Berlin) 68, 223
Gudowius, Col. 250
Gunther, Maj. 250
Günther, Willi 222

Haas, Gen. (also Gen. Haas
  Freikorps) 151, 198
Haase, Hugo 3, 5, 23, 37, 59,
  216
Hagen 193, 199
Halle 91–3, 96, 226, 247
Hallesche Tor (Berlin) 73
Haltern 199
Hamborn 194

Hamburg 23, 88–9, 174, 228
'Hamburg points', the 41–2
Hanover 23, 198, 226, 265
Harbou, Maj. von 44
Harden, Maximillien 228
Harrer, Karl 235
Hasenklaver, Capt. 193
Hauenstein, Heinz 247, 248
Haussmann, Konrad 21
Havel (Berlin) 68
Heines, Edmund 240, 242, 267
Heinz, Friedrich Wilhelm 129,
    135, 187, 212
Held, Gen. (Held Freikorps)
    63–4, 68
Helfferich, Karl 212–13, 219, 224
Helgoland, the 18
Helldorf, Wolf Heinrich, Graf
    von 301
Henke, Deputy 88
Hertling, Georg von 15
Hervest-Dorten 90
Herzen, Maj. 250
Hess, Rudolf 154, 255, 271–4,
    276, 279, 302
Heydebreck, Capt. Peter von 86,
    240, 241, 242, 247, 267
Heydrich, Reinhard 93, 272, 302
Heye, Col. Wilhelm 29, 183, 189
Hierl, Konstantin 247
High Seas Fleet, the 6, 17–23, 27,
    161, 165
Himmler, Heinrich 8, 40, 227,
    255, 272, 302
Hindenburg Freikorps 186, 198
Hindenburg, Gen. Paul von 4, 15,
    16, 26, 29, 31, 33, 36, 41,
    124, 164, 186, 190, 263
Hintze, Paul von 15
Hipper, Admiral Franz von 17,
    18
Hirl, Maj. 151

Hirsch, Lt. 92
Hirschfeld, Oltwig von 214
Hitler, Adolf xiv, 36, 94, 112,
    123, 152, 154–5, 156, 158,
    159, 161, 176, 189, 197,
    198, 199, 206, 207, 209,
    216, 217, 229, 230–60,
    261–7, 270, 271–3, 276–7,
    278
Hoefer, Gen. 241
Hoepner, Erich 302–3
Hoess, Rudolf 303
Hofbrauhaus (Munich) 235,
    242
Hoffmann, Adolf 145, 146, 147,
    149, 151, 152, 157, 189,
    207
Hoffmann, Gen. Hermann von
    63, 68, 73, 79, 168, 174
Hoover Commission, the 87
Hulsen, Gen. von (also von
    Hulsen Freikorps) 64, 68, 94,
    102, 174, 241
Hungary 146–7, 153, 216
Hunstert 217
Hyams, Edward 217

Imperial Palace (Berlin) 30, 42,
    43, 68, 69, 82
Independent Social Democratic
    Party (USDP) 5–6, 16, 19,
    23, 24, 25, 28, 30, 35, 36,
    37, 41, 48–9, 49, 56, 58, 59,
    61, 62, 81, 84, 87, 88, 91,
    141, 148, 183, 216
Irish Republican Army (IRA) 113
Iron Brigade 64, 66, 67, 75, 88,
    127, 175
Iron Division 127, 129, 132, 135,
    136
'Iron Fist' 237
'Iron Host' 186–7

Isar, river 157
Italy 108–12, 211, 245–6

Jade, river 18
Jagow, Traugott von 182, 200
Jahreiss, Maj. von 145
Jena 195, 247
Jerusalemstrasse (Berlin) 68
Jogliches, Leo 103
Jorns, Paul 79, 81
Jugendbewung (Youth movement) 115–21
Jungdeutscher Orden ('Jungdo') 206, 208–9, 241
Jünger, Ernst xiv, 10, 120–2, 208, 267–8, 274–9, 303–4

Kahr, Gustav von 189, 239, 250–3, 254, 256, 267
Kaiser, Helene 224
Kamenev, Lev 115
Kampfbund 245, 251, 252, 266
Kapp Putsch 159, 170–91, 192, 195, 196, 199, 204, 206, 207, 208, 209, 214, 238, 241, 245, 247, 249, 264
Kapp, Wolfgang von 6, 171, 172, 173, 176, 177, 182, 184, 185, 187–8, 189, 193, 195, 238, 241, 242, 244
Kassel 27, 43, 44, 118, 124, 185, 209, 216, 265
Kassel, Lt. von 65
Kaufmann, Karl 304
Kautsky, Karl 5, 114
Keitel, Wilhelm 304
Kerensky, Alexander 31
Kern, Erwin 220–6
Kessler, Count Harry 99–100, 105, 213, 225, 229
Keynes, John Maynard 162
Khune Freikorps 197

Kiel 6, 17–23, 34, 42, 43, 64–7, 81, 88, 127, 140, 150, 175, 188
Killian 91
Killinger, Manfred von 210, 240, 263, 304
Klöppel, Sailor 98
Kluver, Lt. Col. 92
Knilling, Premier von 255
Kohl, Helmut 278
Kolberg 124
König, the 18, 23
Königplatz (Munich) 243
Königsallee (Berlin) 223
Kreuzzeitung, the 214
Kriebel, Herman 207, 245, 251, 261, 262
Krischbin 223
Kristallnacht 279
Krone, Zirkus (Munich) 239
Kronprinz Wilhelm, the 18
Kuhnt Bernhard 88
Kun, Bela 114–15, 147
Kurtzig, investigator 79
Kustrine 249

Landauer, Gustav 146, 155
Landesjägerkorps, Freiwillige 52–5, 63, 66, 68, 69, 86, 92–3, 166, 205, 241
Landeswehr, Baltic 127, 129, 130
Landsberg 262, 266, 272
Landshut 239, 257
Landwehr Canal (Berlin) 68
Langemarck, battle of 119, 275
Ledebour, Georg 58
Legien, SPD union leader 183
Leipzig 5, 24, 93, 195, 200, 247
Lenin, Vladimir Ilyich 3, 5, 7, 22, 30, 48, 58, 59, 108, 115, 146, 148, 149

Lettow-Vorbeck, Gen. Paul von 115, 174
Leupold regiment 198
Levien, Max 115, 148, 149, 150, 153, 157
Leviné, Eugene 60, 66, 115, 138, 148, 149, 157, 232
Liabou Freikorps 197
Lichtenberg (Berlin) 99–102
Lichtenrade (Berlin) 67
Lichterfelde (Berlin) 66, 67
Lichtschlag, Capt. (Lichtschlag Freikorps) 89, 193
Liebknecht, Karl xii, 4, 5, 12, 24, 25, 29–30, 30, 31, 35–8, 42, 47–8, 50, 57, 61, 70–83, 95, 100, 101, 127
Liepmann, Lt. 76, 79
Lindner, Alois 145
Lindner, Lt. 74
Lipp, Franz 146, 149
List, Wilhelm 304–5
Lloyd George, David 160, 162
Lorenz, Werner 305
Lorraine 160
Lossow, Gen. Otto von 252, 253, 256
Löwenfeld, Lt. Cmdr. Wilfried von 34–5, 81–2, 88, 136, 175, 186, 197, 198, 200, 248
Lübeck 23
Ludecke, Kurt 243, 244
Ludendorff, Gen. Erich von xi, 4, 6, 8, 9, 11, 12, 13, 16, 17, 24, 38, 171, 172, 173, 178, 181–2, 189–90, 204, 218–19, 245, 251, 254–64
Ludwig, King of Bavaria 141
Luisenstift, the (Berlin) 59, 60, 63
Luitpold Gymnasium (Munich) 149

Lüttwitz, Gen Walther von 48, 55, 63, 68, 69, 96, 98, 103, 167, 172–9, 182, 183, 185, 186, 188–90, 193, 200
Lutzow Freikorps 156, 197
Luxemburg, Rosa xii, 4, 5, 12, 24, 30, 31, 38, 49, 60, 61, 70–83, 101, 114, 127, 148

Maercker, Gen. Ludwig von 50–1, 63, 66, 68, 69, 82, 86, 91–4, 165, 166, 168, 174, 184, 185, 190, 195, 201, 202, 205, 212, 241
Magdeburg 5, 24, 93, 207
Magnis, Col. 151
Mahler, Horst 279
Mahraun, Artur 209
Malcolm, Gen. Noel 171
Mann, Lt. Rudolf 187
Manner, Emil 153
Mantel, Karl 255
Manteuffel, Baron von 128
Marienplatz (Munich) 258
Marinetti, Fillipo 109
Markgraf, the 18–19
Marloh, Lt. von 103–4
Marstall, the (Berlin) 42–4, 48, 49, 50, 57, 58, 61, 98
Marx, Karl (and Marxism) 3, 5, 86, 115
Maurras, Charles 113
Max, Prince of Baden 15–16, 17, 24, 25, 27, 28, 32
Mayr, Capt. Karl 233, 234, 236, 267
Mecklenburg 225
Medem, von, Freikorps 248
Mein Kampf 262, 272
Meissner, mountain 118
Milch, Erhard 305
Mitau 127, 129, 132

Mitterand, François 278
Moabit (Berlin) 64, 80–1, 105
Mohl, Gen. von 151
Moltke, Graf von 2
Morgern, Lt. Gen. von 51
Mühlheim 90, 194, 198
Mühsam, Erich 145, 149, 157
Munich xiv, 24, 138–58, 160,
    175, 179, 185, 189, 192,
    200, 231, 232, 261, 267
Munich Post 256
Munster 185, 193, 197–8
Mussolini, Benito 111–12, 245–6
Muthmann, Gunther 248

National Assembly 41, 84, 87,
    96, 103, 162, 165, 175, 185
National Liberal Party 16
National Party (DNVP) 94, 177,
    208, 213
National Socialist German
    Workers' Party (National
    Socialism-Nazis) xii, xiv,
    115–18, 128, 136, 145, 152,
    189, 203, 206, 209, 210,
    217, 227, 228, 233–40, 242,
    248, 251–60, 262, 264,
    271–3, 275, 276–8
Neanderstrasse (Berlin) 68
Neukolln (Berlin) 68, 73
Neuring, Minister 94
Niekisch, Ernst 277
Niemoller, Martin 198, 305–6
Nietzsche, Friedrich 116–18, 126
'Night of the Long Knives' 34,
    86, 227, 239, 240, 263, 266,
    270, 277
Noske, Gustav xii, 20–3, 31,
    48–9, 50, 55, 58, 59, 60,
    62–3, 64–7, 69, 70, 75, 78,
    81, 85, 87–8, 89, 95, 96, 97,
    101–5, 127, 147, 151, 152,

    157, 163–5, 167, 171–2,
    173, 174–5, 177, 178,
    179–80, 181, 183, 184, 200,
    206, 265
'November Criminals' 36, 262
Nuremburg 258, 265, 273

Oberg, Karl 306
Oberland Freikorps 198, 216,
    241, 242, 245, 252, 256, 258
'Obleute', the 30, 35, 50, 56
Odeonplatz (Munich) 259
Oder, river 241
Oertzen, Friedrich Wilhelm von
    73, 136, 137, 157, 199
Ohrdruf 152
Oldershausen, Gen. von 177, 179
'On the Marble Cliffs' 268,
    277–8
Orbis, Heinz 248
Organisation Consul (O.C.)
    209–12, 216, 220, 222, 228,
    240, 248, 265
Organisation Escherich
    (ORGESCH) 206–8
Organisation Kanzler (ORKA)
    206
Orkney islands 161
Oven, Gen. von (von Oven
    Freikorps) 94, 152, 157, 174,
    179, 198
Owen, Wilfred 275–6

Pabst, Capt. Waldemar 40, 73,
    75–83, 127, 167–9, 170,
    171–2, 173, 176, 185, 187–9
Parcus brothers 257
Paris 11, 160
Pelkum 199
People's Naval (Marine) Division
    42–5, 48, 49, 57, 61, 68,
    97–8, 102–3

People's Party, German 94, 177, 204
Perlach 156
Pernet, Heinz 257, 261
Petri, Capt 78
Petrograd 58, 59, 128, 130
Pflugk-Hartnung, Heinz von 75, 79
Pflugk-Hartnung, Lt. Horst von 75, 77, 79, 80
Pichelsdorfer bridge (Berlin) 181
Pieck, Wilhelm xii, 50, 57, 74, 74–6
Pittinger, Dr. Otto 244–5
Pöhner, Ernst 210, 216, 239, 257, 261, 262, 265
Poincaré, Raymond 246
Poland 7, 123, 161, 241, 263
Pölzing, Lt. Georg 156
Popolo d'Italia, il 111
Popp, Artur 19
Posen (Poznan) 40, 124, 161
Potsdam 43, 63, 65, 172, 208
Potsdamer Platz (Berlin) 66, 68
Progressive Party 16, 21
Prussia 2, 9, 29, 31, 124, 138, 161, 164, 168, 179, 184, 204

Radek, Karl 61, 72, 114
Rapallo, treaty of 219
Rathenau, Walther xiv, 87, 212, 217–28, 243, 265
Rechberg, Arnold 172
'Red Front', the 209, 269
Reichs Chancellery (Berlin) 32, 43, 47, 58, 63, 66, 68, 177, 182, 188
Reichsbanner, the 209, 267, 269
Reichstag, the 2, 3, 5, 16, 21, 25, 68, 83, 200, 212, 213, 216, 222, 224, 264, 270

Reichswehr, the 34, 94, 105, 152, 161, 166–9, 170, 174, 176, 179, 180, 183, 185, 189, 190, 194, 200, 202, 204–6, 207, 232, 237, 249, 252, 258, 264, 267–70
Reinhard, Col. Wilhelm (Reinhard Freikorps) 63, 64, 66, 67, 98, 100, 103–4, 166, 205
Reinhardt, Gen. 179–80, 181, 183, 200, 201
Reitzenstein, Col. von 91
Remarque, Erich Maria 275
Remschied 193, 198
Renn, Ludwig 306
Rhine, river 12, 161
Rhineland, the 165
Ribbentrop, Joachim von 272
Riga 128–30, 135
Roden, Col. von 64, 88
Roeder, Gen. von (von Roeder Freikorps) 63, 66, 68, 102
Röhm, Ernst 86, 115, 136, 205–10, 227, 236–7, 240, 245, 251, 252, 254, 256, 257, 259, 260, 261, 262, 266–7, 306–7
Rosenburg, Alfred 239, 244, 252, 258, 262, 266
Rosenheim 258
Rossbach, Gerhard (Rossbach Freikorps) 115, 119, 135–6, 187, 189, 197, 202, 204, 206, 241, 242, 247, 248, 252, 255, 258, 266
Rote Fahne, the 23, 48, 56, 58, 62, 70, 71, 72, 73, 74, 95–6, 148
Ruhr xiv, 89–90, 188, 192–200, 203, 246–9, 250
Ruhr Echo 194

Runge, Otto 75–6, 78–81
Rupprecht, Crown Prince of
    Bavaria 140, 255, 256

S.A. (Storm Abteilung) xiv, 94,
    112, 128, 136, 208–9, 227,
    240, 242–5, 249, 251, 252,
    257–9, 266–7, 269, 270
Saale, river 92–3
Saaleck, castle 226–7
Saar, the 161
St Quentin 8
Salomon, Ernst von 122, 123,
    125, 126, 127, 131–5,
    195–6, 220–2, 227–8, 248,
    267, 307
Salomon, Pfeffer von (von
    Salomon Freikorps) 128–9,
    197, 240
Sassoon, Siegfried 275
Saxony 195, 212, 222, 240, 251
Scapa Flow 161, 165
Schächt, Hjalmar 262
Scheer, Admiral Reinhard von
    34
Scheidemann, Philipp 24, 28, 29,
    37, 38, 62, 64, 65, 72, 96,
    100, 121, 160, 162, 164–5,
    200, 216, 220, 265
Schellingstrasse (Berlin) 172
Schiffer, vice-Chancellor 181,
    183, 185, 188
Schirach, Baldur von 273
Schlachtensee (Berlin) 68
Schlageter, Albert Leo 248–9
Schleicher, Major (Gen.) Kurt von
    33–4, 41, 43, 45, 183, 190,
    200, 204, 264, 307
Schleissheim (Berlin) 153
Schlossplatz (Berlin) 56
Schmargendorf (Berlin) 68
Schmidt, Lt. 92

Schmidt-Pauli, Edgar von 129,
    133
Schneppenhorst, Minister 147
'Schnitzler', Dr. 172, 177, 183
Schönfelderstrasse (Berlin) 255
Schultz, Heinrich 216
Schultze, Walther 'Bubi' 259,
    307–8
Schulz Freikorps 197
Schulz, Lt. Paul 247, 250
Schulze, Sgt. Maj. 67
Seeckt, Gen. Hanns von 170, 174,
    176, 177, 179–80, 183, 189,
    190, 200–2, 204, 219, 220,
    246–7, 249, 256, 264
Seisser, Col. Hans von 252, 253,
    256, 258
Seldte, Franz 121, 207, 208, 308
Severin Freikorps 198
Severing, Karl 182, 197, 247
Siegesallee (Berlin) 56, 62, 179
Siewert, Capt. 132
Silesia xiii, 161, 175, 186, 205,
    241, 247
Sinclair, Admiral 125
Sinn Fein 113
Sklarz, Georg 72
Smuts, Gen. Jan Christian 162,
    174
Social Democratic Party (SPD)
    xii–xiii, 3, 4, 5, 6, 16, 20, 21,
    24, 25, 27, 28, 30, 36–8, 40,
    41, 48, 50, 55, 56, 58, 60,
    70, 71, 72, 78, 84, 87, 94,
    96, 99, 100, 140, 142, 145,
    147, 149, 152, 164–5, 167,
    180, 182, 183, 189, 190,
    192, 196, 197, 200, 204,
    207, 208, 209, 216, 242,
    247, 255, 264, 267
Soden, Count von 255
Somme, battle of 3, 275

Souchon, Admiral 18–20, 22
Souchon, Sub. Lt. 76
Spa 14, 17, 26, 28, 31, 39, 43
Spandau (Berlin) 65, 68, 97, 273
Spartacus League (Spartacists) xii,
    xiii, 4–5, 9, 12, 25, 30, 36,
    38, 39, 42, 48, 49, 56, 60,
    61, 63–83, 85–7, 98, 100,
    133, 142, 146, 148, 175,
    183, 269
Speer, Albert 272, 273
Speiro, Sgt. 39
Sperrle, Hugo 308
Speyer 248
Spree, river (Berlin) 68
S.S. (Schutz Staffel) xi, xiv, 34,
    227, 255, 264, 267
'Stab in the Back' legend 9, 38,
    136, 171, 268
Stahlhelm, the 94, 121, 205, 206,
    207, 208, 238, 241, 269
Starnberg 152, 153
Steinhauser, Lt. 19–20
Stennes, Capt. Walther 249, 250
Stephani, Maj. von (Stephani
    Freikorps) 63, 65, 66, 172,
    208
Sternecker Beerhall (Munich) 233,
    235
Stinnes, Hugo 172
Stock, Lt. 128
Strasser, Gregor 239, 257, 260,
    262, 266, 267, 308–9
Strasser, Otto 239, 250, 266
Streicher, Julius 258
Stresemann, Gustav 204, 249,
    256, 262, 269
Stubenrauch, Hans 222
Stuckart, Wilhelm 309
Stuttgart 27, 184, 185

Tannenberg, battle of 4, 124

Tanschik, Brig. 103
Techow, Ernst Werner 223,
    225–7
Teltow Canal (Berlin) 68
Tempelhof (Berlin) 67–8
Theresienweise (Munich) 140,
    142, 149
Thorensburg 135
Thuringen, the 18
Thuringia 195, 251
Tiergarten (Berlin) 56, 75, 181
Tillesen, Heinrich 216
Times, The 101
Tirpitz, Admiral von 6, 17
Toller, Ernst 145–57, 232
'Totenkopf', the (Death's Head)
    xi, 8
Traunstein 232
Trebitsch-Lincoln 172, 238
Trotha, Admiral von 177–9
Trotsky, Leon 30, 48, 58, 115,
    148
Türkenstrasse (Munich) 232

Uffing 260
Ukraine, the 7, 123
Ulmanis, Premier 128–30
Unter den Linden, the (Berlin) 56,
    100, 190, 222

Verdun, battle of 3–4, 128,
    236
Versailles, treaty of 87, 124, 133,
    159–69, 170, 171, 190, 201,
    210, 216, 217, 219, 221,
    236, 241, 242, 246, 263
Vienna 109
Viking Bund, the 251
Viktoriastrasse (Berlin) 173
VNS (Association of National
    Soldiers) 208
Vogel, Lt. Kurt 76, 77, 79, 81

Volkischer Beobachter, the 235, 238–9, 252
'Volksgemeinschaft' (People's Community) concept 119–20
Vörwarts xiii, 56, 60, 65, 66, 72, 78, 85, 101, 106, 140
Vossische Zeitung 101

Wagener, Capt. Otto 132
Wagner, Gerhardt 309
Wagner, Richard 266
Wall Street Crash, The 263, 269
Wallottstrasse (Berlin) 224
'Wandrevogel', the 116, 118, 209
Wangenheim, Freiherr von 182
Wannsee (Berlin) 68, 224
Warnemunde 225
Wasserburg 152
Watter, Gen. Oskar von 89, 90, 193, 194, 197
Weber, Christian 244
Weber, Dr. Friedrich 242, 245, 261, 262
'Wehr' – Republican militias 74, 85, 93, 97, 100, 149
Weimar (and Weimar Republic/regime) xii–xiv, 47, 86, 88, 91, 92, 94, 95, 96, 103, 105, 158, 163, 166–9, 173, 195, 200, 201–2, 204, 210, 211, 212, 216, 219, 247, 249, 262, 265

Weissenstein Freikorps 194
Wels, Otto 36, 39–40, 42, 43, 44
Wenden 130
Werderstrasse (Berlin) 68
Weser, river 88
Weygand, Gen. 27
Wilhelm, Crown Prince 29, 68
Wilhelm, Kaiser 1–4, 15–17, 25, 27–8, 29–31, 99, 161, 213, 218, 228, 230–1, 258, 263, 279
Wilhelmshaven 88, 96, 175, 188
Wilhelmstrasse (Berlin) 63, 69
Wilmersdorf (Berlin) 74
Wilson, President T. Woodrow 15–16, 17, 160–3, 165
Wirth, Joseph 219, 220, 224, 265
Wissel, Gen. von (von Wissel Freikorps) 64, 68
Wolff, Karl 309–10
Württemberg 31, 152

Young Plan, the 262
Ypres 119
Yudenich, Gen. Nikolai 131

Zehlendorf (Berlin) 67
Zeller, Max 199
Zinoviev, Grigori 115
Zoo (Berlin) 76, 222
Zossen 50, 55–6, 63
'Zukunft' 228